How to Run a Small Business

How to Run a Small Business

J. K. Lasser Institute

Seventh Edition

McGraw-Hill, Inc.

New York   San Francisco   Washington, D.C.   Auckland   Bogotá
Caracas   Lisbon   London   Madrid   Mexico City   Milan
Montreal   New Delhi   San Juan   Singapore
Sydney   Tokyo   Toronto

Library of Congress Cataloging-in-Publication Data

How to run a small business / J.K. Lasser Institute.—7th ed.
    p.   cm.
    Includes index.
    ISBN 0-07-036576-8
    1.   Small business—Management.   I. J.K. Lasser Institute.
HD62.7.H68   1993
658.02'3—dc20   93-26166
                                                CIP

1 2 3 4 5 6 7 8 9 0 DOC/DOC 9 9 8 7 6 5 4 3

ISBN 0-07-036576-8

The sponsoring editor for this book was Caroline Carney, the editing supervisor was Olive H. Collen, and the production supervisor was Suzanne W. Babeuf. The book was set in Palatino by McGraw-Hill's Professional Book Group composition unit.

Printed and bound by R. R. Donnelley & Sons Company.

Contents

Chapter 4. Deciding on the Location of Your Business   29

Chapter 5. Choosing a Form for Your Business   39

Chapter 6. Control through Accounting and Record   57
   Systems

Chapter 7. Basic Tax Management Decisions   83

Chapter 8. Operating the Retail Store   101

Chapter 9. Profit Pointers for the Wholesaler   127

Chapter 10. Service Firm Management   143

Chapter 11. A Basic Guide to Franchise Operation   153

Preface

For over 40 years, *How to Run a Small Business* has been a popularly accepted guide to business operations. The seventh edition of this book reflects changes in the past few years which affect small business. Since the last edition, more and more Americans have become interested in becoming entrepreneurs. Large corporations have retrenched, forcing many executives to consider small business opportunities, especially in the expanding franchising field. An unprecedented surge in computer and telecommunications technology has placed efficient, time-saving equipment within reach of almost all businesses.

This new edition of *How To Run a Small Business* incorporates these and many other important changes. Whether you are planning to start a new business or are operating an existing one, *How to Run a Small Business* will assist you in making decisions and organizing your thoughts, as well as aid you in solving your business problems by suggesting possible solutions you may have overlooked in the course of a busy workday. Accepting the challenge of running a small business can be rewarding, but you must meet the challenge with knowledge and understanding. We believe that this new edition of *How to Run a Small Business* will contribute to the success and growth of your enterprise.

The J. K. Lasser Institute

1
Entering the Business World

We constantly make economic and financial decisions that affect our lives. Many of these decisions are made on a whim or after superficial appraisal. We can purchase, say, a car because we like the way it looks or think it reflects our status in life, and can drive it without much mechanical knowledge of how it works. But buying, starting up, or operating a business is too major a financial commitment to be casual about.

The failure of a business is usually disastrous to the owner(s). If disaster is to be averted, the person going into business must learn all there is to know about a particular business before investing time, energy, and financial resources into the business. Learn about the experience of other small business operators before you start your own. Once you're in business, there is little time to learn what to watch closely and control and what to leave alone. This requires time, intelligence, and patience.

If this is your first venture into business, get to know the business you want to enter from beginning to end. Get help in your fact finding. Talk to people who are already involved in the business in which you are interested: the owners, employees, suppliers, association directors and members, and, certainly, prospective customers, local bankers, and realtors.

Here are some of the questions you should find answers to:

1. What are the economic trends in your chosen industry (is it growing, stable, declining)?
2. Who will your competitors be?

3. Who will your customers be?
4. What financial level of success have they achieved?
5. Why do you think you will succeed?
6. Are you planning to fill a marketplace niche or take market share from established businesses?
   a. If a niche, are you sure that it can be filled?
   b. If market share, do you have a strategy for taking business away from established firms?
7. Do you know what the downside risks are?
8. Do you have the financial backing to sustain reverses, to wait to succeed?

Your Personal Preconditions of Personal Success

If you are going into business for the first time, it is important to evaluate your attitudes and abilities in the areas of decision making, assuming responsibility, and taking risks before you spend a great deal of time gathering and analyzing information about a prospective business.

Do not confuse the urge to be in business by yourself with the ability to make it on your own. Wanting to succeed is one thing, the ability to succeed another.

Give yourself every chance to succeed. Successful entrepreneurs, aware of the various chances for failure in a new venture, work hard to shift the odds in their favor by thorough investigation at the outset. The person destined for failure is the one who is carried into a business on the euphoria of going it alone without doing the essential preparatory work.

As an introduction to the complexity of making business decisions, consider the experiences of Mr. and Mrs. Smith, who are contemplating buying a business. They illustrate how those who move carefully have the best chance of profiting from the purchase.

John and Marie Smith have some free time on their hands now that their children are in college. Marie, from a restaurant family, has dreamed of recapturing the joy she knew from being involved in the operation of a restaurant. John, a full-time executive, can use his business contacts to help fulfill his wife's ambitions. Marie will handle the operational details, such as hiring talented people to staff the operation. Knowing Marie's background and her decision-making ability, and realizing that restaurants can be very profitable, John believes this type of venture will be right for them.

The Smiths choose to investigate restaurants in a coastal resort area about an hour from the city. A large, year-round tourist population guarantees a sizable group of people who regularly dine out. John and Marie proceed carefully, arranging for both a lawyer and accountant to help them. They are undecided whether to build the restaurant and develop the clientele from scratch, buy an established restaurant and run it their own way, or buy a franchise from a restaurant chain whose meals must be prepared as specified by the franchise.

The attorney first discovers that the local zoning board is against the construction of a new restaurant because of the existing urbanization. However, the board is receptive to the construction of the nationally known franchise, deciding that the addition to the existing overdevelopment would be outweighed by the diners the franchise would bring to the town. An attempt to fight the zoning board's prejudice would be costly, time-consuming, and hurtful to the restaurant's business when it finally opened. These considerations convince the Smiths to drop the idea of building their own restaurant and concentrate on the other two possibilities: buying an existing restaurant or buying into a franchise.

A check of local real estate brokers reveals that there are two restaurants on the market. One is on the shore, available at a bargain price, and the other is farther inland, with a good reputation and a high asking price. John and Marie obtain from the franchise a disclosure statement, an earnings claims document, and a copy of the franchise contract. The papers are forwarded to the attorney for evaluation. Because each state has different laws pertaining to franchises, the attorney must study what effect the contract will have on the operation.

Meanwhile, the Smiths concentrate on evaluating the potential of the two restaurants that are for sale. The proprietors of both restaurants grant interviews and access to the documents John and Marie want to see.

The owners of the successful inland restaurant are selling because, as the Smiths discover at the interview, they are beyond retirement age and are tired of the hectic life of food preparation. However, their pride in what they have accomplished is visible as they discuss recipes, cooking tips, and the preparation of the house specialties. They provide copies of 3 back years of income tax returns, which John and Marie forward to their accountant for analysis.

When John and Marie visit the shore restaurant, they observe that too much of the restaurant's floor space seems devoted to the bar. The dining room is not crowded, and they witness one of the few diners complain to the waitress that the chowder is too salty to be eaten. The owners, a couple in their forties, seem anxious to get out of the business. They also provide copies of their tax returns.

At home, John and Marie discuss the two restaurants. Both operations buy their raw food from the same markets. The kitchen equipment of each is in good condition, although the facilities of the inland restaurant are a little older. County health officials state that there has never been a problem with either restaurant. The employees of the inland restaurant seem to be about a generation older than the staff of the shore restaurant. The shoreline restaurant has a smaller parking lot than the inland restaurant, but more of its customers walk to dinner. There is an empty lot next to the shoreline restaurant that the owners have offered to include in the sale. The lot could be graded and paved to provide additional parking, but it is not clear if the local zoning board would allow the improvement.

The next day John and Marie meet with their accountant to go over the figures presented by the two restaurants. The inland restaurant shows good, consistent profits. The income and expenses are in a ratio normal for restaurants, indicating an efficient operation. The tax deduction for repairs is small, so presumably the machinery is in good working order. The payroll records show little turnover. The inland restaurant seems to keep everyone happy—customers, employees, and owners.

Marie notes that the menu prices at the inland restaurant are moderate for an eatery with a good reputation. The accountant confirms that the restaurant would be even more profitable if the menu prices were raised to keep up with inflation. The accountant and the Smiths postulate that the restaurant's reputation would survive modest increases without losing many customers. Since the asking price of the business seems to be composed of the value of the assets and 2 years' profits, raising prices might considerably shorten the time needed to recover their investment.

In respect to the shoreline restaurant, casual conversation with local residents did not turn up anyone who had eaten there. The figures for the restaurant seem to confirm the emphasis on tourists, with little effort to attract repeat customers. The accountant points out that an unusually high percentage of the restaurant's income is from the sale of liquor, a ratio more akin to a bar and grill. The couple and the accountant agree that they must consider, in addition to the purchase price, the cost of renovations necessary to deemphasize the cocktail lounge. This is still a relatively inexpensive purchase since the asking price for the shoreline restaurant is a figure representing the value of all the assets and less than 1 year's profit, a profit that was low to begin with.

After meeting with the accountant, John and Marie go to their attorney to complete the investigation of the two restaurants and compare these opportunities with the franchise offer. The attorney says the owners of both restaurants have clear title, free of legal attachments and mortgages. Also, the attorney sees no obstacle to obtaining a building permit to remodel the shoreline restaurant. However, because zoning boards can be unpredictable, the attorney recommends that an escrow clause be written into the purchase contract so that John and Marie do not buy the lot unless paving is approved. The part of the restaurant purchase price to be paid to the seller for the empty lot would be placed in escrow, in trust of a local bank, until the zoning board reaches a decision. A contract escrow clause protects the buyer from paying for something unusable, while the rest of the sale goes through.

According to the attorney, the franchise offers the usual entanglements, although it is no fly-by-night scheme. King Craw, the Louisiana-based seafood chain, is rated highly by business credit bureaus even though it has been in business only a few years. The attorney attributes King Craw's success to the direction it gives to franchise operators, as evidenced by the guidelines and restrictions contained in the contract. Other King Craw owners contacted by the attorney (from the list provided in the disclosure statement) confirm that controls are tight. However, the attorney points out that there is no way to tell whether the failures of some outlets were really due to the tight controls or to the public's mixed reactions to seafood restaurants. To judge the possible effects of the company guidelines, the contract has to be studied very carefully.

In return for the franchise fee, King Craw provides the basic supplies and a completed building ready for operation. The franchise purchaser has no say in the location other than to select the town to do business in. The company then sends professionals to choose the exact site and to see that the building is constructed according to company specifications. According to the contract, the company arranges for all licenses and permits, provides publicity for the grand opening, and handles all advertising, national and local.

The franchise purchaser must pay all other costs of day-to-day operation, including freight charges for the shipment of genuine Louisiana crawfish. Most of the specialized foodstuffs must be bought directly from the company at the company's price. Certain seafood can be bought locally if it meets company specifications; lobsters, for example, must weigh between 2 and 2 $\frac{1}{4}$ pounds. The menu itself is limited to the dishes sold at all the other franchise locations. The contract allows the company to set menu prices, restaurant hours, and even the design of the employees' uniforms. The attorney thinks these guidelines are reasonable to protect the integrity of the King Craw image.

In addition to a one-time franchise fee, the operators must also pay King Craw a percentage of the receipts. The attorney points out that there is no minimum sales provision; the contract cannot be canceled if a monthly sales quota is not met.

Of greater concern is that the company does not protect the location; it has the right to put up new outlets wherever it pleases. If the sales volume from John and Marie's outlet is heavy, the company could open another King Craw nearby. The figures on the earnings claim document state that a typical King Craw makes a 10 percent profit on sales that average $500,000 a year, a decent return on the $250,000 franchise fee. However, if the company can limit John and Marie's profit by licensing competitors, the value of the contract is reduced.

The Smiths decide that, given the measure of Marie's faith in her skills, the franchise would be too limiting to her. Buying one of the restaurants would allow more freedom and more opportunity. The inland restaurant would offer the chance to buy in on a successful, on-going operation with low risk. However, the shoreline restaurant has the greater profit potential in the long run because of its favorable location, if its earnings picture can be turned around. After comparing the specific benefits, costs, and drawbacks of the two restaurants, John, Marie, and the attorney arrive at the conclusion that the shoreline restaurant appears to be a bargain purchase, even after the cost of redesigning the interior is factored in.

Although the Smiths decided to buy the shoreline restaurant, another couple, with different skills, could easily have reached a different conclusion. A less well-financed investor might have chosen the inland restaurant because it would produce income right away.

To sum up, good business decisions are not easily made—especially the decision to enter into a new business. Do not be rushed. Obtain all the facts and be objective. You must know not only what you want, but also what you may win and what you may lose. Make a decision— then abide by it.

2
Financing the Small Business

Financing is critical for starting a new business and keeping a business going and growing. You may be able to start on your own capital. But you may not survive for long on internal financing alone. Growing companies need more money to acquire additional assets and to pay for the increasing wages, supplies, merchandise, normal operating expenses, and credit extended to customers that company growth brings. Financing is also important because it is not prudent to place all your personal resources into a business.

Your effort to get outside financing will give you a sobering glimpse of reality. Lenders can be brutally negative about the prospects of survival for new ventures. Because you are asking them to share your risks, they will force you to prove that you have a chance to succeed. You have to prepare marketing and financial projections, and pro forma financial statements are required. Not only must you produce evidence that the products or services you will offer can be sold and provide information about where and to whom they will be sold, but you will also have to describe existing competition and estimate the costs of your undertaking in the form of *capital, fixed,* and *variable* expenses.

Checklists which can assist in drawing up the statements follow.

Capital Expense Checklist

Capital expenses include:

- Land, building, machinery, office equipment, delivery and material-handling equipment, display signs and fixtures

- Professional fees incurred in organizing the business and purchasing facilities such as legal fees, real estate commissions, architects' fees, building permits, and zoning changes

- Physical improvements such as parking lots, landscaping, paving, sewer connections; payments for right-of-way or access routes; remodeling or redecorating, including process piping and duct work; plumbing and heating; and air-conditioning systems

- Cost of patents or copyrights necessary to the business

- Promotion or advertising costs related to the start-up of operations

- Security systems such as burglar alarms, antitheft devices, sprinkler systems, safes, strong boxes, and window gratings

- Rent for premises and for leased machinery and equipment

- Lease of rights for patents, copyrights, rights-of-way, or other rights that must be obtained in order to conduct business

- Insurance: comprehensive business interruption, fire, liability, crime, theft, casualty, disaster, worker's compensation, malpractice, extended coverages for vandalism and malicious mischief, flood, marine, etc.

- Yearly registration fees and certain taxes that are fixed annually such as local property taxes, state automobile license and registration, state certification, professional accreditation, federal highway use tax, etc.

- Retainer fees paid to accountants, lawyers, collection agencies, and credit services

- Contractual fees for garbage collection, snow removal, landscaping, building maintenance, security protection, exterminators, and heating contractors

- Regular membership dues paid to professional associations, chamber of commerce, Rotary Club, and business-related fraternal organizations

- Salary costs for positions that must exist independent of sales levels—in all companies these will include the manager of the business; in some companies these may include research and development staff, personnel departments, secretaries, bookkeepers, and production supervisors

Variable Expense Checklist

These costs include:

- Production-related salaries (including overtime pay)
- Commissions paid to sales personnel
- Federal and state payroll and unemployment taxes
- Contributions to employee health and medical plans, company profit sharing, and other welfare programs
- Rental of extra equipment to service peak production demands
- Customer services such as warranties, repair, and complaints
- Raw materials and supplies necessary for production
- Advertising
- Telephone, postage, and office supplies
- Heat, utilities, etc.
- Repairs
- Uniforms, work clothes, safety shoes, and equipment provided by employer
- Travel and entertainment that are business related
- Compliance with federal, state, and municipal regulatory agencies such as the Environmental Protection Agency, including disposal of industrial wastes and other special handling of materials

One can usually estimate expenses with some precision given a set of assumptions. But it is far more difficult to project income over a period of time unless you can rely upon commitments from reliable sources. The harsh reality is that many businesses open and then close because they are not capable of developing and retaining sufficient sales volume to meet expenses, much less return a profit. Although it is difficult to reliably project income, particularly for a new business, you must, nevertheless, make the effort employing your own and the experience of others. If you are unable to project income with recognizable plausibility, you are risking ultimate business failure.

One of the advantages of buying a going concern is that your income projection can be based upon the past experience of the business. However, do not take the figures at face value. You should check their accuracy to determine whether there were any unusual circumstances during the period they were compiled, such as a price reduction to liquidate excess inventory. You should also determine whether a change of ownership will adversely affect customer relationships, thereby affecting the forecast.

Even when you are experienced in business and optimistic about the firm's prospects, you should make an in-depth appraisal and have another qualified person check your projections of business prospects. In some cases, you can make your own survey, or you can hire a market research firm to perform studies to determine your business's customer base and potential sales.

Your projections should encompass the time it will take you to develop sufficient volume to make a profit. During the initial months, while you are attempting to build a customer base, there will be little or no cash flow generated. The longer it takes for you and your product to be recognized, the greater the chance your business will fail. Eventually, the cost of keeping the business running may overwhelm your ability to finance it. You must be frank in your assessment of the prospects for generating sales and the inherent expenses that will be incurred even with diligent control over cash outgo.

Statistics show that most new businesses lose money during the first year of operation and even through the second year. You must recognize these facts in determining the amount of capital required to finance your business.

Facing Temporary Losses

When projecting the extent of possible losses, you may not be out of pocket by as much as you estimate. Do not overlook the fact that the federal government shares in your risk. Should your business have losses, especially in the early start-up years, you may be able to write them off against other income. If it were not for the tax write-offs, you would have to shoulder the entire loss. By permitting the write-offs, the government shares your loss by forgoing part of the tax otherwise due on your other income. In states which impose income taxes your risk is further reduced to the extent of state tax reductions.

If you have large losses and insufficient income from other sources to absorb them, the excess loss will not go unused. Excess losses may be used to obtain a tax refund from prior years or to reduce taxes in certain future years. These excess losses, called net operating losses, help to minimize your risk.

The ability to reduce your risk by writing off losses is not restricted so long as you "materially participate" in the business. But if you do *not* materially participate, your "passive loss" can only offset "passive income" from other business interests or rental activities.

When organizing your business, you have several choices of business form: proprietorship, partnership, Subchapter S corporation, or corporation. Your choice will affect your entire tax picture. Bear in mind that the ability to write off losses is just one factor that will influence your ultimate decision. The consequences of your choice are explained in detail in Chapter 5.

Source of Equity Capital

Equity financing involves sharing the profits and, to some extent, the control of your business with other investors. In times of tight money, however, when the cost of bank loans is prohibitive if available at all, equity capital may be your primary means of raising the funds to begin your operation.

Relatives, friends, employees, or people you have contacted through advertisements or brokers may want to invest in your business. Your accountant or lawyer, seeing that you have a potentially profitable venture, may also contact possible investors.

The key to obtaining outside capital is convincing potential investors that you have the ability to run a successful business and that your projected venture has a good chance to succeed. Investors may not necessarily want a current return of income, but they will want to be assured that, within a period of time, their capital will have appreciated.

If you do have offers of capital from outsiders, consider their personalities and business reputations. They may prove to be incompatible business associates. Some may demand a voice in the business and its management, others may fight for greater control, and some may be dishonest. If you have to take in associates, make sure you keep the majority equity interest in your business.

Short-term venture capital may be available from companies whose sole business is taking a gamble on a new business with the expectation of a sizable profit. Venture capital is advanced for a short term, usually 5 years, at which time refinancing is necessary to retire the venture capital company's interest. Sources of venture capital (other than small business investment companies) are usually known to bankers, lawyers, and accountants. The U.S. Small Business Administration issues a pamphlet, *A Venture Capital Primer for Small Business,* which may be of assistance to you in securing capital from a venture capital company.

Seeking Financial Advice and Funds through the Small Business Administration

The Small Business Administration (SBA), an independent federal government agency with field offices across the country, seeks to help small business owners by giving advice and guaranteeing business loans. Although you may not want or be eligible for SBA support, you can take advantage of their financial counseling services by writing or visiting a field office. The SBA tries to give special assistance to minority businesses, and its offices will have information on aid programs which are current at the time of application. The SBA does not charge for advice.

Not all businesses are eligible for SBA aid. Newspaper, radio and TV stations, and liquor stores are not. You cannot obtain SBA funds to pay off inadequately secured creditors; to provide payments or distributions to owners, partners, or shareholders; or to replenish working-capital funds which you have already used to make such payments.

The largest proportion of SBA aid is in the form of guaranteed loans. Before you can qualify for such assistance you must show that you cannot obtain other financing. If your request is approved, you can borrow up to $750,000 from a bank and the SBA may guarantee up to 85 percent of the loan. Guaranteed loan applications are processed faster if your bank has been certified by the SBA. Some other financial institutions, including certain stockbrokers, have been given permission to make SBA-guaranteed loans.

In addition to general business loan guarantees, the SBA provides specialized loan guarantee programs, including export revolving lines of credit, international trade loans, seasonal lines of credit, small general contractor financing, lender incentives for small loans of less than $50,000, loans for Vietnam veterans and disabled veterans, handicapped assistance loans, pollution control loans, and community economic development loans.

Businesses involved in the creation or distribution of ideas or opinions, such as newspapers, magazines, and academic schools are not eligible to receive SBA loans. Other types of ineligible borrowers include businesses engaged in speculation or investment in rental real estate.

A number of organizations offer aid to minority business owners:

Minority Business Enterprise Legal Defense and Education Fund, 220 I Street N.E., Suite 280, Washington, DC 20002; (202) 543-0040. The organization provides information and legal assistance for minority-owned businesses.

National Association of Minority Contractors, 1333 F Street N.W., Suite 500, Washington, DC 20004; (202) 347-8259. Identifies procurement opportunities, offers education and training, publishes bulletin on legislation of interest to minority contractors.

National Minority Business Council (NMBC), 235 (205 for in-person visits) East 42d Street, New York, NY 10017; (212) 573-2385. Provides data on procurement opportunities for minority-owned firms, offers training and education.

Even if you qualify for an SBA loan, be aware that funds may be delayed by—or strangled in—red tape. For this reason, you may decide not to ask for SBA help. However, the SBA, aware of this common criticism, has recently taken steps to speed up its loan application process. For example, it has increased its pool of lenders, reduced the documentary paperwork required to process loan applications, and called for advance meetings with lenders before the loan application begins. In addition, the SBA is also likely to be the source of assistance should your business suffer damage in a disaster, such as a flood or hurricane.

Financial Aid from Small Business Investment Companies

Under the Small Business Investment Act, small business investment companies (SBICs) are licensed by the SBA to supply equity capital to companies unable to raise funds from other sources. The SBICs are chartered under state law; they are privately owned and operated for profit. Under the SBA guidelines defined by federal law, SBICs usually will take greater risks than banks. Negotiations between an entrepreneur and an SBIC are private business arrangements and are not supervised by the SBA.

If you are a sole proprietor or in partnership, with no intention of incorporating, SBIC financing is available in the form of long-term loans (over 5 years), secured by real estate or other collateral. If you are incorporated, you may seek long-term loans or equity financing. Equity financing may come through purchase of stock in your company, through loans with stock-purchase warrants attached, or through convertible debentures. The SBIC supplying equity capital may demand board representation and a voice in your business. For that reason some small businesses refrain from seeking SBIC financing. But, given a mutually satisfactory arrangement, the SBIC can be a source of valuable business counsel.

Your choice of SBIC will be determined by the type of financing you are seeking. If you want equity financing, be prepared to show your company's history, current status, and projections for the future. Your financial statements should be comprehensive. Be ready to describe how the equity financing (or term loan) would relate to your financial projections. SBICs are profit-motivated, and you have to convince the SBIC representatives of your company's growth and profit potential.

You may have to apply to several SBICs before you find one prepared to take a risk with you.

Finally, some SBICs are bank-related. Inquire whether your bank has such a connection. You may obtain backing more readily from a company that can check on your financial status and prospects through data at the bank than from one that cannot.

Borrowing from a Bank

A bank makes money by lending money and will generally lend you funds if your business reputation is good and your business venture is profitable. It will seldom lend money on prospects alone.

Banks are conservative lenders as far as new enterprises are concerned. However, in certain circumstances, your project might merit a bank's consideration. The bank will spell out the conditions of lending. Although a bank loan may not currently be available, the loan officer may be favorably impressed with you and your project and may suggest other sources of capital or be willing to extend aid at a later stage in your business's development.

From the start, set up a good working relationship with your bank. Personal contact with the manager, officers, and staff will be helpful. You want to earn the bank's confidence in your business so that you can establish and increase a line of credit. Look ahead to the time when you will be expanding your business. Your banker should be kept abreast of your plans and financial developments.

Bankers generally prefer to limit their loans (especially in hard economic times) to businesses that are not pressed for funds to meet current obligations. They prefer to make loans to a problem-free business which needs funds to expand operations to a new city or to develop a new product. The bank will readily consider such a loan because, if the new venture fails, the company continues to operate its regular line and has the resources to pay off the loan.

A bank loan will not be forthcoming if the bank suspects that the money is needed to pay off your debts to other creditors. The bank does not want to pay off other creditors and be left as the only remaining risk taker. A bank wants its funds put to a constructive use.

Preparing for Borrowing

Regardless of the source you will seek to borrow from, prepare your application well. When applying for your loan, you will have to provide business and personal credit data for yourself and any partners or other associates or stockholders. The application form may require information about life insurance, business and civic organizations in which you are involved, the organization of your business (corporation, partnership, or single proprietorship), indebtedness to other banks or lending institutions, outstanding contingent debts, and, most important, the purpose of the loan and how you plan to repay it. For example, is the loan needed to finance the purchase of merchandise which can be sold before the loan is due? How did you arrive at the amount of the loan requested? Is it the minimum amount necessary for the intended purpose?

The loan officer will discuss your prospects. You should be ready to:

- Give a brief account of the future of your business. Discuss such questions as the probable demand for your product or service and the competition likely to be encountered.

- Demonstrate your ability to obtain raw materials or supplies of merchandise in the future and what the costs will be.

- Show what you think future price levels will mean to the value of your present inventories.

- Provide a balance sheet, listing your business assets and liabilities, and a summarized statement of prior sales, costs of doing business, and net profit before income taxes. At least 1 previous year must be shown for established businesses. Several years' data are even more desirable. Your figures should include the amount you and your partners are drawing from the business, and how much has been paid and put in dividends in recent years.

If you are starting a new business, you will not be able to furnish much of the foregoing information. What, then, should you present?

- Present a detailed business plan to show how you will use the financing to operate your business.

- Prove that you have a reputation for paying your obligations when due.

- Show that you have had adequate business experience in this or a similar area.

- Show that you have sufficient financing of your own to warrant a lender's taking a reasonable risk by advancing part of your financial needs.

- Show, if possible, that you have unfilled orders on hand or business prospects which are likely to produce sufficient income to repay the loan.

Informal Venture Capital

Another source of venture capital is the private sector. Private investors fund more ventures each year than all the venture capital firms organized for that purpose—an estimated 20,000 companies annually. The reason is that if you need less than $500,000 or cannot project sales of $20 million or more in the first decade in a business venture, capital firms are not likely to be interested in you, but private investors may be.

Types of Business Loans

1. *Character loans.*   This term is used for short-term, unsecured loans made without collateral. Only a company or an entrepreneur with the highest credit standing, business integrity, and ability to manage a company is likely to be eligible.

2. *Line of credit.*   A banker extending a line of credit makes an advance commitment to lend money up to a certain maximum and on specific conditions. A credit investigation will precede the arrangement; then, when loans are called for, they are usually granted on a revolving basis so that not more than one may be outstanding at any time. Approved customers usually find the arrangement highly adaptable to their financial needs, especially when those needs are seasonal in nature. When short-term bank notes are due, the customer may protect the line of credit by borrowing elsewhere to meet the obligation. If an annual clearance of debt is part of the arrangement, the business will ensure a buildup of funds by refraining from other outlays until that line of credit is cleared up.

3. *Term loans.*   Short-term loans cover periods of less than a year, perhaps only 30 to 60 days; and long-term loans run over 5 years, sometimes for as long as 10 or 15 years. Collateral as well as a high standard of credit may be necessary to secure a term loan. A bank will review the current financial position of a business, and it may require an equal ratio of equity capital to debt. It may require payments each month, each quarter, every 6 months, or annually. A series of notes due at specified times may be the method of payment.

4. *Collateral loans.*   Inventory may be accepted as collateral for short-term loans. Longer-term loans may be secured by chattel or real estate mortgages, by stocks and bonds, or by life insurance. Since forced sale of collateral may not repay the lender in case of default, the demand for a good credit background and for sound prospects in the business will also be required.

5. *Cosigner loans.*   If a cosigner or comaker joins with the borrower on a loan, that person is equally obligated to see that the loan is repaid. A cosigner with good credit standing at a bank carries some weight when a loan is authorized.

6. *Warehouse and field warehouse loans.*   A bank or commercial finance company may lend funds to a small business on the basis of a warehouse receipt delivered directly by the lender. The staple or standard merchandise of a readily salable type is placed either in a public warehouse or in the proprietor's own warehouse where a warehousing company takes over responsibility and places a bonded employee in control. There are variations in field warehousing, some of which involve interbusiness financing. The basis of this type of loan is that the bank or other lender has security and legal possession of the merchandise while the loan is in effect. Use this method of financing when you want to take advantage of favorable buying conditions or when you anticipate a seasonal drop in business. It enables you to obtain more working capital if cash is short at a time when production and operating costs are high.

7. *Equipment loans.*   Equipment may serve as collateral for a loan, or the cost of new equipment may be financed through installment purchases.

8. *Accounts receivable financing.*   Commercial credit or finance companies accept accounts receivable as security for loans; so do some banks. With this type of financing, you remain responsible for the repayment of the loan when the proceeds of the accounts receivable do not cover the advance. In factoring, the factor purchases accounts receivable at a discount for cash. Unless other arrangements are made, the factor assumes all collection responsibilities.

There are two plans used by finance companies, banks, factors, and other lenders that deal in accounts receivable financing. Under the notification plan, customers are asked to pay the lender directly. But many businesses prefer not to reveal to their customers that they are financing through accounts receivable. Unless state law requires that the notification plan be used, they therefore use the nonnotification plan, accepting payments as usual and channeling them to the lender.

Trade Credit

A business short of working capital may find it financially expedient to delay payments to suppliers—in effect, taking short-term loans through trade credit. However, to encourage you to pay within 10 days, suppliers will usually give you a small cash discount which you may deduct from your bill if you pay within 10 days. It may be advisable to take advantage of the discounts rather than delay payment. For example, if you order merchandise and the invoice reads "2/10, n/30," a 2 percent discount may be deducted from the bill if you pay in 10 days. If you delay payment until the end of the 30-day period, you are incurring an "interest" charge by not taking the discount. This interest charge is 36 percent, calculated as follows: Each credit period is 20 days. During the year, there are eighteen 20-day periods during which a 2 percent discount is not taken. Two percent multiplied by 18 equals 36 percent a year.

Some newcomers to small business eagerly seize on trade credit to acquire fixed assets, a mistaken course which may compound financial troubles. If the credit is used, it should be to generate more business, to satisfy customers, and to build up a cash flow so that you can pay bills within the discount period.

3

Buying an Existing Business

Buying an established business is a quick and direct way to get into business. In doing so, you may avoid some of the hazards of having to start up a new business. On the other hand, if you don't thoroughly investigate the business, you may end up having bought somebody else's troubles. How much investigating you will need to do depends on the size and nature of the enterprise.

Find out, if you can, why the present owner is selling. It may be because of age, failing health, or other reasons independent of economic results. But, if the owner is eager to unload the business because it's failing (which is not always revealed by financial statements), you do not want to be left holding the bag for the mistakes of the previous owner.

If the business is failing, investigate the effect that poor management has had. If you can correct past management mistakes, you may have an opportunity to buy the business at a bargain price. For example, if the owner's poor choice of equipment, unwise inventory purchases, or unattractive floor layout seems to be the cause of failure, the situation may be correctable. Investigate the reputation of the business among former and present customers. If the previous owner's practices drove off customers, you may be able to change them and thus attract former customers. Recognize, however, that turning a business around takes time. People are slow to forgive poor service, merchandise, or treatment. It usually takes a long time before people will look again in the direction of a business they have proscribed. Extra publicity steps can help make people aware that the business has changed hands or changed methods.

Evaluating the Product or Service

Determine if the business has a broad or narrow foundation. A business with a narrow product or service base may be riding the crest of a trend which will come to a sudden stop. Find out from the industry associations if the product or service is special; if so, learn how long it has existed, whether it is currently in or out of favor, if it is driven by fashion or style, or whether certain conditions must exist in order for the business to maintain or gain momentum and what they may be.

All products or services have life cycles. Find out what cheaper, better, or newer alternatives may exist or have been recently announced which could threaten the business. If the product is produced with specialized skills and equipment, it may require a whole new set of capabilities to compete in the marketplace. Determine what you could get for the machinery and inventory if you had to sell it.

If the business offers diverse products or services, understand why the company considers it necessary to offer the particular product mix. Analyze the contribution to profit and cost for each business segment and the degree of managerial attention required.

In a brand and product business, determine the effect of overseas business, the age and sophistication of equipment and personnel, the attractiveness of the package, the acceptance in the marketplace, the sensitivity to price, and the way it is perceived by customers.

In a service business, determine the effect of automation, the age and sophistication of equipment and personnel, the acceptance in the marketplace, the sensitivity to price, and the way this business is perceived by customers. In instances when you cannot determine the value of the inventory (for example, a bottle of wine), try to accept the inventory on a consignment basis or arrange a contingency agreement where you pay a small part of the inventory's value at the time of purchase of the business and the balance when the inventory has been sold.

Evaluating the Business

Determine exactly what you are buying. Purchasing a business is much more complicated than buying a single piece of investment property, such as a building. Many different assets are involved—equipment, trucks, machinery, facilities, inventories—and their physical condition will have to be examined and their value to the business determined. Agreements with employees and customers must be reviewed, and the existence of liens and other liabilities must be researched. You will need the assistance of an attorney and an accountant.

A lawyer will check (1) the chain of legal title, leases on machinery, patent arrangements; (2) registration of patents, trademarks, formulas, copyrights, franchises, and their transferability; (3) the existence of any encumbrances on the property, such as mortgages, liens, or chattel mortgages against machinery and fixtures; (4) restrictions, either in zoning or on ownership, and any rental or building regulations; and (5) unfulfilled contract commitments.

An accountant will ascertain receivables and liabilities and will check whether the company endorsed or guaranteed any obligations of others, including negotiable instruments sold or discounted; whether there are any disputed assessments or possible tax liabilities; and whether there are cumulative dividends in arrears. The accountant will review records going back at least 3 years, preferably 10. If the company is a relatively new one, the accountant should familiarize you with its entire record.

Your accountant will determine the gross profit margin of the company and will calculate whether it is high enough to give you a comfortable profit. You want to know the growth rate of the company over the past 5 years and whether there are any factors which indicate that the rate will not continue.

A valuable source of information will be the firm's federal income tax return, which the owner should show you. You can be fairly sure that the receipts are not overstated, although expenses may have been exaggerated and the inventory may have been adjusted for tax purposes. Sales tax records can be used to double-check the receipts. Property taxes can be checked with the county treasurer. Insurance expenses can be verified with the company's insurance agent. Production costs can be reviewed by examining freight costs, vendors' invoices, records of merchandise payments, bills of lading, and inventory records. Payroll and Social Security records can be used to determine salary costs. At the same time, consult union officials to find out when the labor contracts expire; there may be future wage increases on the horizon with the possibility of prolonged wrangling over other pay benefits. Salespersons' reports will give a good indication of the size of the clientele and the volume from the geographic sales area. Sometimes the company's suppliers or bankers will help you estimate the amount of the company's business.

Find out how the inventory is appraised. Is it valued at the price of the oldest item bought awaiting sale, or is the inventory valued at the price of the most recent item purchased? Both methods are acceptable, and each gives a different value depending on price fluctuations. Examine the inventory; there may be items in the storeroom which cannot be sold or that have no value to you.

Also have these points checked out to avoid unexpected future costs and liabilities:

- Are invoices discounted? Old customers will expect you to continue this policy, which may affect your cash flow.
- Are there unfulfilled contracts? Check what projects are ongoing against what receipts are due for them. Are there penalties for late completion?
- Has the company guaranteed the obligations of others (like being the cosigner on a loan) which may produce unexpected debts later?
- Will key personnel leave if the owner leaves?
- Consider labor relations and employee morale. Find out what benefits will continue after you buy the business, such as holidays, paid vacations, sick days, and health insurance.
- Are there any pending damage claims, lawsuits, disputed assessments, or possible tax liabilities?
- Are there pending matters before government agencies, such as a suit for equal opportunity claims or over minority hiring practices?
- Are there any problems with government regulations or the Underwriters' Laboratory concerning the design of the product?
- Are there any new environmental standards that will affect the way the company does business?
- Are any changes needed to comply with building, health, or sanitation codes?

Setting Your Price

The seller will offer you the business for a price and give you an opportunity to examine records and check up on promises. The seller is, of course, trying to get the most from the business. The price will be based on the fair market value of the assets of the business plus an amount set for the value of its capacity to provide profits. The excess value is usually viewed as goodwill. You must accurately determine the value of the assets and the expected yearly profit. Once you have determined these factors, you can determine a fair price to offer for the business. After your review, you may agree with the seller and still try to pay less through negotiations, or you may disagree with the values set and the seller's claim of sales, production costs, profit margin, and goodwill.

Set your price for the business from your financial perspective, by considering your earning power as compared with that offered by the business:

1. Start with the investment required to buy the business.

2. Figure how much this amount would earn if invested elsewhere.

3. Take the figure on line 2 and add the amount of your current salary that you would be giving up to run the business. This is your total earning power.

4. Compare the projected business profit claimed by the seller with your total earning power.

5. The excess is the earning power of the business.

6. Multiply the excess earning power by 5 for a well-established business or by 3, if you have any concern about the stability of the business, and add the result to the value of the assets of the business. For example, a business with assets of $200,000 earns $80,000 a year. If you invest $200,000 in bonds at 7 percent, you would get a return of $14,000. You are now earning a salary of $40,000. Your total earning power is $54,000 ($40,000 salary *plus* $14,000 return on bonds). Therefore, the excess annual earning power of the business is $26,000 ($80,000 − $54,000). Five times that figure is $130,000. According to the formula, a fair price for the business might be $330,000 ($200,000 + $130,000). If you used 3 years as your measuring rod, the price would be $278,000 ($200,000 + $78,000).

Another method bases price on the capitalized value of future earnings. The rate used coincides with rate of return realized on investments involving a similar amount of risk. To find the capitalized value, divide annual profit by the expected rate of return. Assume, for example, that the estimated profits over the next 5 years will average $40,000 per annum, as they would in the foregoing example ($80,000 minus salary of $40,000). If the business is considered as safe as an investment in corporate securities earning 7 percent, an offering price would be $571,428 ($40,000 divided by 0.07). However, the risk factor in a small business is considerably higher than the risk in a stock market investment, so a rate of 20 to 25 percent might be applied. A rate of 20 percent gives a purchase price of $200,000. Of course, a low offer might not be realistic. Yet, if the proprietor is eager enough to sell, he or she may agree to it and you would be able to recover your investment in about 5 years. In any event, this figure provides you with a starting point in your bargaining. Another formula uses the value of inventory at cost plus profits of 1 year.

Whatever formula you use to set a price, there is bound to be a gap between the asking price and your bid price at the onset of negotiations. The amount you offer for the business is one thing, the actual sales price of the business is determined after negotiations between the seller and you, or the agents who represent you. How badly does the owner want to sell? How badly do you want to buy? What are other businesses going for? Are there other prospective buyers for the business? What are the possibilities of expanding the existing operation?

In arranging payment terms, it is not unusual for a seller to accept one-third down, the balance payable over a 5- to 7-year period. You should also negotiate warranty protection against false statements by the seller, a covenant preventing the seller from competing with you, and a provision giving you protection from the time the contract is signed until the actual settlement takes place. This prevents a dishonest seller from depleting assets or inventory with a "going out of business" sale or destroying goodwill that you had agreed to pay for. You should have full access to the premises and records. You may even require a good faith deposit in escrow for 6 months or longer to back up the warranty.

Getting Your Best Tax Advantages

Tax planning should begin before any purchase is completed to determine how the purchase agreement will affect future tax liabilities. The liabilities will vary between the purchase of an incorporated or an unincorporated business.

Even though you buy the business as a whole (you can buy only the assets of a business, its specific assets, its name, etc.), for tax purposes the purchase of an unincorporated business is viewed as a purchase of individual assets. The total purchase price must be allocated over the various assets. You generally get your greatest tax advantage by negotiating with the seller to allocate the purchase price to those assets that give you the greatest tax deductions during operations and the largest capital gain on disposal. Be aware that the allocation process is not as straightforward as it may appear, because the seller may prefer a different allocation. Negotiate the allocation vigorously with the help of your attorney or accountant.

Value the following at a *high* price:

- *Merchandise inventory.*   A high cost reduces taxable profit.
- *Supplies and similar items not used in the manufacture of your product.* These supplies are fully deductible as expenses.
- *Accounts receivable.*   If some go bad, the loss is fully deductible.
- *Patents, copyrights, franchises, and amortizable intangibles.*   If the remaining life is short.
- *Machinery, equipment, and buildings.*   The cost of these assets is recovered under the accelerated cost recovery system over periods and at rates fixed by law.
- *Covenant of seller not to compete.*   This is discussed more fully below.

The following should be valued at a *low* price:

- *Land.*   You get no depreciation deduction to recover cost.
- *Stocks, bonds, and securities.*   You get no annual depreciation.
- *Goodwill.*   You generally get no annual deduction for depreciation and must wait to recover your expenditure until the business is eventually sold. The IRS and courts typically disallow annual deductions on the grounds that goodwill has no measurable life. However, the deduction rules could change. When this book went to press, Congress was considering legislation that would allow an annual write-off over a 14-year period for goodwill and certain other acquired intangibles (the 14-year period could be changed in the course of Congressional deliberations). Even if this legislation is not enacted, the Supreme Court made an important breakthrough in a 1993 decision which held that client or customer lists can be depreciated under the current law if it can be proved that they have specific values and limited useful lives. Although the Court held that a deduction should be allowed as long as the value of the items and their useful lives can be shown, it emphasized that a taxpayer has a difficult burden of proving value and useful life.

The tax law provides a specific method of allocating the purchase price among the transferred assets; goodwill is taken into account last. Both the buyer and seller must use the allocation method, which is shown on IRS Form 8594.

Covenants Not to Compete

A business purchase usually includes agreements not to compete for a specific time or in a specified area or both, but the buyer will seek to characterize the "noncompete" agreement in one way, and the seller in another, because of the different tax consequences attached to each characterization.

As the buyer, you should seek deductions for your payments to restrain the seller from competing. The seller will usually resist your demands because, under the tax law, if you deduct the payments, he or she must report the payments as ordinary income. The seller will try to avoid this. To get the deduction, you may have to do some hard bargaining and possibly allow for an adjustment of the price.

To get a deduction for the covenant, the sales contract must include the covenant and allocate a specific amount to it. Further, the contract should state that the agreement not to compete is not part of the transfer of goodwill. Retain other evidence to corroborate the agreement. Show that it has an independent value and that its chief function is not to assure the beneficial use of goodwill. The rules for covenants not to compete could be changed by Congressional legislation. When this book went to press, Congress was considering legislation that would provide a fixed write-off period of 14 years for amounts paid under a covenant not to compete.

Purchasing a Corporation

When you are interested in acquiring an incorporated business, you have two choices. You can buy the stock of the corporation and thereby acquire control of its assets, or you can buy the assets themselves, either directly from the corporation or from the shareholders, if the corporation is liquidated and its assets distributed in the liquidation process.

As a buyer, you would generally prefer to acquire the assets of the corporation, rather than its stock. By buying stock, you may inadvertently acquire hidden or contingent corporate liabilities, such as unpaid withholding taxes. While you can protect yourself from such liabilities by guarantees or by placing part of the purchase price in escrow to cover potential problems, these protections may be costly and may be unacceptable to the seller. Also, you may not want or need all the assets and might prefer a selective purchase. On the other hand, you may want the corporation as it is because it has rights or contracts that may not be transferred. Your desires, however, may run counter to those of the seller. The seller typically prefers a stock sale; it is a clean one-step transaction subject to capital gains treatment and avoids tax problems of a corporate liquidation. Stockholders may no longer take advantage of tax-free liquidation rules.

Purchase of Assets

When you buy the assets, the price you pay becomes the basis for those assets. If you assume liabilities when you buy the assets or if the assets are subject to liabilities, the liabilities also become part of your basis. The basis is the figure upon which depreciation will be figured and against which gain or loss on a future sale will be measured. When you acquire assets, your attorney will, of course, check for any preexisting liens or mortgages on the property.

When you have acquired the assets, you may then choose to incorporate or not. The corporation from which you acquired the assets is completely independent of your business.

Purchase of Corporate Stock

When you buy the stock of a corporation, the corporation remains intact and you step into the shoes of the former owners. Your stock basis is the amount you paid for it. This amount should reflect the present value of the corporation's assets. The corporation's basis for its assets does not change as a result of your acquisition. Several assets may have appreciated, but depreciation deductions are still figured on the old basis. As a buyer, you are forsaking important deductions unless you liquidate the corporation as discussed below. Also, you face the possibility of contingent or undisclosed liabilities.

Stepping up the Basis of Assets Following a Stock Purchase. If the basis of corporate assets differs from the market value, you may step up the basis of the assets by acquiring the stock and liquidating the corporation. This will provide you with larger tax deductions for depreciation, an operating cost. Normally, when a corporation is liquidated, the stockholders pay tax on any gain (the difference between the value of the property received on the liquidation and their stock basis). But when you buy stock and immediately liquidate the corporation, little or no gain results; your stock basis approximates the value of the assets. However, a liquidating corporation is subject to tax on the distribution or sale of appreciated property.

Buying a Company with Its Own Funds or Earnings. Sometimes a business can be purchased in part with its own funds or future earnings. This may be possible where a corporation holds substantial cash which can be used to redeem part of the seller's stock from the company. You buy from the seller only a portion of stock. The corporation redeems the balance of the stock from the seller with the cash it has. As you have the remaining stock, the only outstanding stock, you are in full control of the purchased corporation. In planning such a transaction, both you and the seller must arrange the steps of the transaction to avoid an IRS challenge that dividend income has been earned.

Checklist for Closing Title

Your attorney and accountant should cover and acquaint you with these facts:

- The total contract price and assets you are receiving on closing date
- Steps you must take to comply with state or city bulk-sales acts on the purchase of merchandise, stock-in-trade, and fixtures
- How you or the seller is to satisfy any chattel mortgages, liens, and conditional bills of sale
- Adjustments for all payments of real estate taxes or water taxes; payments to mortgages; payments for utility services, such as electricity, gas, and telephone; and insurance payments
- How the sale affects employees' pension or profit-sharing plans
- How accounts receivable are being transferred—you may wish to acquire these accounts to continue doing business with the customers
- Adjustments for uncompleted contracts with unions and sales or service agencies which must be notified (for example, the IRS, Social Security Administration, state unemployment insurance agencies)

Your attorney must see that all legal documents (titles, leases, mortgages, etc.) show the change of ownership. You should see that insurance policies are converted to provide for proper coverage under your new ownership. Finally, you must notify customers, suppliers, and employees of the change in ownership.

4

Deciding on the Location of Your Business

Location is important to all firms; it is the character of the location which varies. Different kinds of businesses require different kinds of locations. For the typical retail store it is vital that it be central to the shopping patterns of its potential customers. A mail-order business, on the other hand, need only be near a post office and sources of low-cost but literate labor. A distributor needs to be in a low rental area with the shortest cumulative travel time to the customers.

The appropriate location for a manufacturing plant will vary with its nature; with whether it serves a regional, national, or international market; and with the costs of delivering its product. For example, a concrete block plant must be at the center of a large population of block users (blocks cannot profitably be shipped long distances and are not universally employed in construction businesses across the country), on very cheap land (since it must have ample room for storing its ungainly output), and with access to cheap labor. On the other hand a manufacturing plant serving a national market should be located in accordance with the economics of its products and the logistics of its marketing. For example, if it is a manufacturer of semiconductor chips or other high-unit-cost items, it can be located almost anywhere as long as the area has ample skilled labor and is near an airport. By contrast, a producer of chicken parts needs to be on cheap land close to chicken farms and in an area with abundant cheap labor.

Using Population Data to Determine Market Location

Sales are made to people, and the number of people in a particular area can be counted. Of that number only a percentage are potential customers. Before you decide on a location, you should estimate the number of people in the area who may be your potential customers.

You can obtain population data from the following sources: a local chamber of commerce, a town office, the Small Business Administration, the Department of Commerce, and, of course, the Bureau of the Census.

Other statistics can be found in the *Statistical Abstract of the United States*, published by the Bureau of the Census. This book contains a wealth of data, including the average hourly wage for each state, which a manufacturer may look at to locate a plant in an area with low payroll costs. Statistics for the educational level of a state's residents may also give clues to a pool of skilled labor or a market for consumer computer products.

Let us assume you have done your research in connection with your plan to start a florist shop. You have the following information:

1. Population of the community: 120,000

2. The number of stores in it similar to the type you want to open: 11 plus your store makes 12

3. The average number of people in the town per store: 10,000

4. Based on government statistics, the average national number of inhabitants needed to support the store: 9000

A comparison of the averages under points 3 and 4 tells you the margin for another florist shop is narrow. In addition, you estimate that for 5 months of the year private gardens are in bloom and business declines. You might decide to supplement the new store with a seed and garden department which would produce business in the spring and summer, or decide to consider another community where you would have about 15,000 inhabitants per store.

Determine the growth trend in the market. Assume a town has grown from 10,000 to 120,000 people in the last 2 years. New plants are going to open in the next year, bringing in workers and new residents. You might consider opening your store here if you believe your abilities are impressive enough to claim the patronage of an expanding market. Also consider population shifts. For example, will the plants increase the percentage of executives, middle managers, and professionals in the community or, quite the opposite, increase the percentage of blue-collar workers? Will the population shift you foresee aid or hinder your business prospects?

Researching the Location

Before deciding what kind of site you need, research the issue. The first thing to do after you have decided on your target customer(s) is to discover what you can about their buying patterns. Make firsthand observations at regular intervals to determine the flow and destination of pedestrian traffic. Note the proportion of men to women and their relative ages. Chart whether they fit the profile of the clientele you seek for your store: young adults for a music store, professionals for a men's shop, affluent women for a jewelry store. If pedestrians seem to be hurrying to bus stops or train stations, the chances are that the location you are considering will not attract passersby to a store which requires more leisurely shopping. On the other hand, a stationery store, newspaper stand, or convenience store might do well there. Perhaps your area contains other businesses which may draw trade during a lunch hour. Consider the entire work and leisure cycle of a neighborhood before you accept or reject it as a likely spot for your firm.

Some stores will succeed wherever they are located because their uniqueness serves to draw the customers to them; for example, a piano dealership or a furrier. Other stores actually benefit from being near the competition. Apparel stores frequently locate in the same district, offering shoppers a choice and comparisons. Together, they attract more buyers and can offer more items. The customer can usually find what is desired, so there is more overall spending. However, two nearby specialty shops, such as pet stores, will end up dividing trade to the detriment of each.

If you have to rely on customers who will come to a location by car, you must consider parking facilities. Drivers will avoid areas where parking space is not convenient or where parking may be subject to overtime fines. Sometimes, to make an area attractive to shoppers, retailers can persuade authorities to reset the time periods on nearby parking meters to better coincide with an owner's business hours. A local merchant's association can often help take steps to improve parking conditions for retail customers.

If you plan to provide parking facilities, you must have at least 200 square feet of parking lot per car. That takes into account the dimensions of the car, room to open doors, and sufficient turnaround space. A lot for 10 cars would need 2000 square feet. However, in estimating the amount of space, you must also consider the length of time customers spend in your store and the availability of other parking space in the area. Also, consider the eventual need to expand parking facilities as business improves. Sometimes adjacent stores can share the investment for customer parking.

Location of the Retail or Service Shop

Visibility may or may not be an important factor in the choice of location. Stores which attract customers through the senses need to be where they can present people with opportunities to see, hear, and/or smell the goods in the stores. Corner locations are preferable because they are passed by pedestrians coming from two different streets. A major intersection also may increase trade, especially if it is regarded as a landmark or a general meeting place. Another productive location may be close to a store that generates a lot of traffic, such as a supermarket. Customers attracted to such a store will also pass your location.

Service firms depending less on impulse buying, such as beauty parlors, travel agencies, and investment counseling firms, rely less on visibility of location and more on accessibility, decor, and interior comfort to attract customers.

Locating the Wholesale Business

In this day and age of energy efficiency, the location of the wholesale business should be determined with an eye toward minimizing transportation costs. Centrally locate your warehouse to cut costs of delivery to the most frequent customers. Easy access to major transportation arteries is an important consideration. If snow or other local weather conditions could make it difficult for you to receive and ship goods by truck, you might consider locating the warehouse near a railway line. A wholesaler of frozen foods, desiring a constant supply of electricity for freezing, should not locate in an area where power interruptions are frequent (unless the warehouse has a generator of its own).

For many urban wholesalers, delivery costs are raised by perpetual double-parking problems. Your location should have ramps or bays to ease your receiving problems. Your location may enable you to reduce shipping costs as well, if you can organize goods well enough to use smaller vehicles for better maneuverability in the streets.

Locating a Small Plant

When choosing a location for a small plant, consider the proximity to your market, availability of labor, local wage scales, and access to raw materials. Before deciding between a metropolitan, suburban, or rural location, analyze your particular needs. If you require few skilled workers, especially at the outset, and if your process relies mostly on purchased parts, you may thrive in a small town. Wages are often lower outside the metropolitan area. An operator who prefers locating in a small town will have to consider the availability of repair service for machinery and the expense of bringing in raw materials and supplies from a distance. The plant that needs to be near big labor pools, with skilled workers, specialists, and consultants, will be more likely to prosper in the large city. This is also true of any factory that needs to be near customers and suppliers, such as those concerns which also maintain a retail factory store outlet.

Many areas of the country have an abundance of manufacturing space available. Especially tempting for beginning businesses are low rentals offered on space found outmoded by a former tenant. Furthermore, an owner of such a factory building (particularly abundant in the northeast) may be willing to make improvements to suit your needs in order to gain an occupant. If a municipality owns the building, the offer may be even more generous.

Enterprise zones or industrial parks may offer attractive plant sites. Designed to be near transportation lines, water access, and sewage facilities, they may have solved many of the problems you have in choosing a site. Again, as enterprise zones or industrial parks are usually organized under a state or municipal development plan, there may be tax breaks and other incentives for locating there.

If your plant creates noise, odors, or other pollution problems, the community may be hostile to your presence. Even if zoning regulations allow a plant to make certain environmental incursions in an industrial area, near a residential area, or in a retail zone, you will never feel secure or comfortable when popular opinion opposes you. Sound out potential opposition before you move in. Local newspapers and town meetings provide forums for local approval. If your desire to see your company expand coincides with the community's growth plans, there should be few problems.

The Location of an Existing Business

Location is just as important when you are buying a business as when you are starting one from scratch. Just because the business being bought is a going concern does not mean the location problem has been solved. Location may be the very reason the business is being sold, in which case even the best business expertise may be unable to turn an unprofitable situation around. Consider the following when buying an existing business.

1. *Has the composition of the immediate neighborhood population changed so as to be adverse to the business?*   A farm nursery may be unable to function in an area where local farms are being converted to suburban developments. Northern cities may be losing population to the south, in which case there may no longer be enough people in the immediate area to buy your goods. A change in the average income of your neighborhood can spell doom for a yacht basin. As families move out and singles move in, a store that sells maternity clothes can fail. If the crime statistics for your area increase, the cost of insurance and security can make it hard for you to do business.

2. *Have the suppliers of materials important to your business moved farther away?*   Many clothing factories were once located near New England textile producers. Once the textile concerns moved nearer southern cotton fields, the clothing makers could no longer make a profit. A snack shop will fail if the factory that provided lunchtime customers goes out of business.

3. *Have transportation arteries passed the business by?*   A new interstate highway means that a formerly viable roadside cafe is now on a secondary road. New mass transit facilities encourage customers to make an easy trip to the city instead of finding their bargains locally.

Locating in a Shopping Center

Malls and shopping centers radically changed shopping habits, draining business from the old, established districts in the center of towns and cities. In fact, at least 40 percent of the nation's retail transactions take place in shopping centers.

Before you sign a lease, investigate the center carefully. What competition would you face from similar businesses within the center? Has the center fulfilled the promoters' stated expectations? Check for yourself on its potential in relation to competition, traffic patterns, and the big-name stores scheduled to open on the site.

Can you afford occupancy in a shopping mall? Developers extract the highest rents they can get, and the small shop is usually the victim.

Although a full-line department store may be able to drive a bargain because it is the main tenant, small stores have less leeway in negotiating rents.

Suburban homeowners, the country's biggest spenders, do gravitate to the shopping centers. Attractions at many centers gain shoppers' interest. Some feature video arcades, rides, art shows, modern bazaars, fashion shows, or sports car rallies. Consider what value such gimmicks might have for your type of business. Music shops, ice-cream franchises, and moderately priced fashion boutiques often thrive in lively surroundings. But if you are running a conservative gift shop or a women's half-size dress store, a carnival atmosphere is not likely to enhance your business. Also, if your business is highly prone to pilferage, losses are likely to be greater in a shopping center.

Shopping centers can be classified under three headings: neighborhood, community, and regional. The neighborhood center, perhaps a few minutes' drive from a specific residential area, will feature a chain supermarket and shops selling drugs and sundries. Ideally, it will also offer such personal services as laundry, dry cleaning, and shoe repair. Ample parking space is available on the premises. If space is available and consumer interest is high, you might find the neighborhood center a good location for your small hardware or meat store or delicatessen.

A community center is likely to be dominated by a branch department or discount store. It may serve a population of 40,000 to 150,000 people. In the regional center, one or more full-line department stores exert the major drawing power. The trading area may extend outward as far as 10 to 15 miles in all directions. The most ambitious of these centers are climate-controlled, enclosed malls with fountains, gardens, and supervised play areas to lure customers. Several department stores usually exert a cumulative attraction and powerful traffic pull. Many malls include theaters, restaurants, bowling alleys, game rooms, and all the facilities possible to encourage a family not to leave the shopping area.

Leasing in a Proposed Shopping Mall

Use caution in signing a lease for space in a shopping mall that has not yet been constructed. Such agreements usually work to the advantage of the contractor, not the store owner. If the contractor should decide that the shopping mall venture is not attractive after all, he or she can usually default on the agreement without penalty. The courts seldom compel the contractor to proceed.

If you do lease before the premises are constructed, be sure the agreement states the dimension of your area, its exact location in the mall, its position in relation to other firms, and all its specifications.

Be aware of the various interpretations that can be given your "finished" facilities. Try to avoid the shell specification which requires the developer to supply you only with four walls, a roof, and a dirt floor. You will have to furnish all the internal construction on this bare cavern—a considerable contracting job. A half-shell will provide you with certain other items: front and rear doors, gypsum wallboard, concrete floors, and perhaps a toilet and heat. Ideally, you should arrange for key specifications. With this plan, the developer supplies the tenant with complete facilities ready for the addition of fixtures and decor.

What other types of retail stores will be included in the center? The designation *retail* can include insurance offices, service stores, theaters, and bowling alleys. Be sure you know exactly which establishments plan to locate in your center and what effect they might have upon your business.

Locating in Town

If rent costs are prohibitive in the shopping centers, you may find as large a clientele in the proper downtown location. With the government offering programs of financing assistance and tax abatements, real estate developers have been revitalizing downtown areas, building high-rise structures for offices, parking garages, and shopping facilities. These downtown areas seem to attract many older couples. With the increase in renovations and affordable housing alternatives many young families and an increasingly large group of single people are moving back into the cities as well.

The variety of merchandise your store carries will help you decide the type of shopping area in which to locate. For example, clothing, jewelry, and department stores are more likely to be successful in the main or outlying central shopping district. On the other hand, grocery stores, drugstores, gasoline stations, and bakeries succeed on principal thoroughfares and neighborhood streets outside the main shopping districts.

Deciding on a location in a small town is sometimes secondary to the determination of the economic health of the community itself. What is the shopping pattern of the inhabitants? Are they inclined to travel to the city for major purchases, or do they rely on shopping centers situated on their route to work?

Beware of some of the inducements promised by local governments. Mayors and council members change with each election. Even the obvious has a way of not occurring. For example, the West Side Highway, a major automobile artery in Manhattan, collapsed in 1973. Downtown merchants were led to believe it would be rebuilt. Since all commerce would suffer without it, rebuilding seemed inevitable. But after 20 years the West Side Highway has still not been (and may never be) completed.

Highways are not the only transportation services that fall into disrepair. Regional airlines are chronic money losers and do occasionally go bankrupt. If your business is going to rely upon air supplies or deliveries, investigate the financial condition of the local carrier before commencing operations. Railroads may also cut back services or drift into bankruptcy. Either arrange for alternate shipping methods at the first sign of trouble, or, at extra cost, insure your business against service interruption.

Other municipal problems that may cripple your business include police, fire service, or sanitation strikes; municipal water shortages; and civil disorders. Any one of these disturbances occurring during the crucial Christmas season can spell failure for a retailer. Again, there is no inexpensive protection from these problems, but you should make every effort to gauge well the local mood before commencing business in a community.

Location and Design of Your Facilities

Appearance influences customers, and locations influence design. Whether an architect is planning your building from scratch or you are renovating an existing structure, the aesthetic or functional appeal of the design will be influenced by the location. For example, a location in a mall, redevelopment plan, or industrial park limits your design to something conforming to the tone set by the development.

Another example of design limited by location is a building conversion, for example, a barn converted into a restaurant or an abandoned factory turned into a roller-skating rink. If your intention upon securing a location is to radically alter the interior, consider the cost of these alterations in planning for what you must spend to start or purchase a business.

Ideally your design will project the personality of the business in such a way as to attract customers. For example, a drug manufacturer might wish to create a clean-cut, antiseptic look, whereas the owner of an exclusive women's dress shop might add glamour with some roco-co flourishes on the store exterior. Your basic design can be traditional, contemporary, neoclassical, or very modern. Just be certain that your architectural style matches the nature of your product.

You will be able to choose from many building materials: stone, brick, wood, glass, cast concrete, ceramic tile, plastic, aluminum, and steel. Which is most practical and attractive for the terrain or street on which your property is located?

If you can afford it, hire a consultant to direct studies for your interi-or design. An industrial engineer can plan the layout, a general con-tractor can direct the building operation, and an interior decorator can advise you on interior finishing. Some store architects specialize in doing an entire job from site selection to decor. Be sure to find one whose tastes and objectives are compatible with yours. Also, do not fail to estimate energy costs. Many business facilities are now designed to minimize energy costs.

5
Choosing a Form for Your Business

Before choosing a form of running your business, you should consider:

1. *Your options.* If you are doing it alone, your choice is between operating as a sole proprietor or incorporating. If you are going to operate with associates, your choice is between a partnership or corporation, which may for tax purposes be either a C or S corporation.

In certain states, you may also consider organizing your business as a limited liability company (LLC). LLCs are a comparatively new business form devised to get around S corporation restrictions. If allowed by state law, an LLC gives the advantage of corporate limited liability without the requirement of structuring the business as an S corporation, which is subject to restrictions such as the 35-shareholder limitation. If an LLC is treated as a partnership, investors benefit from the pass-through of income and deductions without incurring a corporate tax. Professional malpractice liability generally cannot be avoided. LLCs have grown in popularity in recent years, but they are not yet recognized in all states and many issues related to their operation are in a state of flux.

2. *The advantages and disadvantages of each form.* The simplest way to operate is as a sole proprietor, but if you are concerned with limiting your personal liability, incorporation is generally advantageous.

3. *The tax cost of each form.* If taxes were the only test for a business form, you would choose an unincorporated form of doing business,

such as a sole proprietorship or partnership. The tax cost of operating a corporation that reports as a C corporation is generally more than that of operating as a sole proprietor or partnership because the corporation is subject to tax and because corporate income received by you is also taxable on your personal tax return. If you must incorporate, an S corporation election can approximate the tax cost of an unincorporated business.

For purposes of comparing tax costs, you can put a partnership, sole proprietorship, and S corporation into one category, since only one tax is paid by the proprietor, partner, or S corporation stockholder. In the other category is the regular C corporation. This business form involves double taxation, first to the corporation and then to the stockholder when the after-tax profits are distributed. However, the effect of the double taxation can be minimized or sometimes eliminated by income-splitting methods. As a general rule, in splitting income between yourself and a corporation, you must try to place into two low tax brackets income that would normally be taxed in one high bracket. You split business income between yourself and a corporation by drawing from the C corporation amounts which it then deducts from its gross income. Drawing salary as a stockholder-employee is the usual method of splitting income. Sometimes you can also get income-splitting by drawing interest on loans you have made to the company; but this method is far more susceptible to IRS disallowance than salary withdrawals. Another means is payment by the company of expenses you incur in entertaining customers and traveling on business trips. This, too, is subject to IRS review and possible disallowance. However, in all cases, to the extent a corporation can deduct payments to you, there is only one tax.

The choice of business form is not irrevocable. You are not bound by your initial choice, nor subsequent ones. You can change form as circumstances change. You can start out in business as a sole proprietor, later take on a partner, and, as business expands, choose to incorporate, which will allow you to raise additional capital. On the other hand, going in reverse—incorporating first and then converting to a partnership or sole proprietorship—can be costly, primarily because of the tax cost of liquidation.

In coming to your decision, you have to consider not only current objectives but also future projections for expansion, retirement, and a later sale or liquidation of the business. Because of these complications, consult with an accountant or attorney who has experienced the various phases of business life. This chapter provides an overview that will help you discuss your decision with a consultant.

Now let's take a look at each business form.

Sole Proprietorship

A sole proprietorship is a business owned and operated by one person. To operate as a sole proprietor you do not have to get special permission or pay an attorney to prepare a charter or special papers. However, you may have to get certain local licenses and, if you are doing business under a business name other than your personal name, you may be required to file a notice of that business name at your local county office. You may also have to place a notice in a newspaper, noting your business name. Your county clerk will give you the requirements.

The business operations of a sole proprietorship are considered an integral part of your personal activities. Therefore, as a sole proprietor you are personally liable for your business debts; your business creditors can force payment from your personal assets.

Business income and expenses for the year are reported in Schedule C on your personal income tax return. The net result of entries on Schedule C, profit or loss, is combined with your other income. If you incur business losses, the losses will reduce the amount of your active nonbusiness income subject to tax.

In addition to paying regular income tax on business income, you must also pay self-employment tax for social security and medicare coverage. Self-employment tax liability is figured on Schedule SE of Form 1040. A 12.40 percent rate has been set for the social security part of self-employment tax, and a 2.90 percent rate for the medicare part. The amount of net earnings subject to each rate changes annually. For example, in 1993 the 12.40 percent rate applied to earnings of up to $57,600, and the 2.90 percent rate applied to earnings of up to $135,000. Before the rates are applied, self-employment net earnings are reduced by a percentage. Finally, 50 percent of the self-employment tax is deductible when figuring regular tax liability on Form 1040.

Partnership

A partnership is an unincorporated business owned and operated by two or more persons. For some purposes, the partnership activities are attributed to the individual owners as if they were sole proprietors. For other purposes, the partnership itself is treated as a unit divorced from the individual partners. For example, the tax law requires the partnership entity to compute and report income and losses but does not require the partnership itself to pay taxes. On the other hand, it requires the partners to report their share of partnership income or loss on their personal returns. Thus, the individual partner for tax reporting purposes is in generally the same position as a sole proprietor.

The advantages of a partnership are:

1. *Division of profits.* Profits may be divided in accordance with both the capital and services contributed. Moreover, each class of contribution may be rewarded separately, a certain return for capital investment and a different return for services or abilities contributed.

2. *Freedom of action.* There are usually no limitations on what a partnership may do, other than those self-imposed by the partnership agreement.

3. *Division of responsibilities.* The partnership permits specialization in management. Each partner can handle that aspect of the business for which he or she is best suited by experience and knowledge.

4. *Flexibility of operation.* Since the partnership is a contractual relationship, its objectives, capital, and membership may be changed to meet changing needs.

5. *Increased sources of capital.* The resources of several individuals are naturally greater than those of one individual. As larger capital becomes necessary, partners may be added. Also, the combined credit resources of existing partners afford greater possibility of expansion.

6. *Retention of individual control.* Even though risk and responsibility are divided among partners, the individual partner retains some control. If dissatisfied, a partner can withdraw and thus dissolve the firm, or force the other partners to buy out his or her interest.

7. *Personnel advantages.* The partnership can offer more incentive to the key employees than can the individual proprietorship. Reward for efficiency or excellence of service may be admission to the partnership, either as a general partner or as a special partner, according to the partnership agreement.

The disadvantages of a partnership are:

1. *Unlimited liability.* Partners are usually jointly and severally liable for all debts of the firm. Generally speaking, the more numerous the partners, the greater the risk of each individual partner. The larger the scale of the partnership operation, the greater the potential liability.

2. *Impermanency of existence and ease of disruption.* Partnerships are usually terminated voluntarily, by agreement of the parties, but they may be terminated involuntarily, by the acts of the partners, by cer-

tain events (such as death, insanity, or insolvency of a partner), or by court action.

The impermanency of a partnership may also lead to another serious problem—the ease with which the whole organization may be disrupted or disorganized. Personality or policy clashes between partners, the death of a partner, dishonesty, or unfair practice may cause difficulties which can be served only by dissolution of the partnership.

3. *Capital limitations.* When an enterprise needs large amounts of capital, the partnership form is usually impracticable. A partnership with too many partners becomes clumsy.

4. *Limited marketability of interest.* A partnership interest is usually not readily marketable. Generally, the partnership agreement provides that the partner must sell to a co-partner or to an outsider only with the consent of the partners.

5. *Difficulty of centralizing authority.* It is difficult to centralize or circumscribe authority in a partnership. So far as third persons are concerned, one partner may have as much authority as another on each question. Any partner generally has authority to act as an agent for the partnership, and the acts of a single partner may render the partnership liable for damages. A partner can usually make contracts which, within the scope of the partnership business, are binding on the partnership and the other partners. Generally, a partnership cannot sue, or be sued by, one of its partners.

A written partnership agreement defines the rights and obligations of each partner. While you and your partners will be on amicable terms during the formulation of the partnership and all may agree to have one attorney act as the partnership attorney in preparing the partnership agreement, you should have your own personal attorney review the agreement to ensure that your interests have been protected in the event of the death, bankruptcy, or retirement of any partner. The agreement should also anticipate how certain tax obligations are to be treated when they arise.

Partner's Share of Special Income or Loss Items

Generally, a partner's share of partnership income (or loss), deduction, or credit is fixed by the partnership agreement. Partners can agree to any division of income, deduction, or credit items unless the formula does not have substantial economic effect. (This means that you can't allocate these items solely for the purpose of cutting the tax bills of the parties involved, unless there's also a business reason for the allocation.)

Gain or Loss on the Sale of Contributed Property

A partner may contribute property to the partnership instead of investing cash. If there is a difference between the partner's cost (basis) for the property and its present market value, the partnership agreement must provide for methods of adjusting the calculation of profit.

Interest and Salary Payments to Partners

Partners' salaries and interest payments on capital can be treated (1) as distributions of profits or (2) as guaranteed payments. The partnership agreement can determine which method is to be used.

Buy-Sell Agreements

To provide for the possibility of a partner's death, a partnership agreement should include a buy-sell provision. Under partnership law, the death of a partner causes automatic dissolution unless state law or the partnership agreement provides otherwise. A buy-sell agreement may name either the partnership or partners who agree to buy the deceased partner's interest in the business. The agreement should be funded; that is, it should provide funds for the buyer to carry out his or her part of the agreement. Generally, insurance is used to fund a buy-sell agreement. Insurance may be carried by individual partners on one another's lives under a cross-purchase plan. Sometimes, the partnership owns the policies, pays the premiums, and acts as a conduit through which insurance proceeds pass to the estate of a deceased partner in exchange for the partner's interest. In either case, the premiums are not deductible. When there are several partners, the cross-purchase plan may be too cumbersome. Instead, insurance is used to fund a redemption of the deceased partner's interest. A buy-sell agreement should also fix the price of a partner's interest or provide a formula for determining the price.

Dissolution of the Partnership

A partnership is automatically dissolved when any of the partners is expelled, sells his or her interest, withdraws, dies, or is declared bankrupt. When partners cannot agree on dissolution, a court will dissolve the partnership in certain situations. A court will act if a partner has been guilty of misconduct that makes it impractical to carry on the business with the partner, or if the business can be carried on only at a loss. Also, a court will dissolve the partnership if a partner is shown to be of unsound mind or otherwise incapable of carrying on his or her duties.

The Corporation

A corporation differs radically from a partnership or sole proprietorship because it is treated as a separate and distinct unit from its owners. Legally, it is treated as an artificial person having rights and duties all its own. The tax law adopts this legal principle and treats it as a separate taxpayer (unless an S election is made), thus creating the problem of double taxation: (1) The tax paid by the corporation on its earnings, and (2) the tax paid by the owners when they receive these earnings in the form of dividends.

The advantages of a corporation are:

1. *Limited liability.* Liability of a stockholder is usually limited to the amount of his or her capital investment.

2. *Continuity of existence.* Change of ownership through transfer of stock has no effect on the existence of the corporate form.

3. *Continuity of management.* Change of ownership through transfer of stock need not affect management.

4. *Acquisition of new capital.* A successful corporation may seek as much capital as it needs. Investors have greater confidence in the securities of a corporation than in those of other forms of doing business.

5. *Personnel advantages.* The corporation can offer more opportunity to the efficient and ambitious employee and thus secure top-flight personnel. Opportunity to secure stock in the corporation is an incentive for employees.

6. *Limitation of power to bind.* Power to bind the corporation is limited to designated directors, officers, and agents. Any one partner can bind all partners, perhaps disastrously.

7. *Control of minorities.* If minority stockholders have adequate representation, a dissident minority group is usually not as difficult to manage as in partnerships.

8. *Transfer of interests.*   Corporate shares provide a means of investment that can be transferred to heirs with comparative ease. A partner's heir cannot succeed to his or her status as a partner without the consent of the other partners.

The disadvantages of a corporation are:

1. *Startup expenses.*   Forming a corporation involves following certain formal steps and can be expensive.

2. *Control and regulation.*   The corporation is subject to governmental control and regulation. It has to file reports and tax returns.

3. *Interstate limitations.*   If a corporation wants to do business in states other than the one in which it is organized, it must usually qualify in the other states and pay their fees and taxes.

4. *Charter limitations.*   The scope of activity of the corporation is limited by the purposes set out in the corporate charter. This difficulty may be eliminated by making the original charter broad or by amending it. The corporation's outstanding stock may not be more than the amount authorized by its charter.

5. *Inflexibility of operation.*   Some types of transactions must be authorized by the directors or stockholders. It may be difficult to get quick action on many important transactions.

6. *Possible liability of stockholders.*   The corporate form has sometimes been disregarded. Stockholders may be held individually liable where the corporation is sued for fraud, evasion of the law, monopoly, or personal gain of a dominant stockholder.

7. *Division of profits.*   In a partnership, profits can be divided in proportion to capital or services contributed. If the corporation divides profits, it must do so in proportion to stock holdings. Profits can be distributed only after a declaration of dividends by the directors. Limitations are often placed upon the amount of distributions. These vary with states. Generally, the laws try to prohibit impairment of capital by the payment of dividends.

8. *Minority stockholders.*   If you are a minority stockholder, you sometimes have no means of protection against acts of majority stockholders.

9. *Separate ownership and management.*   The divorcing of management from ownership may lead to abuse. Constant change of management is dangerous when continuity of effort is needed.

10. *Dissolution.*   Dissolution of the corporation may be an involved process.

11. *Retirement plan changes.* If you incorporate a sole proprietorship, you are no longer allowed to contribute to your Keogh plan. You must set up a new plan for the corporation.

Organizing a Corporation

You create a corporation by filing certain legal papers. Once you have made out these papers, filed them, and paid fees to the state which has chartered the company, you have a corporation which is recognized by law as a legal entity separate from you, the owner.

As a general rule, you will set up a corporation in the state in which you will do all or most of your business. It is usually not advisable for a small business to incorporate outside of the state in which it does business. If you do, your corporation will be considered a foreign corporation and will have to pay additional taxes and fees. Sometimes there are advantages to incorporating in another state because of favorable state taxes and less restrictions on corporate powers and capital requirements. However, foreign corporations must pay a fee for a certificate to do business in states other than where they were incorporated. Failure to do so may prevent the company from taking certain legal steps in the state and subject the company to penalties.

Filing for incorporation is not difficult. You may do it yourself with the help of kits available at a local office supply store. If you want to use an attorney, call several law offices for the cost of setting up a corporation. You will probably find that the fees quoted will range from a low of $250 to over $1000 for the same service!

Do not pick a name for the corporation which may be confused with the name of any other corporation doing business in the state. The state may reject your choice and delay incorporation. You can determine the acceptability of the name through the state office which receives certificates of incorporation or employ a service company to make the check.

After the company receives its certificate, the stockholders must meet to adopt the corporate bylaws and elect a board of directors who elect the officers who will run the corporation. Directors may elect themselves as officers.

Bylaws will cover such items as location of the principal office; time, place, and required notice of annual and special meetings of stockholders; quorum and voting privileges of the stockholders; number of directors, their pay, their term, elections and meetings; the election of officers and their duties and salaries; the issuance of stock certificates and transfers and the declaration of dividends.

In your choice of directors, remember that they have the power to run the business without interference from the stockholders. The power of a director usually cannot be taken away by an agreement to act merely as a "dummy." Directors and officers should know that minority stockholders have a legal right to injunction or damages in cases of the following:

- Fraudulent, illegal, or negligent acts of directors or officers
- Violation of their rights in reorganization, liquidation, merger, etc.
- Losses sustained through acts not authorized by the charter
- Wrongful withholdings of dividends

Restrictive Agreements

Stockholders frequently enter into agreements restricting the sale or other disposition of their stock. There are many business reasons for doing this—to ensure continual control of the corporation, to prevent outside interests from becoming stockholders, to fix the price on disposition of stock after death of a stockholder, and to define the mechanics for disposing of a stockholder's interest.

There are difficulties in making these agreements. For example, the disposal price should not be set at a figure out of the survivor's reach. Neither should it be set so low that it injures the family of the deceased. Unless the agreement is completely effective, a dissatisfied executor may contest it. Ask your attorney how restrictive agreements should be drafted so as to limit estate and gift tax valuations to the agreed price.

Multiple Corporations

Business reasons may require you to form more than one corporation. For example, the owner of several restaurants may want to limit the liability of each one. The use of multiple corporations can also have these tax advantages:

- Corporations may be able to elect different tax years and accounting methods.
- The use of two or more corporations may facilitate the future sale of part of a business.
- The losses of one corporation can be offset with profits of another corporation, provided that the corporations are members of an "affiliated group" and file a consolidated return.

Capitalizing Your Corporation

An important step in setting up a corporation is proper capitalization. You can base your corporation's capital structure on common stock, preferred stock, and debt, such as bonds and notes. Not only legal and financial considerations but also tax consequences will influence your choice. For example, the S corporation rules (discussed later in this chapter) limit an electing corporation to only one class of stock. This might be sufficient reason for a decision not to issue preferred stock despite other reasons in favor of such issue. If an S election is not desired, the issuance of preferred stock is useful as an income-splitting or estate-planning device.

You may want to capitalize partially with long- or short-term debt. The corporation deducts interest paid on loans, avoiding the double tax on income paid to the stockholders on the debt. When the debt is finally repaid, no income is realized as usually occurs when stock is redeemed.

You may also want to use Section 1244 stock which allows you to convert a long-term capital loss into an ordinary loss if the corporation fails. A Section 1244 loss is advantageous. Even though the same rate of tax is imposed on capital gains and ordinary income, under the tax law, the annual deduction for capital losses is limited to capital gains plus up to $3000 of ordinary income.

Issuing Debt

Here are two advantages to setting up stockholder debt in structuring the capital of a corporation:

- *Deductions for interest.* This is preferable to payment of dividends which are not deductible by the corporation.

- *Tax-free repayment of debt.* If you are anticipating a future repayment of part of your capital, you may plan a tax-free distribution through a repayment of the debt. A repayment of debt is tax-free whereas a redemption of part of the stock is generally taxable.

To achieve these advantages, companies have been set up with more stockholder debt than equity capital. However, the Internal Revenue Service resists attempts of businesses to set up substantial debt structures for the foregoing tax advantages and is aided by the tax law which sets down restrictions to the creation of debt obligations.

Stockholders may lend money to the corporation in proportion to their equity interests. However, the debt must be closely monitored.

The debt must carry a reasonable interest rate, and interest must be paid currently.

If stockholder debt is held substantially proportionate to stock, it may also be treated as stock when (1) the debt is excessive, (2) the debt is not issued for money, or (3) the debt is payable on demand. However, even if loans initially qualify as debt, they may be reclassified as equity if the company fails to pay interest or principal when due.

Complex regulations set down certain permissible ranges of debt obligations to stock. These ratios should be discussed with an experienced tax practitioner who may decide whether and how much debt obligations should be issued.

Issuing Section 1244 Stock

If your corporation fails, the loss on your stock investment is treated as a capital loss. A capital loss deduction is not as favorable as an ordinary loss deduction. Ordinary losses are fully deductible from ordinary income. A capital loss is fully deductible from capital gains but is not fully deductible from ordinary income. If you do not have capital gains to offset your loss, you can deduct only up to $3000 of a capital loss from ordinary income.

To avoid to some extent this capital loss limitation, you can designate stock as Section 1244 stock. If the stock meets certain legal tests and you do suffer a loss on the stock, you may claim an ordinary loss of up to $50,000 ($100,000 on a joint return). Losses in excess of these limits are deductible as capital losses.

To ensure that the designation of Section 1244 stock will be respected, make sure that the stock is common stock and that it is issued only for cash or property other than stock and securities. Finally, see that your attorney describes the issue as Section 1244 stock.

Dividend Distribution

The power to declare dividends rests with the board of directors who can declare them only out of the firm's surplus funds. Know the law of your particular state on this point. Generally, past deficits from operations must be made up before a dividend can be declared. In most states, directors are personally liable to creditors if capital is impaired by declaration of a dividend not out of surplus. These are some of the dividends that can be paid:

- *Cash dividend.* Paid in cash
- *Stock dividend.* Additional stock that is issued to stockholders on a pro rata basis
- *Dividends in property (dividends in kind).* For example, capital stock or bonds of the distributing company; other shares of stock or bonds owned by the company; dividends in property will result in income to your company if the value of the property exceeds the cost basis
- *Liquidation dividend.* Paid out of the assets of the corporation upon dissolution
- *Scrip dividend.* Paid in notes that are to be redeemed at a later date, usually in cash
- *Consent dividend.* Stockholders consenting to be taxed as if they had received a stated sum of money, but getting no actual payments of any kind
- *Elective dividend.* Stockholders taking cash or a stock dividend at their option

Corporate Tax Reporting

You have the choice of paying no corporate income in one of two ways:

1. The corporation reports taxable income and pays a corporate income tax on that income (regular C corporation). You pay tax on your receipts of salary, dividends, and interest from the corporation.
2. The corporation reports its taxable income (or loss) as an S corporation. But you, as a shareholder, report and pay tax on this income on your tax return, whether or not you withdraw money or property from the corporation. An S election may be advisable for a new corporation which anticipates losses at the start. The shareholders may deduct their share of these losses on their personal tax returns. S corporations are also advisable when the corporate rates for regular C corporations are higher than the top personal tax rates for stockholders.

In a C corporation, income which you do not withdraw in the form of deductible items, such as salary, interest, or similar expenses, is subject to corporate tax, and when you withdraw the amount as a dividend, it is again subject to tax on your return. The S election avoids this possible double tax by allowing you, as the stockholder, to pay a tax on corporate income directly.

If you decide to operate a C corporation subject to tax, drawing salary as a shareholder-employee is the usual and preferred method of reducing or avoiding the double tax. The corporation deducts the salary payments, which offset an equal amount when you report the salary on your return.

When you fix salaries, including your own, be aware that the corporation may deduct salary payments only to the extent that they are "reasonable" in amount. In determining reasonableness, consider duties, complexity of the business, pay in comparison with gross and net, income salaries paid in similar businesses, and the special abilities that make your services, and those of your executives, valuable.

Peg salaries at an adequate level from the beginning of the operation. Fluctuating salaries, high salaries in high earning years and low salaries in lean years, will attract a review of salary payments by the Internal Revenue Service. A charge might be made, for example, that the high salary payments were in fact dividend payments.

S Corporations

For S corporate reporting, you make an S election. You may take advantage of the election as long as it benefits you, for as little as 1 year or indefinitely.

On your personal return, you report your share of corporate earnings and losses. Your share of corporate operating losses reduces your other income. You report your share of the corporation's long-term capital gain. The corporation files only an information return, Form 1120S, instead of the regular corporate return. To qualify for the election, your corporation must meet certain requirements:

1. It must be a domestic corporation which is not
   a. A financial institution that takes deposits and makes loans
   b. An insurance company (other than certain stock casualty insurance companies)
   c. A corporation electing the Puerto Rico and possessions tax credit
   d. A DISC or former DISC; DISCs (Domestic International Sales Corporation) are characterized by 95 percent of its gross receipts, and 95 percent of its assets, being export-related
   e. A member of an affiliated group, whether or not eligible to file a consolidated return (unless it is an inactive subsidiary that has not begun business and does not have gross income)

2. It does not have more than 35 shareholders. A husband and wife are counted as one shareholder, regardless of how the stock is owned.
3. It must have only individuals, bankruptcy or decedent's estates, or certain trusts as shareholders.
4. It must have only one class of stock. However, differences in common stock voting rights are allowed. Also, if shares are divided into two or more groups which are identical in every respect except that each group has the right to elect directors in proportion to the number of shares in each group, they are considered to be one class of stock. Straight debt is also not considered a second class stock if all of the following conditions are met:
   a. The debt is evidenced by a written unconditional demand to pay a fixed amount on demand or on a specified date
   b. The interest rate and payment dates are not contingent on corporate profits, discretion, or similar factors
   c. The debt is not convertible into stock
   d. The creditor could qualify as an S corporation creditor
5. It must not have a nonresident alien as a shareholder.

Before electing S corporation status, you should discuss these points with your attorney.

Electing S Status

An S election may not be filed before a corporation is formally incorporated. A tax year of a new corporation does not begin until it has shareholders, acquired assets, or begins to do business. However, if under state law corporate existence begins with filing articles of incorporation, the first date of the tax year begins on the day of such filing. This procedure should be followed even though the corporation has no assets and does not begin doing business until a later date.

The election does not have to be renewed each year. It may continue until it is revoked.

Incorporating a Sole Proprietorship or Partnership

In time, you may find disadvantages in operating as a sole proprietor or as a partnership. Your personal assets remain at risk for business losses and liabilities. You may find it difficult to get long-term financing. To limit liability and to attract other financial support, you may want to incorporate your sole proprietorship or partnership. Further, a corporation offers these benefits, which are not available in a sole proprietorship or partnership.

- Fringe benefits in the form of accident, health, and life insurance protection can be made available.
- Corporate form may facilitate saving income and estate taxes by gifts of stock to children.
- Members of a family may be stockholders without the restrictions of family partnership.

You can transfer your proprietorship or partnership assets tax-free. If you meet both of the following requirements, you may incorporate without tax:

- Assets are transferred to the corporation solely in exchange for stock and securities of that company.
- Immediately thereafter you (and your partners, if any) own 80 percent of the voting power and 80 percent of all other classes of nonvoting stock of the corporation.

In a tax-free exchange, the corporation uses the basis of the assets that it had in the unincorporated business as its basis for depreciation and resale. This is so even if they are worth considerably more (that is, the fair market value of the assets exceeds their basis, after reductions for depreciation).

Securities received need not be proportional to one's interest in the unincorporated business before the exchange. However, although a disproportion between the value of the property transferred and securities received will not make the exchange itself taxable, part of the deal may be taxed as a gift or compensation. If more than 20 percent of the stock is received as compensation, the entire transaction is taxable.

Transfers of liabilities may result in tax. Often assets transferred to a corporation in exchange for stock are subject to liabilities, as, for example, a building subject to a mortgage. Whether the corporation takes assets subject to liabilities or assumes the liabilities, the tax-free nature of the transaction is not usually upset. However, you may realize taxable income on transferring property subject to liabilities when the transfer is part of a tax-avoidance plan, or when the liability exceeds your basis (tax cost) for assets transferred to the corporation.

If you incorporate you may no longer contribute to your Keogh plan. You must set up a new qualified plan for your corporation. Consider this expense before incorporating.

Limited Liability Company (LLC)

Limited liability companies (LLCs) are a relatively new form of business entity devised to get around S corporation restrictions, such as the 35-shareholder limitation. In recent years, LLCs have been authorized by a growing number of states as a means of combining partnership and corporate benefits. If the LLC qualifies as a partnership for federal tax purposes under IRS tests, the LLC investors benefit from the pass-through of income and deductions without incurring a federal corporate tax (state law treatment varies). At the same time, LLC investors obtain the corporate benefit of limited liability, which is personal liability protection for LLC's debts without having to structure the business as an S corporation. However, professionals cannot avoid liability for personal malpractice. LLCs are not subject to S corporation eligibility restrictions, such as the 35-shareholder limit and the one class of stock requirement.

Given the recent emergence of LLCs, there are uncertainties concerning their use. An LLC may be formed only in a state that has adopted LLC legislation. States that do allow the organization of LLCs differ as to LLC regulations and the business flexibility provided to LLCs. Furthermore, LLCs that do business outside the state in which they are organized face risks; other states need not tax the LLC as a partnership or respect the limited liability of the owners.

At the time this book went to press, the following states permitted the formation of LLCs: Alabama, Arizona, Colorado, Delaware, Florida, Iowa, Louisiana, Maryland, Minnesota, Nevada, Oklahoma, Rhode Island, Kansas, Texas, Utah, Virginia, West Virginia, and Wyoming. Most other states are expected to follow with their own LLC legislation.

Given the varying state LLC rules, and the possibility that Congress may pass federal legislation establishing national guidelines, you should consult an experienced tax practitioner concerning the advantages and disadvantages of organizing your business as an LLC.

6
Control through Accounting and Record Systems

Too often, fledgling businesses fail to hire an accountant. Some are concerned about cost; others do not understand the importance of accounting controls. The value of accounting services far outweighs their cost. Many accountants offer services to small businesses at reasonable fees. As for the need of such services, basic business sense tells you that keeping good records is essential to the conduct and control of your business. Current federal, state, and municipal tax laws impose periodic reporting requirements on all types and sizes of businesses. Those alone justify creating a system which ensures that all the firm's transactions are recorded and retained in such form that government reporting obligations can be efficiently met. When the need to measure and control the operations of your business on an ongoing basis is added, a good record-keeping system becomes absolutely necessary.

If for some reason you do not start with professional aid, make sure that you keep a separate ledger account for all of your business transactions and keep a file to store all of your business records such as invoices and receipts. In addition, keep separate business and personal checking accounts. Do not use a cash card to withdraw cash from your business; write checks which show to whom payment is made. Also, deposit only business receipts in the business account. When the volume of checks written during a typical month exceeds 25, it is perhaps time to consider the type of accounting plan discussed in this chapter.

All record-keeping systems designed and maintained to meet basic business needs contain information essential to the following functions: order entry and fulfillment, billing and paying, costing and estimating, payroll, cash control, inventory management, fixed asset management, expense control, and debt management.

A well-designed accounting system serves two needs. The first is *bookkeeping*, which involves the recording of all transactions (income and expenses). The second is *analysis* of these accounts. Bookkeeping without analysis is of little value to you as a business manager. It is *analysis* of the records that produces the periodic statements you need in order to assess the status of the business and to measure its progress. Such statements include:

- *Weekly statements of your cash position, accounts receivables, and accounts payable.*   This will give you an opportunity to feel the current pulse of your business and to detect problems as soon as they arise. An accounts payable list will help you take action on slow payers.

- *Income statement.*   The income statement shows the profit or loss for the period by matching income received against the expenses incurred to generate that income.

- *Balance sheet.*   The balance sheet shows the picture of your business at a point in time broken down into categorized assets (what you own), categorized liabilities (what you owe), and the capital section (the owner's position in the business).

- *Aged accounts receivable.*   This statement recounts monies owed to the company by customers and how long it has been from the date of sale to the date of this statement.

- *Aged accounts payable.*   This gives an analysis, by vendor, of monies owed for purchases of materials or services from the date of actual receipt of the purchases to the date of this report.

- *Expense analysis.*   The expense analysis gives a detailed listing of expenses incurred for the period, shown in total dollars; the percentage relationship of each expense item to sales; and a comparison of expenses with the budget for these items.

- *Inventory reports.*   These can help you see which products are selling well and which are not, and help you to identify inventory shortages quickly. Inventory reports identify which products "turn" the fastest and which are slow movers. You may also set up your reports so that they classify your inventory into "ABC" categories; for example, A items include inventory which is critical to your operation, whereas C items are the least important to the running of your business.

Bookkeeping and the Double-Entry System

You will probably use the double-entry system of bookkeeping. Although you can keep a record of business transactions in a notebook or a "day" book, you will soon discover how inadequate this method of record keeping is. Obtaining management information from such a record-keeping system is difficult, because analysis is required before any accounting schedules can be prepared. Some small businesses still operate with a checkbook as the only record of transactions. However, this method provides no internal checks or balances to prove the accuracy of the input or of any subsequent analysis or accounting reports.

A system of record keeping was adopted centuries ago by merchants in response to the need to have a logical organization of accounting data with its own internal checking capability. It is called the *double-entry* system of bookkeeping. In this system a business transaction is entered both as a debit and a credit item. For every debit entry there must be a corresponding credit entry. As a result, when you properly record both parts of a transaction, your books are in balance. If both sides do not balance to the penny, an error has been made, and you, your bookkeeper, or your accountant is alerted to track down the discrepancy. Further, accounts and adjustments are so arranged that various accounting statements can be made periodically and systematically.

Example

Transactions:

1. You start your business with $50,000 of your own money and $120,000 of borrowed funds.
2. You buy $25,000 of merchandise and $25,000 of equipment and fixtures for cash.
3. You rent a building at $1500 per month, putting down a 2-month security deposit.
4. You sell some of your merchandise that cost $12,000 for $13,000 cash.

Under the double-entry system the transactions would be recorded as follows:

Debit side		Credit side	
1. Cash	$170,000	1. Capital	$50,000
		Liability (loan payable)	$120,000
2. Merchandise	$25,000	2. Cash	$50,000
Equipment	$25,000		
3. Security deposit	$3,000	3. Cash	$4,500
Rent expense	$1,500		
4a. Cash	$13,000	4a. Sales (income)	$13,000
4b. Cost of sales	$12,000	4b. Merchandise	$12,000

Although the example is a simplification, it reflects the principles and advantages of the double-entry system. Note that each transaction is balanced: For each debit there is a corresponding credit entry and vice versa.

Bookkeeping starts with sales and purchase invoices, register tapes, check stubs, and deposit slips. From these input sources entries are recorded in books of original entry (journals), such as cash receipts and cash disbursement journals or sales and purchase journals. The data in the journals are summarized daily, weekly, or monthly and posted periodically to accounts in a *general* ledger. A general ledger is a compilation of discrete account classifications, each of which has relevance to describing the financial activities of your business.

- *Equipment and fixed assets.* Includes land, buildings, furniture and fixtures, manufacturing equipment

- *Other assets.* Includes security deposits, prepaid insurance, goodwill, and certain amortizable assets

- *Current liabilities.* Includes accounts and loans payable due within the current accounting year

- *Long-term liabilities.* Includes the noncurrent portion of installment payables and obligations due after the current accounting year

- *Other liabilities.* Includes such items as deferred taxes or obligations contingent upon some future event (reserve accounts)

- *Capital or ownership.* Includes those accounts describing the original investment(s) (capital stock, paid-in capital surplus), subsequent earnings (losses) realized (retained earnings), and treasury stock (capital stock that had been previously issued and subsequently repurchased by the corporation)

- *Income accounts.* Includes sales, returns and allowances, sales discounts, interest income, and income realized from other sources

- *Expense accounts.* Includes those accounts describing expenses incurred which are directly related to the creation of income, such as wages, payroll taxes, office, telephone, vehicle expense, and rent

The use of computer programs has not changed these basic principles; computers have eased the input of data and speeded up to an incredible degree the analysis of business data, thereby facilitating the publication of reports and statements. Computers allow you to set up a list or a "chart of accounts." All transactions being entered into the company's books are validated against the chart of accounts to ensure that the account exists, that is, that the account is active and that the debits and credits are exactly in balance.

For less than $100, you can purchase computer software which will provide you with a completely automated accounting program than can handle all aspects of your small business. Most software manufacturers even have a 30-day trial period, allowing you to evaluate the product and determine how it functions in your particular environment.

As your business grows, you may need a computerized accounting program set up by a consultant who can train your staff and implement the accounting system. Consulting fees range from $35 per hour up to $250 per hour, depending upon the consultant's expertise, the complexity of your accounting system, and market demand. A company like Plum Creek Operations [(800)756-7578] serves small businesses by evaluating both your hardware and software requirements, making appropriate recommendations, and training personnel.

In selecting a consultant, check references (at least three) in the same industry if possible and even arrange an on-site visit.

Accounting Reports

At the end of each accounting period (usually monthly) a "trial balance" is drawn which reflects the total debits and total credits. If the double-entry system has been followed correctly, debits will equal credits and hence the trial balance.

Once the accounts are balanced, the bookkeeper or accountant can prepare a statement of income and a balance sheet as well as all the supplementary analytical reports upon which effective management of the business depends. The reports might include a statement which shows changes in financial position and the sources and uses of cash and working capital. Other valuable reports are comparative statements (income and balance sheet) that compare transactions or changes in asset position for this month (or year-to-date) against the same period in the prior year. Probably no accounting report is as vital to the management control of a business as is the cash flow statement (discussed later in this chapter).

Again, computers do not *change* this process. They do, however, automate the posting of the journals to the ledger, with complete cross-referencing in the ledger as to the source of the original transaction.

Figures 6.1 through 6.5 depict typical monthly statements.

Significance and Uses of Accounting Reports

Statement of Income

Profit is a major aim of business. No information is more important than that contained in the income statement. Not only does the statement reflect, in detail, an itemization of sales, cost of goods sold, and expenses, but it also permits calculating the percentage relationship of each item of expense to sales. Such percentage figures help you check efficiency trends. Regular analysis of the percentages provides management with one of the most valuable tools in measuring and controlling individual cost elements.

In following the format shown in Figure 6.1, it is recommended that current period information be compared with that of a similar past period. Percentage figures for growth or decline give valuable clues to sales trends, costs of goods, and other expenses.

The Balance Sheet

The following is the traditional account format for balance sheet statements (note the similarity in the order of accounts to that of the general ledger accounts described above).

Assets	Liabilities
Current assets	Current liabilities
Investments	Long-term liabilities
Fixed assets	Reserves (for contingencies,
Intangible assets	taxes, obsolescence, etc.)
	Capital stock and surplus
	(Ownership)
	Paid-in capital surplus
	Retained earnings

THE CORPORATION
Statement of Income
For the year ended December 31, 19_____

Gross Sales		$.....
Less	$.....	
Sales returns and allowances		.....
Sales discounts		.....
Net sales		
Cost of goods sold:		
Inventory, January 1		.....
Purchases	$.....	
Less: Purchase returns and allowances	.....	.....
Freight in		.....
Goods available for sale		.....
Less: Inventory, December 31		.....
Cost of goods sold		.....
Gross profit on sales		.....
Selling expenses:		
Sales salaries	.....	
Store rent	.....	
Advertising	.....	
Delivery salaries	.....	
Depreciation—delivery equipment	.....	
Delivery supplies used	.....	
Sales supplies used	.....	
Freight out	.....	
Depreciation—Sales equipment	.....	
Total selling expenses		.....
General and administrative expenses:		
Officers' salaries		
Office payroll	. .	
Bad debts	. . .	
Insurance	.....	
Telephone and telegraph	.....	
Legal and auditing	.....	
Printing and stationery	.....	
Depreciation—Office equipment	.....	
Miscellaneous taxes	.....	
Total general and administrative expenses	.....	
Total expenses		.....
Profit from operations		.....
Other income:		.....
Interest income	.....	
Cash discounts on purchases	.....	
Dividends earned	.....	
Total other income		.....
Other expense:		
Interest expense	.....	
Other income less other expense		.....
Income before income taxes		.....
Income taxes		.....
Net income for year		$.....

Figure 6-1. Sample statement of income.

	January 1994	January 1993	Increase or decrease, percent	Percent of total 1994	1993
Gross sales	$50,000	$40,000	25.0	102.0	102.0
Less: Returns and allowances	800	700	14.1	2.0	2.0
Net sales	49,200	39,300	25.0	100.0	100.0
Cost of goods sold	34,100	28,300	21.0	69.3	72.0
Gross profit	$15,100	$11,000	37.0	30.7	28.0
Operating expenses: Selling	$ 4,500	$ 3,200	41.0	9.2	8.1
Administrative and general	5,475	3,400	61.0	11.1	8.7
Financial	140	100	40.0	0.3	0.3
Total expenses	$10,115	$ 6,700	51.0	20.6	17.1
Net operating profit	$ 4,985	$ 4,300	16.0	10.1	10.9

Figure 6-2. Comparative income statement.

January 31, 1994 and January 31, 1993

	January 1994	January 1993	Increase or decrease, percent	Percent of total 1994	1993
Assets					
Current assets	$15,380	$12,200	26.0	43.8	43.0
Fixed assets	18,000	14,100	27.6	51.2	49.6
Other assets	1,750	2,100	16.6	5.0	7.4
Total assets	$35,130	$28,400	23.7	100.0	100.0
Liabilities and net worth:					
Current liabilities	$ 6,000	$ 4,000	50.0	17.1	14.0
Fixed liabilities	10,000	8,000	25.0	28.5	28.1
Capital stock	10,000	10,000	00.0	28.5	35.2
Surplus	5,000	4,000	25.0	14.2	14.0
Reserves for contingencies	4,130	2,400	72.1	11.7	8.7
Total	$35,130	$28,400	23.7	100.0	100.0
Working capital	$ 9,380	$ 8,200	11.4		

Figure 6-3. Condensed comparative balance sheet.

Customer name	Total receivable	Amounts receivable			
		0–30	30–60	60–90	Over 90
Ace Company	1,250	250	500	500	—
Base Company	710	—	480	200	30
Pace Company	465	265	—	200	—
Total	13,240	8,475	3,650	985	130

Figure 6-4. Aged accounts receivable schedule as of January 31, 1994.

Vendor account	Total payable	Amounts payable			
		Current	30–60	60–90	Over 90
ABC Company	750	750	—	—	—
Black Company	450	200	250	—	—
Drop Company	620	350	270	—	—
Public Utility	210	210	—	—	—
Western Supply	1,500				—
Total	6,480	5,260	1,220	—	—

Figure 6-5. Aged accounts payable schedule as of January 31, 1994.

The asset section of a balance sheet roughly follows the order and relative ease with which the assets will be turned into cash.

This explanation of the traditional "order of liquidity" refers to the speed in which cash can be generated by the disposal of the particular asset should a business crisis exist. Therefore, after cash on hand, marketable securities can be readily converted into cash. Most of your accounts receivable can be liquidated, in effect, either by factoring or by borrowings collateralized by the receivables. Inventories normally are not easily converted to cash unless they represent commodity-type items for which there is an established market, such as basic metals or petroleum products.

Financial and Operating Ratios

A ratio is a comparison of one item with another on the balance sheet or operating statement. While some of the commonly employed ratios are of limited interest to a firm's management, they are, nevertheless, important because of the interest investors and lending institutions have in them. Brief descriptions of the nature and implied significance of these ratios follow.

Current Ratio

Current assets divided by current liabilities provides a ratio that indicates the ability of a business to finance its current operations after allowing for payment of its current liabilities. A 2:1 ratio gives the business a margin of safety, since part of the current assets may consist of slow-moving merchandise not yet sold and of accounts receivable which may be subject to discount or are uncollectible.

A current ratio of less than 2 can be satisfactory in certain situations. A ratio higher than 2 should be maintained where the current debt is of an extremely short-term or demand character or where market demand and product lifetimes are of short duration. In any case it is always prudent to try to maintain a ratio of 2 or more and/or a ratio better than that maintained in your particular industry.

Acid-Test Ratio

This ratio is similar to the current ratio but shows cash capacity more sensitively. It expresses the relation between "quick" assets (that is, readily usable assets, such as cash, collectible receivables, and readily salable securities) and the current liabilities. When this ratio is 1 or higher, a business is considered to be in a satisfactory liquid condition.

Ratio of Liabilities to Net Worth

This ratio shows the relative proportions of business ownership belonging to all types of creditors on the one hand, and to the proprietor (stockholders) on the other. For example:

$$\frac{\text{Liabilities}}{\text{Net worth}} = \frac{\$16,000}{\$19,130} = 83 \text{ percent}$$

When computed for several successive periods, this ratio reveals the trend in proportion of debt to ownership. It shows whether a larger share of business assets is being held by the owner, or whether business assets are being acquired through borrowing from creditors.

In general, it is preferable that business operations from year to year produce increases in stockholders' ownership. However, this generalization does not hold for all situations, particularly when adherence to it prevents the firm from seizing opportunities for major growth in sales and/or profits. For example, the company may prefer to increase its debt for expansion purposes. Borrowing for such purposes may be particularly desirable if equity capital is unavailable, surplus earnings are insufficient, and borrowing can be done at favorable terms.

Inventory Turnover Ratios

These ratios are vital for enterprises in which merchandise is purchased or produced as the principal basis for making sales.

The rate of merchandise turnover varies greatly between different types of businesses with differences in the efficiencies of purchasing, inventory control, marketing, and sales. A new business should calculate turnover(s) for each fiscal period, preferably every 3- or 6-month period, and watch closely for any changes in the rates. Once the typical inventory turnover rate is determined, calculations should be made on a monthly basis as the business matures, to enable management to respond faster to negative indicators.

Merchandise turnover is computed by dividing the cost of the goods sold during a fiscal period by the average of the opening and closing inventories. This gives the number of times the average inventory has been "turned" during a period. For example, if the cost of goods sold was $120,000 and the average of the initial and ending inventories was $20,000, the merchandise-inventory-turnover ratio would be as follows:

$$\frac{\text{Cost of goods sold}}{\text{Merchandise inventory}} = \frac{\$120,000}{\$20,000} = 6 \text{ times turned}$$

The average age of the stock would be 2 months. This does not mean that every part of the stock has been sold and new stock purchased 6 separate times during the fiscal year. It does mean that the equivalent of this has been accomplished in terms of the total goods handled during a 12-month period. It is obvious that some parts of inventory stocks may not have been turned at all. Other parts will have been turned more than 6 times.

In the ordinary merchandising concern the inventory turnover may be figured for all merchandise combined. However, separate rates of turnover should be calculated for each department (assuming there is more than one) or for each class of merchandise. It enables management to spot slow-moving goods that should either be pushed more aggressively by sales techniques or be discontinued entirely. For this reason, every business manager engaged in distributing a variety of products should keep informed on the turnover trends.

In the manufacturing concern, inventories normally consist of raw materials, goods in process, and finished products. If the turnover rate is calculated for each of these classes of goods, the ratio is a good indicator of trouble. A lower-than-average inventory turnover ratio is usually an unfavorable sign. The stock may contain so much old merchandise that sales of new goods are slowed up. A very high inventory-turnover ratio may sometimes be attained at high cost: The company may be buying in quantities so small that the best prices are not obtained or may be increasing sales by taking excessive markdowns thereby reducing gross profit.

Ratio of Net Sales to Receivables

This ratio is a valuable index of the ratio of net sales for an accounting period to the amount of unpaid accounts and notes receivable at the end of that period. For example:

$$\frac{\text{Net sales}}{\text{Receivables}} = \frac{\$49,200}{\$5850} = 8.4$$

This means that the annual rate of sales is about 8 times the amount of receivables, or that the average period represented by these receivables is one-eighth of a year's sales, or about 45 days of sales volume. This ratio is most valuable in a business which makes sales exclusively on credit. In companies which do a cash as well as a credit business, the ratio should be calculated only on that portion of sales made on credit. (*Note:* The significance of this type of report will be discussed more fully in the section Cash Management.)

Ratio of Net Profit to Net Sales

The significance of this percentage is that it reflects the efficiency of operations in terms of expense control as well as efficiency in purchasing or manufacturing goods processed by the business. For example:

$$\frac{\text{Net profit}}{\text{Net sales}} = \frac{\$4810}{\$49,200} = 9.8 \text{ percent}$$

Any major variance in net profit per dollar of sales requires close study by management. Since the ratio expresses the difference between the *gross margin* percentage and the *expense* percentage of net sales, obviously either a high markup or a low expense will combine to produce a high net-profit ratio. Bear in mind, however, that a high markup may deprive you of sales volume because your prices are too high. On the other hand, too low an expense ratio might mean you are not spending enough on advertising or selling expenses to produce the sales volume that could be generated.

To summarize this discussion of ratios, it is often instructive for a business to compare its data with those of other businesses in the same line of activity and of approximately the same size (usually expressed in sales volume or asset structure and values). Such comparative data are frequently available through trade associations and organizations such as Dun & Bradstreet. It is important to note that the range of acceptable ratios varies from industry to industry. Make sure that when the comparison is done, it is done against a similar industry; otherwise the results can be very misleading. One caution before making the comparison, however, is to ascertain whether the businesses whose figures are used have a standard or substantially uniform system of accounts. Otherwise, any comparisons would be totally misleading.

Break-Even Point

When starting a new business or planning to increase (or decrease) the productive capacity of an ongoing business, it is critical to calculate the break-even point. To *break even* generally means to obtain a volume of sales equal to (or covering) the total expenses incurred to generate those sales. A conventional break-even chart is shown in Figure 6.6.

Fixed costs are the expenses which do not vary as production or sales volume increases, such as rent, property taxes, insurance, depreciation of assets, and fixed payments on bank notes or installment contracts. Variable expenses are those which vary directly (in direct proportion) to changes in production or sales volume, such as materials, direct labor costs and related payroll taxes, operating supplies, mar-

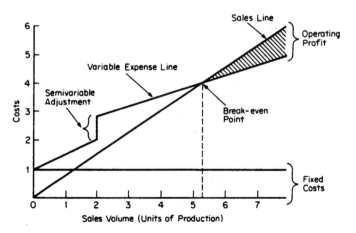

Figure 6-6. A conventional break-even chart.

keting expenses, and commissions. The nature of your business will define these variable costs.

A third category of expenses, semivariable, vary with volume but not in direct proportion. Costs of light, power, or other utilities will increase with greater production but not necessarily in direct proportion. As illustrated in Figure 6.6, at index point 2 of sales volume, it is necessary to add supervisors or additional equipment to be able to generate the additional sales (or production) indicated.

To run a profitable business, every unit produced or sold must absorb (provide for) a share of the fixed and semivariable overhead costs. Selling prices must be established to reflect these facts in order to generate profits.

The experienced business manager uses break-even charts to indicate profit margins at a given rate of production. If the cost factors change or the fixed costs increase for any reason, a new break-even point must be computed. It is readily apparent that if management can reduce variable costs, operating profits can be improved.

Budgetary Control

A startling number of businesses operate without a budget, trusting memory and luck to sort out expenses and income in the months ahead. Occasionally, companies have survived without written budgets, but sooner or later the pressures on their managers become too great and the failure to organize relevant business data brings on disaster.

A new business will probably be forced to feel its way along uncharted financial corridors for a time. Although the entrepreneur may know the amount of capital on hand and most operating expenses, he or she can only make educated guesses about sales. Forecasts at this stage should be cautious. Arithmetical computations can and should be made to determine the break-even point, and the new operator should identify all foreseeable expenses and consider them against available capital.

The purchaser of an existing business can base a budget on records of the company modified by economic expectations. Allow a certain percentage of variation: Will some customers desert the company with the departure of its former owner? Were production and sales continued at an even rate during the negotiation and transfer of ownership? Has the same staff been retained at the same wages? All cash expenditures and debts should be enumerated and considered.

The *sales forecast* is the basis for all budgets. Whether you own a tool plant employing 40 workers or a retail shop with only 1 salesperson, your sales expectations should dictate your company's expenditures and income. The owner of the very small business must assume this responsibility. However, if your operation is larger, your department heads should prepare budgets for sales, production, purchases, costs of goods manufactured and sold, cash transactions, and cash flow. You should prepare the overall selling budget as well as personnel and administrative budgets. (You can decide whether you need the help of your accountant.)

Your master budget should then be broken down, preferably month by month, but at least by quarters, since seasonal sales vary. Do not base your budget on ideal or hypothetical conditions. The prudent manager plans for 5 to 10 percent fewer sales than expected and 5 to 10 percent higher expenses than expected. Your budget should itemize and classify costs by function, such as manufacturing, administration, and selling. Once you have formulated your budget, consult it frequently. Each month, compare your projected income and expenses with the actual figures to detect unexpected losses, to factor in new or canceled orders, or to indicate whether to curtail or increase capital investments. If any decided change should appear, attempt to bring sales into line, adjust the expenses, and, if all else fails, adjust the budget to reflect the revised conditions.

Manufacturing concerns use a budget method called *flex budgeting*, where the budget changes or is flexible with the varying levels of manufacturing. Although most computer systems allow for some type of budgeting function within the general ledger, the most flexible systems allow you to input current budget information from spreadsheets generated by Lotus 1-2-3, Excel, or Quattro. Spreadsheet programs are especially adept at creating, modifying, and analyzing budgets. The ability to import the results back into the accounting system is important so that financial statements with comparative budget results, such as actual to budget variance, can be generated as a standard monthly report.

Your Cash Budget

Companies showing good profits may fail because of cash shortages. Their owners have theorized that cash on hand need only be sufficient to cover a month's rent, while they rely on day-to-day receipts to pay inventory expenses, maintenance, payroll, taxes, dividends, etc.

Remember that cash to meet obligations is not provided by profits tied up in inventory or machinery. Your cash budget consists of cash on hand at the beginning of the month, plus collections expected from past and current receivables, minus planned disbursements. Your cash receipts will be based on sales adjusted for collection. The manufacturing budget is based on the units that will have to be produced to meet projected sales. It is tied in closely to the sales budget. It will include manufacturing materials, purchased parts, direct labor, manufacturing overhead, tools, fixtures, and selling overhead. Costs of marketing and general administration should not be included.

In planning production, consider the capabilities and limitations of your equipment. Make a methodical analysis of material requirements. Is your plant equipped to carry out these operations? Be sure your budget is not committing you to an output which makes unreasonable demands on your equipment or employees.

One of the main reasons for failure of new businesses is the ever-escalating cost of leases and rents. This is especially true in large urban areas like Chicago, New York, and Los Angeles. A recent SBA study showed that in certain industries the new business failure rate was as high as 88 percent. Most of these companies did not fail due to lack of business but to increasing lease costs that were not planned for in the initial budget. Getting a history from your prospective landlord of escalations of property they own and have leased for the past 10 years is one way of understanding and preparing for the potential lease price increases that you may be facing.

Budgeting Capital Expenditures

Capital expenditures should be planned, if possible, for several years in advance. Your equipment should never deplete your working capital. Be sure you are financially capable of meeting long-term investments in equipment. Each year's budget should take into consideration the settlement of long-term debt, not merely the payment of interest.

Forecasting and budgeting may involve extensive figuring, but they are the foundations of your company's stability and future expansion. Your accountant can help you to determine the steps to take in producing your budget, but its actual production and application are up to you.

Control of Cash

For all businesses there are certain fundamental rules which should never be violated:

1. Keep personal cash transactions completely separate from those of the business. Use a specific bank account for business-related cash activities.

2. Record all incoming cash in a ledger or journal—the amounts along with their sources and dates.

3. Deposit all cash receipts each day in the company account.

4. Pay all business bills and expenses by company check. Do not make disbursements out of daily cash receipts. Try to take advantage of bill payments that offer cash discounts for prompt payment. Maintain a ledger or journal for all cash disbursements, making certain to identify the payee and the reason or classification of the expense paid.

5. Make disbursements only when you have received a validated supplier's invoice (matched against some receiving document to prove that the goods or services have, in fact, been received or against a receipted, paid-out voucher dated and signed by the person who is to receive the check).

6. Reconcile bank statements immediately after receiving them. The fact that a bank keeps an account of your cash transactions provides you with an important check of your business's cash records. A bank gives you monthly statements along with canceled checks, and reconciling your bank record and your own cash account should be done to check not only the accuracy of your account but also that of the bank.

7. If you have to make expenditures using personal checks or credit cards, make sure you promptly submit expenses to the business for reimbursement.

Cash Forecasts

Once you have devised a budget and are satisfied that you have employed every practical economy, you will want to consider using a cash forecast. You should always have enough cash available to meet sudden shifts in economic conditions or product requirements. Therefore, when your business is just starting, it is a good idea to keep your investments fairly fluid, to give you a quick source of cash when you need it. Should seasonal fluctuations result in cash deficits, short-term borrowing can tide you over.

Cash forecasts are essential to stabilizing the cash flow pattern for any business. They are the keenest tools for planning. Use them to direct new investments into growing lines or to withdraw capital from declining lines. By forecasting cash needs, a firm can determine the amount of excess cash which can be diverted to short-term investments. A sensible forecast enables an owner to stay on top of every phase of the company's performance and to plan for acquisition of new equipment or expansion of facilities.

To obtain data for forecasting, use your company's projection of sales by item or product line, and trends of your industry as a whole, but particularly in the geographical area where you will be competing. Such statistics can be obtained from your internal records, trade organizations, the U.S. Department of Commerce, local banks, and from the National Bureau of Economic Research, among other agencies.

To create a cash flow forecast requires an analysis of budgeted expenses and sales projections along with a series of educated guesses on the rate of collections of cash and anticipated major expenditures including asset purchases and debt repayments.

Figures 6.7 and 6.8 show a typical cash flow forecast statement. With experience, each company can refine the elements in the cash flow to more accurately reflect the significant items that must be analyzed in greater or lesser detail. As indicated in the figures, you normally forecast for a period of 3 months in advance; however, at the end of each month, the actual results are entered and the variances are calculated. If the variances are significant (usually plus or minus 10 percent), reproject the cash flows for another 3-month period.

Particularly in a new company, sales projections reflect management's best "guestimates" as to when and in what volumes sales will be realized. If this forecast goes amiss, all projected cash receipts will be understated as sales fall short of target; if, on the other hand, sales exceed the forecast, additional cash inflow may be anticipated.

Where sales are made "on account" (open invoices), the collection cycle (the number of days between sale and collection) becomes of paramount importance. If your normal invoice terms are "net 30 days," payment is due from the customer 30 days from the date of the invoice. However, experience will show that a significant percentage of your customers will pay their accounts well after the 30-day term. If, for example, you generate $3000 in monthly sales and only two-thirds of your customers pay their bills when due, you can only reasonably expect to collect $2000 in the month following the sale. The remaining one-third ($1000) should be collected in the following month. Those customers that do not pay then are obviously real credit problems and strong collection effort will be required.

Once your company's collection pattern is determined, you can more accurately project cash income. Table 6.1 shows such a projection assuming a 70 percent collection rate.

CASH FLOW FORECAST
Part I: Receipts and Disbursements
For 3 months ending _____

	Month 1			Month 2			Month 3		
	Estimate	Actual	Variance	Estimate	Actual	Variance	Estimate	Actual	Variance
Projected cash receipts:									
Cash sales									
Collections on accounts receivable									
Other income									
Total receipts									
Projected cash disbursements:									
Raw materials									
Merchandise									
Production supplies									
Payroll									
Utilities									
Rent									
Insurance									
Taxes									
Office supplies and postage									
Administrative									
Telephone									
Advertising									
Selling expenses/commissions									
Travel and entertainment									
Legal and accounting									
Computer									
Notes and loans payable									
Other									
Total disbursements									
Net cash increase or decrease (difference between receipts and disbursements)(To Part II: Summary)									

Figure 6-7. Cash flow forecast worksheet.

CASH FLOW FORECAST PART II: Summary For 3 months ending September 30, 19____						
	July		August		September	
	Estimate	Actual	Estimate	Actual	Estimate	Actual
Expected cash balance at beginning of month						
Add increase or subtract decrease (from Part I Figure 6.7)						
Expected cash balance						
Required cash balance						
Short-term loans needed*						
Cash available for short-term investment†						

* If cash is less than requirements.
† If cash exceeds requirements.

Figure 6-8. Example of cash flow forecast summary.

Table 6-1. Sample Cash Income Projection

	Month 1	Month 2	Month 3	Month 4
Forecast net sales	3000	5000	6000	8000
Collections:				
Current	2100	3500	4200	5600
Prior	—	900	1500	1800

Expenses must also be projected for the forecast period. While some of the expense categories may be educated guesses, others will be based on known factors or key relationships. For example, some of the items that should be fairly accurate include rent, notes and loans payable and their related interest costs, insurance and many administrative costs. Among those that are variably determinable are purchases of raw material and merchandise, factory payrolls (related to budgeted production), advertising, utilities, and certain selling costs. Other expense items can be projected within some reasonable ranges. Of course, with continuing experience of actual costs incurred, future projections can be made more accurately.

While it is difficult, if not impossible, to accurately forecast every expense item, your company will soon discover those elements of significant expense over which management has a degree of control. With a few months of actual experience, you should be able to identify the controllable costs and the approximate percentage relationship of the uncontrollable costs to total expenses.

It is important to compare the actual results, by line item, against the forecast primarily to provide the basis for reforecasting the succeeding monthly periods. Substantial variances should cause management to delve into the reasons behind the differences—both positive and negative. In the example above, lower collections on receivables may indicate a slowdown in payments by customers that may call for additional dunning and collection efforts. More significantly, this situation means that you will have less cash inflow than projected.

Another cause for concern would be increases in expense items that management must examine and correct to avoid any problematical trends.

No business can operate successfully without proper management of its assets. Since *cash* is the life blood of any business, it is readily apparent why cash control utilizing this tool, as previously discussed, and its inherent discipline for planning and controlling a business is so vital.

Inventories

Tax considerations govern the taking of your inventories. The regulations require the use of an inventory in every case in which production, purchase, or sale of merchandise is an income-producing factor.

Any inventory method that conforms with acceptable accounting principles in a balance sheet showing your financial position may be used for tax purposes.

Inventories should include all raw materials and supplies, as well as finished or partly finished goods, but they should not include the following:

- Raw materials and supplies which will not become a part of merchandise intended for sale.

- Materials ordered by you for future delivery, title to which has not yet been transferred to you.

- Assets of a capital nature, such as machinery, fixtures, land, buildings, accounts receivable, cash, or like assets.

- Goods received on consignment (even though inventory control must be maintained on these items).

- Goods (including containers) sold, title to which has passed to your customers.

In taking inventory of your normal goods, a consistent basis of costing must be applied. Where you maintain perpetual inventory records, inventory accounts are:

- Charged with the actual cost of the goods purchased or produced.

- Credited with the value of goods used, transferred, or sold, calculated upon the basis of the actual cost of the goods acquired during the year (including the inventory at the beginning of the year).

The net value as shown by the accounts is accepted to be the cost of the goods on hand, but balances shown by perpetual inventories must be verified by taking physical inventories at reasonable intervals, at which time adjustments are made.

There are other factors to be considered in a discussion of items of which inventory should be kept. Among them are:

- Operating supplies consumed in the normal course of business but not part of the product sold should be inventoried.

- Returned or defective merchandise must be inventoried in a separate control category where the value assigned reflects the cost to be realized upon final disposition.

- Goods in the hands of a "processor" (such as fabrics sent out to be dyed or finished) must be inventoried by the owner. But when a new product is to be returned (for example, refined copper for ore, or flour for wheat), then it is an exchange and must be treated as raw material-out and *new* material-in.

The overriding issue in determining whether merchandise must be included in a business's inventory is ownership. Title usually passes when the parties intend it to pass, subject to local or state laws. Exclude merchandise from the seller's inventory; include merchandise in the buyer's inventory even if goods are in transit or the buyer does not have physical possession. Goods shipped on consignment belong to the seller even though the consignee must account for them until sold or returned.

Inventory Valuation (for Tax Purposes)

You should weigh the merits of all available systems before you choose your method of inventory. Once you elect a method it must be applied in later years, unless you obtain authorization to change it from the Internal Revenue Service.

Table 6-2. How to Find Cost Using the FIFO and the LIFO Methods

Method	Inventory at end of year is computed	Therefore, cost of goods sold in year is
Cost:		
First in–first-out	1500 at $4	{ 1000 at $2 500 at $4
Last-in–first-out	1000 at $2 500 at $4 }	1500 at $4
Cost or market, whichever is lower	1500 at $4	{ 1000 at $2 500 at $4

Cost, and cost or market, whichever is lower, are approved as proper methods for inventorying. To find cost, you may use the *first-in–first-out* (FIFO) or the *last-in–first-out* (LIFO) methods. How each of these works is illustrated in Table 6.2.

Assume that the inventory at the beginning of the year was composed of 1000 units which cost $2 each. They had a market value of $2 on that date. Purchases during the year were 2000 units at $4. Sales during the year were 1500 units. Inventory at the end of the year was 1500 units. The market value was then $5.

Cost or market is used in inventory by many businesses in a falling market. This enables you to choose the lower of the two figures for each individual item. In practice, your inventory records will show three columns of figures: cost of the item, its present market price at a typical volume of purchase, and the lower of the two. Thus, on several items, your choice will vary. The effect upon cost of sales by the various methods of inventory is outlined in the following table:

Unit	Cost	Market price	Lower of cost or market
D	$5,000	$4,500	$4,500
E	6,500	6,800	6,500
F	2,000	1,900	1,900
	$13,500	$13,200	$12,900

What does *cost* mean? In the case of merchandise on hand at the beginning of the year, cost is the inventory price of such goods. In other cases, it is as follows:

1. On merchandise purchased since the beginning of the year, cost is computed as invoice price less trade or other discounts, excluding

strictly cash discounts. To net invoice price, add transportation or other necessary charges incurred in taking possession of the goods.

2. On merchandise produced since the beginning of the year, cost is the sum of the cost of raw materials and supplies entering into or consumed in connection with the product, direct labor, and indirect expenses necessary for the production of the particular article, including probably a reasonable proportion of management expenses, but not including any cost of selling.

3. For miners and manufacturers who, by a single process or a uniform series of processes, derive a product of two or more kinds, sizes, or grades, costs are allocated to each kind, size, or grade of product, which in the aggregate will absorb the total cost of production. Cost must bear a reasonable relation to the respective selling values of the different kinds, sizes, or grades of the product.

4. In any industry in which the usual rules for computation of cost of production are inapplicable, costs may be based upon an established trade practice of the particular industry.

What does *market* mean? Under ordinary circumstances it is the current bid price prevailing at the date of the inventory for the inventoried merchandise in the volume in which it is usually purchased. This rule applies to goods purchased and on hand, to goods in the process of manufacture, and to finished goods on hand. It does not apply to goods for delivery upon noncancelable sales contracts, at fixed prices below the market. These can be inventoried at cost. Or you can use the following rules:

1. If no open market exists or if quotations are nominal because of stagnant market conditions, use evidence of a fair market price at the date nearest the inventory. Or use specific purchases or sales by you or others in reasonable volume and made in good faith. Or use compensation paid for cancellation of contracts for purchase commitments.

2. When prices are falling, the market price may be your sales price, less what it costs you to make the sale. Correctness of this method is found by your actual sales for a reasonable period before and after the date of the inventory.

The use of LIFO is not dependent upon the character of a business. LIFO is generally the preferred method in inflationary times because a high inventory valuation minimizes profits for tax purposes. LIFO should not be used if prices are likely to decline in the years ahead.

The LIFO method would leave you with high inventory valuations of the items acquired at high prices, while your cost of goods sold would be understated. If you use the LIFO method of valuing your inventory for some years and prices drop, see if it is to your advantage to apply to the Internal Revenue Service for permission to change.

Ordinarily, rent, repairs, taxes, depreciation, and other factory over-head expenses are charged to the cost of production. Such expenses would then be included in the value of goods manufactured during the year, some of which will remain in inventory. This conforms to accepted principles of cost accounting.

Equipment and Fixed Assets

Virtually every business employs fixed assets or capital equipment in the conduct of their activities. Whether you only use desks, chairs, typewriters, and filing cabinets or whether you employ manufacturing or delivery equipment or own buildings and other types of property in generating your income, you must keep detailed records on them including at minimum the following data:

- Description or class of equipment.
- Date of purchase.
- Original cost or other basis.
- Costs to install or to improve equipment (if it is used) or to general-ly put it into productive capability.
- Estimated life of equipment, by class, to establish type of deprecia-tion expense to be taken.
- Accumulated depreciation recorded to date for each asset or class of asset.

Selection of a depreciation method or methods should only be done with the advice of your accountant or tax planner. The Internal Revenue Service has published guidelines describing the rules govern-ing acceptable depreciation methods.

Records Storage

Every company requires an organized method of storage for all origi-nal documents created in the conduct of their business. Payroll records, canceled checks, sales invoices, vouchers, purchase orders, etc., must be retained along with your cash books, journals, registers, and ledgers.

Many, if not all, of these records should be filed and saved for a period of time after the accounting year is closed. Specific legal requirements have been set forth by the Internal Revenue Service and other government authorities. Consult your attorney or outside auditor for these regulations and how they may apply to your specific business.

Because storage of old records is time- and space-consuming, the use of microfilm or microfiche can satisfy legal records retention requirements while enabling you to dispose of the space-consuming original documents. Should some future legal or tax problem surface, copies of the original documents can be readily reproduced.

7

Basic
Tax Management
Decisions

In Chapter 5 we discussed the tax aspects of choosing a business form. Tax decisions that affect current business operations are discussed in this chapter.

Several governments are silent partners in your business. The federal government probably takes the largest share of your profits through taxes, and, depending on the revenue needs of the state in which you conduct your business, the state government can also keep an amount of your income through taxes. Local tax authorities, city or county, may not be too far behind. Topping it all off are the costs of keeping the required records and preparing returns.

The word *tax* is inadequate to describe the many taxes to which businesses are subject. Income taxes, payroll taxes, sales taxes, and property taxes are only a few. There are as many others to be aware of and in compliance with.

Large companies usually have special departments for tax research and compliance. Because you are not likely to be big enough to afford your own department, be sure to develop within your bookkeeping and accounting systems a way of seeing that tax liabilities are calculated, documented, and met. You should also take steps to see that your enterprise keeps abreast of changes in tax laws which may affect it, to minimize its tax liabilities and avoid penalties. Because of the complexity of tax law, you probably will have to seek the help of a tax professional. However, having such help does not relieve you of your responsibility for keeping your business in compliance with tax regulations.

Tax Obligations Placed on Business

Income Tax

Sole proprietors and corporations are required to pay income tax to the federal government and, possibly, to city, county, and state governments as well. In addition to income tax, net earnings of a sole proprietorship are subject to self-employment tax on Schedule SE of Form 1040 (see Chapter 5 for further details). A partnership as an entity pays no income tax, but each partner pays income tax on his or her share of the income from the partnership (and gets to subtract certain credits and deductions which are passed through from the partnership). These items are spelled out on the Schedule K-1 every partnership issues to its partners annually.

In many states, income reported for federal income tax purposes is used as the base for computing state income taxes. The due date of income tax depends on the business taxable year and the form of your business. The filing date may be different for state and federal returns.

Employment Taxes

If you have employees, you must withhold and pay employment taxes (covering federal income tax, Social Security, and Medicare), no matter what form of business organization you use. The first step is to obtain a federal employer identification number by filing Form SS-4, a short-form registration.

A basic working definition of an employee is anyone you pay and whose conditions and place of employment you control. You may occasionally hire a consultant or other "contract labor," but such persons are not usually considered employees, and the taxes described below do not apply to them (they are responsible for their own self-employment taxes). Employment taxes should not be overlooked. The tax collector demands cash payment of the total amount of employment taxes. There is no credit. Not projecting and meeting these tax liabilities may cause a business to fail.

Social Security and Medicare Taxes

The tax for financing Social Security programs and Medicare hospital insurance, also known by its legislative initials FICA, must be withheld from the pay of all employees. The FICA withheld, the employer's FICA contribution, and the income tax withheld from employees' wages are all reported to the IRS on Form 941, usually quarterly.

The employment taxes due on employees' wages are usually paid directly to a designated depository bank. The frequency of the payments depends on the size of your employment tax liabilities over a 12-month "lookback" period. The amount is entered on a simple deposit coupon, Form 8109. A booklet of these forms is automatically issued to you when you obtain your employer identification number, along with instructions and a reorder form. Be careful to make these deposits on time, as the penalties for being late or making underpayments are severe.

If you are a sole proprietor or a partner, your personal Social Security liability is paid to the IRS in the form of self-employment tax, which you include along with your income tax. Your personal Social Security is not entered on Form 941 with your employee taxes unless you are an officer-employee of a corporation.

Unemployment Taxes

Unemployment taxes are paid to both the state and the federal government. The IRS gives partial credit for unemployment taxes paid to the state.

You register your business with your state bureau of labor. The state then assigns an identification number (to credit your deposits to your account) and an experience rate. The rate is determined by how often you and other businesses hire and fire people. The higher your turnover, the more demand is placed on the state unemployment fund and the more you will have to pay into the fund. The better you are at retaining employees, the less unemployment taxes you will be required to pay. Finally, the state will inform you how and when to deposit unemployment taxes with them.

The Federal Unemployment Tax

This tax, also known by its legislative initials FUTA, will be smaller than the state tax. One month after the close of your tax year you file Form 940 with the IRS to show how you calculated the unemployment tax that is due. The tax money is sent with the Form 940 if the amount owed is less than $100. If it is more, you use Deposit Form 8109 to pay the tax to an authorized bank. It usually takes three full-time employees before a business exceeds $100 in FUTA taxes.

Excise Taxes

The IRS also collects federal excise taxes. Currently, the taxes must be paid by producers of coal, truck parts, tractors, firearms, tires, and lubricating oil. The tax also is imposed upon telephone services, transportation of freight or passengers by air, and the use of international air travel facilities. Reported quarterly on Form 720, the tax can be sent with the form if it amounts to less than $100; otherwise, the tax must be paid to a depository bank, again using Form 8109.

Other Taxes

Some states also levy taxes on business property and inventory. Your state should automatically send you the necessary forms when you register the business. In the case of inventory tax, it's to your advantage to minimize your inventory at the assessment date, by running "preinventory clearance sales" or by postponement of incoming merchandise shipments, if that is possible.

If your business imports or exports products, you may have to pay customs duties in the United States and/or abroad. Contact the U.S. Customs Bureau, a reputable freight forwarder, or the foreign embassies or consulates for the countries in which you do business for information about applicable fees and product restrictions.

Related Tax Obligations

In addition to your obligation to collect or pay the correct taxes, you may be required to file other tax forms, even though no money is due. If your company has a pension plan, for example, it probably has to file a report every year. You must provide a Form W-2 to every employee to whom you pay wages and send Form 1099 to firms and individuals for certain payments made during the year by your firm. A copy of each Form W-2 and 1099 issued must be sent to the IRS. If you file over 250 forms, they must be filed on magnetic media unless you can prove doing so is a hardship. You must also receive and keep on file a Form W-4 (withholding allowances) for each employee. Your outside accountant can give you further help in meeting these various tax-related responsibilities.

Choosing Your Accounting Period

Income taxes are generally computed on transactions occurring during a 12-month period. If the period ends on December 31, it is called a calendar year; if it ends on the last day of any month other than December, the IRS refers to it as a fiscal year. In any event, a reporting period (technically called a taxable year) can never be longer than 12 months except when (1) it is the year in which you start or end your business, (2) it is the year in which you change your taxable year, or (3) your business reports on a 52- to 53-week fiscal year basis.

Businesses may not establish just any fiscal year they choose. A business year generally must correspond to a calendar year unless you have a good business reason for choosing otherwise. The business year of a partnership or S corporation must be that of the majority of the partners or stockholders.

The following factors should be taken into account when considering making an application for a fiscal year:

- *What is your natural business year?* The year you select should be the one which gives you an undistorted picture of your business. This is especially important if you operate a seasonal business. It should encompass your entire business season, and *it should end when you have the minimum amount of incomplete transactions,* for example, when your inventories and accounts receivable are at a minimum. Having such a year greatly facilitates the preparation of your financial statements and tax return.

- *When will your tax payments be due?* If you choose a tax year which ends at a time when your cash reserves are low, you may find it difficult to pay your taxes. It usually is advisable to end your tax year when substantial cash is on hand to pay your taxes.

Tax Accounting Methods for Reporting Business Income

Your business income is reported on either the accrual or cash basis. You may figure your business income on the accrual basis even if you report your nonbusiness income on the cash basis. If you have more than one business, it is possible to have different accounting methods for each business.

If you have inventories, you must use the accrual basis for business sales and purchases.

Cash Basis

On the cash basis, you report income items in the taxable year of receipt; you deduct all expenses in the taxable year in which they are paid. Under the cash basis, income is also reported if it is "constructively" received. You have "constructively" received income when an amount is credited to your account, subject to your control, or set apart for you and may be drawn by you at any time. For example, in 1993, you receive a check in payment of services, but you do not cash it until 1994. You have constructively received the income in 1993 and it is taxable in 1993.

In general, you deduct expenses in the year of payment. Expenses paid by credit card are deducted in the year they are charged. Expenses paid through a "pay by phone" account with a bank are deducted in the year the bank sends the check. This date is reported by the bank on its monthly statement.

The cash basis has this advantage over the accrual method. You may defer reporting income by postponing the receipt of income. For example, if 1993 is a high-income year or income tax rates will be lower in 1994, you might extend the date of payment of some of your customers' bills until 1994. But make certain that you avoid the constructive receipt rule. You may also postpone the payment of presently due expenses to a year in which the deduction gives you a greater tax savings.

The following may not use the cash method: a regular C corporation with average annual receipts of more than $5 million, a partnership with a C corporation as a partner, a tax shelter, a tax-exempt trust with unrelated business income, and a business with inventories.

Accrual Basis

On the accrual basis, you report income that has been earned whether or not received, unless a substantial contingency restricts your right to collect the income. Where you are prepaid for future services that must be completed by the end of the next tax year, you may defer the reporting of the income until you earn it.

For example, you report business income as a calendar year accrual taxpayer. You sell several products on December 27, 1993, and bill the customer in January 1994. You report the sales income on a 1993 tax return even though payment is not made until 1994. Under the accrual method, you are considered to have the income when the products were sold and delivered to the customer.

Expenses under the accrual method are deductible in the year your liability for payment is fixed, even though payment is made in a later year. To prevent the manipulation of expense deductions, there are technical tests for fixing liability which in doubtful cases should be left to your accountant to interpret. They are listed in IRS Publication 538, which is available without charge from the IRS. However, the basic operation of the accrual expense rule can be understood from the following example.

Example

You report business income as a calendar year accrual taxpayer. In December 1993, you order and receive supplies with an invoice for payment. You pay the bill in 1994. You deduct the expense on a tax return reporting 1993 income and expenses. Liability was fixed in 1993, and the supplies were delivered in 1993. What if delivery was not until 1994? The expense is deductible in 1993 if the timing of the order and the delivery follows your normal business practice.

Change in Accounting Method

When you file your first business return, you may choose any permitted accounting method (subject to the previously discussed restrictions) without IRS consent. The method you choose must clearly show your income and the same method must be used from year to year. However, if after your first return is filed you want to change your accounting method, you must first obtain permission from the IRS. Apply for consent by filing Form 3115 with the Commissioner of Internal Revenue, Washington, DC 20224, within 180 days after the beginning of the tax year in which you wish to make the change. Thus, if you report on the calendar-year basis and want to change from the cash method to the accrual method for 1994, you should file by June 30, 1994.

Depreciation Elections

Depreciation is an expense deduction that allows you to recover your capital investment in business assets. There are two methods of claiming expense deductions for your purchases of machinery, buildings, equipment, fixtures, autos, and trucks (land itself is never depreciable) used in your business:

- First-year expensing (Section 179 deduction), which allows you to deduct a flat amount; check with your tax adviser.

- Regular depreciation, which allows a prorated deduction over a period of years. Most business equipment is depreciable under the modified accelerated cost recovery system (MACRS) over a 6-year period. The objective of MACRS is to provide rapid depreciation and to eliminate disputes over useful life, salvage value, and depreciation methods. Useful life and depreciation methods are fixed by law; salvage value is treated as zero. If you do not want to use MACRS accelerated rates, you may elect the straight-line method. MACRS applies to new and used property.

Capital investments in buildings are subject only to depreciation using the straight-line method.

In general, you may depreciate property if it meets all of the following requirements:

1. It must be used in your business or held for the production of income.

2. It must have a determinable useful life which is longer than one year.

3. It must be something that wears out, decays, gets used up, becomes obsolete, or loses value from natural causes.

Specific annual depreciation rates for each class of property are provided by IRS tables and are subject to change by Congress.

When choosing a depreciation method, remember that the total amount of depreciation for any piece of property cannot be greater than the cost of the item. Accelerated methods give you greater deductions early and lesser deductions in later years. They may be helpful where the increased deduction will give you more cash for working capital. However, in starting a new business in which you expect losses in the beginning, the accelerated methods are likely to give you deductions that you do not need now but which would be of more benefit later, when the business starts generating more taxable income. If you plan a program of regular replacement of equipment, an accelerated method will probably work to your advantage.

Splitting Business Income with Family Members

Tax on your business income may be reduced by shifting it to family relatives. Income shifting is possible by giving a relative a partnership interest or stock in a corporation. As in all tax-saving plans, there are restrictions:

- Income splitting with children will not provide any significant tax savings unless a child is 14 years of age or over. Investment or unearned income of a child under age 14 is subject to tax at a parent's top bracket under the kiddie tax rules. However, wages paid to your child are not subject to the kiddie tax. You may also deduct the wages as a business expense if the payments are reasonable. Set the wages at the scale that you would pay an outsider; keep records of your child's work; withhold tax; and provide the child with a Form W-2. If your child is age 17 or under, you do not have to withhold FICA taxes on the wages. FICA taxes are due on wages paid to your child age 18 or over.

- With a partnership, income shifting is possible if capital is a material income-producing factor in the business. But in a service partnership—real estate or insurance brokers, for example—a gift of a partnership interest to a family member will not shift partnership income, unless he or she actually performs services for the partnership.

- A minor child will be recognized as a partner if he or she is competent to manage his or her own property, or control of the property is exercised by an independent fiduciary for the minor's sole benefit. To accomplish this objective, a trust may be set up to hold the partnership interest.

- Stock of a corporation may be given to a minor child by setting up a custodian account or a trust for the child's benefit. However, a transfer of stock in an S corporation to a trust must be carefully drafted. The trust itself must be an S trust. If not, the transfer will terminate the S election.

- In an S corporation, pass-through items must reflect the value of services rendered or capital contributed by family members of the shareholders. In an S corporation, if you do most of the work, your income from the company must reflect the value of your services. You cannot deflect your income to family members who are stockholders.

- If you keep within the annual gift tax exclusion of $10,000 for each donee, there will be no gift tax consequences. However, the estate tax advantages of "estate freeze" techniques have been limited, making it difficult to avoid estate tax on the appreciation in capital interests transferred to children. To discourage estate tax freeze plans, a complicated gift and estate tax law was passed in 1990. The rules affect common and preferred stock holdings within the family, partnership interests, the deferral or dividend payments on preferred stock, life and remainder interests, and buy-sell agreements in family businesses. The estate freeze rules impose gift tax and estate tax values for property transfers subject to the law. Because of the complexity of these rules and their effect on gift and estate values, we suggest that you seek professional advice in the following situations: (1) As an owner of a family business, you plan to give common stock to family members while retaining preferred stock or recapitalize with common and preferred stock; (2) you plan to give up a voting interest or liquidating rights attached to preferred stock in a family business; (3) you defer payment of dividends in preferred stock in a family business; and/or (4) you plan to give stock to a family member in a company in which you have a buy-sell agreement.

Fringe Benefits

The law prohibits you from deducting most personal expenses, such as food, life insurance protection, your children's education, and vacations, from taxable income. However, payment for some personal items may be shifted to your business, thereby freeing personal funds for additional investment, etc.

Owning a business in the form of a regular C corporation enables you to take full advantage of several fringe benefits sanctioned by the tax law. *Fringe benefits* is a term designed to cover all benefits supplied by your corporation beyond salary. It includes such benefits as health and accident insurance coverage, group-term life insurance, discounts on company products, transit passes, meals and lodging on company premises, and dependent care assistance.

The main attraction of fringe benefits is that they come to the recipient partially or wholly tax-free. What this means in terms of dollars and cents depends, of course, on your tax bracket. For example, say your personal income is taxed at 40 percent (federal and state combined), and your corporation pays $1000 per year to provide you with tax-free group-hospital coverage. That insurance is worth $1670 in personal pretax dollars to you. Stated another way, you would have to earn $1670 before taxes in order to have the $1000 to pay the premium yourself.

Partners and S corporation shareholders owning more than a 2 percent interest are not allowed tax-free treatment for certain important fringe benefits. For example, accident and health insurance coverage and the first $50,000 of group-term life insurance coverage, which are not included in the taxable income of C corporation employees, are treated as income for partners and more than 2 percent S corporation shareholders.

The availability of fringe benefits becomes meaningful only when the business is profitable enough to provide such benefits. To be a deductible business expense, the same fringe benefits available to you must generally also be available to your employees on a nondiscriminatory basis.

Check with your tax advisor as to which benefits currently qualify for partial or total tax-free treatment. The list of qualifying benefits is subject to change by Congress and the IRS.

Retirement Plans

Retirement plan coverage for yourself and your employees is a major fringe benefit. If you set up a *qualified* pension profit-sharing or stock bonus plan, the following tax advantages are obtained: (1) you and your employees are not taxed on contributions that are within the limits fixed by law; (2) the contributed funds compound tax free within the plan; and (3) distributions on retirement may be rolled over tax free to an IRA (individual retirement account). Distributions from the IRA may be spread over your retirement years for further tax savings. For plan participants who were born before 1936 and who are in the plan for at least 5 years, a special averaging method may be available to reduce the tax on a qualifying lump-sum distribution that is not rolled over to an IRA.

To obtain these tax benefits, a retirement plan must meet technical legal requirements, including nondiscrimination rules aimed at preventing owners from discriminating on their own behalf. Plans meeting the technical requirements must be approved by the IRS to be considered qualified plans. Most employees adopt prototype plans that have already been approved by the IRS, but an individually designed plan may be submitted for IRS approval.

In general, the qualified plan rules are the same for corporate plans as for *Keogh* plans, which are plans used by self-employed individuals and partnerships. However, there are certain special contribution and nondiscrimination rules for self-employed Keogh plans. Furthermore, loans from Keogh plans to owner-employees are generally prohibited, whereas loans from a corporate plan are allowed subject to specific limits.

A corporate or Keogh retirement plan can be in the form of a defined benefit pension plan or a defined contribution plan.

A *defined benefit pension plan* is the traditional type of pension, providing for a fixed benefit upon retirement, typically keyed to a percentage of compensation based upon years of service. With a defined benefit pension plan, contributions are not based on profits. Depending upon the benefits formula, contributions must be actuarially determined to ensure that there will be adequate funds to pay the projected pension benefits. A defined pension plan can be costly if you have older employees for whom you must fund proportionally high benefits.

There are three types of *defined contribution* plans: profit-sharing plans, stock bonus plans, and money purchase pension plans. All three types of plans require a formula for determining contributions to the plan, such as a percentage of compensation. There is no fixed or predetermined amount of benefits. The amount to be received at retirement depends on the level of contributions and how they have been invested.

A stock bonus plan can be set up only by a corporation; contributions are made in the form of company stock.

A profit-sharing plan allows your employees to share in your business success. Generally, you contribute a percentage of each participant's compensation each year. The percentage can be changed as business conditions require. In loss years, you may contribute nothing. For regular employees, the maximum profit-sharing contribution is 15 percent of compensation, subject to an annual dollar limitation, currently $30,000. If you are self-employed and have a profit-sharing Keogh plan, the maximum contribution percentage for yourself is 13.0435 percent (instead of 15 percent) and that percentage is applied to net self-employment earnings (from Schedule C) after being reduced by 50 percent of the self-employment tax liability figured on Schedule SE of Form 1040.

A money purchase plan requires fixed annual contributions, without regard to profit. Contributions of up to 25 percent of compensation are allowed for regular employees; for self-employed individuals, the maximum contribution percentage is 20 percent of net earnings, after such earnings are reduced by 50 percent of self-employment tax liability.

A self-employed individual can maximize contributions by setting up a flexible profit-sharing plan and supplementing it with a smaller, fixed-contribution money purchase plan. Your tax advisor or Keogh plan trustee can help you arrange separate plans while staying within the overall contribution limit of 20 percent of net earnings.

If your company has a profit-sharing or stock bonus plan, it has the opportunity of giving additional tax sheltered pay. The tax law allows the company to add a cash or deferred pay plan, called a 401(k) plan, which can operate in one of two ways:

1. Your firm contributes an amount for the employee's benefit to a trust account. The employee is not taxed on the employer's contribution.

2. The employee agrees to take a salary reduction or to forgo a salary increase. The reduction is placed in a trust account. The reduction is not considered taxable pay because it is treated as the employer's contribution. In 1993, the limit was $8994 and is subject to annual inflation adjustments. To satisfy special nondiscrimination requirements in the law, salary reduction deferrals of highly compensated individuals may have to be limited below the generally applicable annual ceiling.

Making salary deferrals is an ideal way to defer income and get a tax-free buildup of earnings. Although there is no income tax, the contribution is subject to Social Security tax. Withdrawals before age $59\frac{1}{2}$ are restricted. A 401(k) plan does not permit distributions except for retirement, death, disability, termination of employment, attaining age $59\frac{1}{2}$, or financial hardship. The plan does allow employees to borrow from their accounts, but such loans must generally be paid back within 5 years. Qualifying lump-sum distributions are eligible for special averaging tax treatment if the employee participated in the plan for 5 years or more and was born before 1936.

Another retirement plan option for corporate or self-employed business owners is the *simplified employee pension* plan, or SEP, which is a special type of IRA. The advantage of an SEP is that it is flexible and easier to implement than pension or profit-sharing plans. With an SEP, an employer makes contributions to the IRAs of all eligible employees and the contributions can exceed the regular $2000 IRA limit. Most employees must be covered under the law's strict eligibility requirements. You do not have to make contributions every year, but when you make contributions, they must be based on a written allocation formula and must not discriminate in favor of yourself, other owners with more than 5 percent interest, or employees who are considered highly compensated under the law. SEP contribution limits are similar to those for profit-sharing plans: 15 percent of pay for regular employees and 13.0435 percent for self-employed owner-employees. If your business has no more than 25 employees, you can also offer a salary reduction feature to an SEP. The salary deferral limit is generally the lesser of 15 percent of compensation or the annual deferral limit for 401(k) plans (for example, $8994 in 1993).

Distributions from an SEP are taxable unless rolled over to another IRA, and distributions before age 59½ are penalized unless you are disabled or payments are received under an annuity-type schedule. Special averaging, which may be available as discussed above for lump-sum distributions from qualified defined contribution plans, does not apply to SEP distributions.

Recommendation: The kind of retirement plan you choose will depend on the probable future of your business and the kind of benefits you want your employees to have. Given the technical retirement plan rules and the frequency with which they are changed by Congress, you need to consult with your tax and financial advisers before committing yourself. You need to know the cost commitment and how much flexibility you will have in annual contributions. Your consultants can give you cost estimates based on 20- or 30-year projections.

Home Space Used for Business

You may operate your business from your home, using a room or other space as an office or area to assemble or prepare items for sale. To deduct home expenses allocated to your business, you, as a self-employed person, must be able to prove that you use the home area *exclusively and on a regular basis* either as a place of business to meet or deal with clients or customers in the normal course of your business, or as your principal place of business.

Note the terms *exclusively* and *on a regular basis.* The exclusive-use test requires use of a specific section of a residence solely for the purpose of carrying on business. The use of a room for both personal and business purposes does not meet the exclusive-use test. But a part of a room can qualify, if you can show that it is exclusively and regularly used as the principal place of business or for seeing clients or customers. A separate structure not attached to your house can qualify if it is exclusively and regularly used for business; it does not have to be your principal place of business or used to meet with clients or customers.

Under the regular-use test, expenses attributable to incidental or occasional trade or business use are not deductible, even if the room is used only for business.

The previously discussed tests will generally not present problems in deducting home expenses when the home is the principal place of business. Problems arise when you have an office elsewhere and use a part of your home for some business transactions. If your deduction is questioned, evidence that you have actual office facilities and records of business visitors are important. For example, a woman operated a road stand a mile from her home and used her home to prepare items for sale at the stand. Although she used the home space for a business purpose, she was not allowed to deduct home expenses because her home was not considered her principal place of business. Her principal place of business was the road stand; the home area was not used for seeing customers.

A home office deduction is allowed for a second, or sideline, business even if you are employed or have another business elsewhere. Each separate business may have its own principal location.

A deduction for home business use may include real estate taxes, mortgage interest, operating expenses (e.g., home insurance premiums, utility costs), and depreciation allocated to the area used for business. Household expenses and repairs that do not benefit that space are not deductible. For example, the cost of painting and repairs to rooms other than the one used as a business office is not deductible. However, a pro rata share of the cost of painting the outside of a house or repairing a roof may be deductible. Costs of lawn care and landscaping are not deductible.

Expenses allocated to the business use of an area in your home may not exceed the *net* income derived from that use (i.e., gross business income minus all other expenses attributable to that income). Follow this order in deducting expenses:

1. Deduct allocable taxes and interest (and casualty losses, if any).

2. From the balance of income, deduct materials, supplies, salary paid to employees, and other business expenses not allocable to the use of the office space.

3. From the balance of income, deduct operating expenses allocable to the office; this includes heat, power, insurance, and any other utilities used by your business. Also deduct any repairs and maintenance to the business area and the allocable percent of whole-house repairs.

4. If a balance still remains, deduct allocable depreciation up to the amount of remaining net business income. Any amount disallowed because of the net income limit may be carried forward to later tax years, subject to the same net income limitation then. The allocation percent is determined by the ratio of business-use space (square footage or number of rooms) to total space in the home. The amount of taxes, interest, or casualty losses not allocable to the home office may be claimed as itemized deductions.

Tax Problems of a Sideline Business

A sideline business poses a special tax problem when it loses money. If your return is examined, deductions claimed for these losses may be disallowed on the grounds that you do not operate with the expectation of making a profit.

If your sideline venture is running into the red, take your loss deductions, but at the same time be prepared to produce evidence of business or profit-making intentions. This may be evidence that your activity is in a field of personal expertise; you devote considerable time and effort to the activity; losses are due to unexpected events, such as casualties; you employ experts or consultants in the field; you run the activity in a businesslike manner, maintaining complete and accurate books and records; or the element of pleasure or recreation is not dominant. A reasonable expectation of profit is all you must show.

If your return is examined and your losses are questioned, there are special tax rules that may help you. If you show a profit in 3 or more years during a 5-year period, you are presumed to be in an activity for profit. The Internal Revenue Service may rebut this presumption. If it does, you must then show facts that support your claim of being engaged in an activity for profit. Similarly, if you do not show 3 profitable years in the 5-year period, you have to prove your case. If you anticipate profits in later years, you have this option: You may elect to delay a determination of the issue until the fifth taxable year from the year you first entered the activity. If you have by then realized at least 3 profitable years, the presumption of profit will apply to the loss years. In making the election, you sign a waiver of statute of limitations for the taxable years involved. The waiver keeps those years open to possible deficiency claims. In the case of horse racing, breeding, or showing, the presumption is based on 2 profitable years during a 7-year period.

If you are a passive investor in a business in which you do not take an active management role, your share of the business's loss is treated as a "passive loss" which may be deducted only from income of other passive activities. A passive loss may not be deducted from other income such as salary, self-employment earnings, interest, dividends, or other investment earnings.

Reviewing State Taxes on Business Activity

If you are planning to do business across state lines, you must consider the taxes that may apply to your business in each state in which you will do business. Each state has the right to tax, and a company doing interstate business will pay taxes to more than one state. In some situations multiple state taxes can be as costly as federal taxes.

Check with your accountant and attorney. Tell them how you plan to handle sales, billing, accounting, and warehousing. Include any activities that may involve other states even indirectly. One trivial activity may subject you to tax liability. Your lawyer may seek information from a service company that will keep him or her posted on legislation and court decisions affecting businesses in each state. After a review with your counselors, you can decide in which states you will apply and qualify to do business.

Your books should reflect in which states income and expenses arose. Otherwise, you may have to pay state taxes on income that legally should escape. The way you render your bills may also affect sales tax liability.

Some states will hold you responsible for unemployment taxes and other levies if you use traveling sales representatives who solicit orders, even though final acceptance of the orders comes from the head office. One method of avoiding this type of tax is by limiting your sales in such states to independent agents.

If you sell equipment that requires installation or maintenance, you may be able to avoid tax liability in some states by turning the work over to local businesses and letting them handle it for their own accounts.

8
Operating the Retail Store

The independent retailer who feels overwhelmed by chain-store buying power and diversity may be cheered by knowing that about 60 percent of retail sales in the United States take place in independent stores. There are close to 2 million retail firms in the United States, most of them single-unit, independent stores.

The success of chain retailers depends a good deal on establishing and adhering to standard methods of buying and merchandising, inventory, and cost control. Small, independently owned shops cannot compete with the chains in costs of goods, variety of merchandise, or price. However, that does not leave them defenseless. They can concentrate on uniqueness of merchandise, the quality of the shopping environment, and the personal attention which makes shopping more pleasurable than in a large chain store.

Since the small retail firm cannot serve the broad needs of the buying public, it must seek to profit from specialization. Magazines and paperback publications, tobaccos, maternity and half-size clothing, gourmet and health foods, upholstery and upholstery materials, picture framing, greeting cards and novelty items, and automobile accessories are examples of lines or activities ideally suited to small-store operations. Patrons of small stores are in the market for items and services not commonly available in chain stores. If your lines and services are designed to match their needs, you can draw them from department-store trade. Know and meet your customers' tastes and habits, and you may win their regular patronage.

Location

"Location, location, location" is the chant of just about everyone who has gone into or acts as an advisor to the retail trade. Location is a powerful factor in retailing. Although restaurants sometimes prosper in a seemingly poor location (seemingly, because even in such cases, remoteness or "poor" location can be an attraction in itself—to those who want a ride into the country before dinner, for example), thanks to superlative food and atmosphere, a store selling goods had better not be difficult for its customers to reach.

A clear example is a gas station located near two other gas stations on or near a business intersection with traffic lights. The station that gets the most customers—assuming rough equality between prices and products—is the one with the easiest means of access and departure. The spiffy major station right on the corner may well lose out because during rush hours (and even during a significant part of the business day) potential customers pass it by as they try to make the lights or, if they have entered the station in the past, found it impossible to leave without a long wait. However, the service station in the middle of the block suffers neither of these problems and, therefore, enjoys more business than its competitors (and probably lower rent, too).

Appearance and Atmosphere

Ideally, if your store is a specialty shop, it should be the only one of its kind in the immediate area. However, if there is competition, your store can succeed by capitalizing on the weaknesses of competitors. You might offer better selection in your merchandise, use more aggressive and focused sales promotion, carry higher-priced quality goods or lower-priced lines, arrange better displays, offer more attractive packaging, and stress departments neglected by your competition.

It is good practice to clue the public into the nature of your store by its exterior appearance, display, and window advertising. Travelers, for example, are often attracted to chain restaurants on highways because they know what to expect. Your sign and your show windows should give some indication of the store's price level and type of service. If you attract customers through misleading displays, their dissatisfaction may result in unfavorable publicity for your shop.

Try to arrange displays for dramatic effect. The seasons and events offer opportunities. At very little expense you can decorate and arrange your store windows to represent a theme: the season, school reopening, religious holidays, vacation time.

Location of sales items should receive careful consideration. For example, keep staples near the back of the store (except when they are on sale or the objects of special promotions). Place impulse items at the front of the store to attract the attention of customers who must pass by these items on the way to the staples. This creates more customer exposure to impulse items and makes selling these goods easier.

Consider the location of other areas in your store. Place your stockrooms behind your sales area. You should have adequate space to accommodate the items that cannot be easily stacked behind counters. If necessary, make arrangements for an alteration room or repair room. In a clothing store, you will need fitting rooms with good lighting, mirrors, and doors or curtains for privacy. A rest room can be a goodwill builder for shoppers, particularly if you cater to elderly shoppers or if your store is located in a relatively remote location.

The casual shopper's opinion of your store's merchandise and its quality, price, and style will be formed on the strength of your window displays. Arranging attractive selling displays is a challenge to any dealer, but attractive displays can be produced without large expenditures of money. You or someone in your family may have a talent for designing appealing window displays, or you may find a free-lance designer who works for several store owners in your vicinity. Local schools with good commercial art courses are a possible resource; arrangements are sometimes made for promising students to give part-time help in window display.

Your front show windows can be open- or closed-back, depending on your preference, the size and nature of the merchandise, and the type of image you hope to create. With an open-back window, pedestrians on the sidewalk can look into the body of your store. This style of storefront helps create the impression of a friendly environment where shoppers are free to browse without a purchase in mind. A closed-back window gives greater prominence to merchandise on display but is less likely to invite the casual shopper into your store.

To attract attention to your displays, try to make the exterior of the store distinctive in some way, whether by use of an attractive awning, a distinctive sign, or simply a well-painted door and trim. Lighting is also an attention-getting factor, particularly in attracting the interest of evening passersby. Integrate lighting with window displays and the store's exterior, but do not forget the store's interior. Fluorescent lighting sometimes gives a washed-out look to merchandise, so use lighting which brings out the true colors of the items. Not only will this promote sales, it will also reduce the return of merchandise by customers who have found that the colors did not look the same under normal lighting conditions. Lighting is a factor deserving of professional advice.

Color is an important key in creating a mood conducive to sales. If your retail shop is large enough, you might try a different color scheme for each department, such as bright colors, a peppermint stripe awning or colorful wall decorations for children's wear or toys.

Many times it is the atmosphere offered by a restaurant, not its food, that is the critical factor in determining its success. Reduced lighting and muted colors give an air of intimacy and encourage leisurely dining. If you are relying on quick turnover of trade, bright lighting and clearer colors will probably better fit your mode of service.

Balancing Your Space

In most stores space is at a premium, and the good store operator manages space as well as he or she manages product selection, buying, and pricing. The greatest volume of profitable sales is produced by well-balanced departments. Space cannot be added to one department without proportionately reducing another. For this reason, do not overdevelop one department at the expense of another unless you are convinced that overall sales volume will be increased.

Placement of departments is of major importance. If you plan structures within the store that cannot be easily moved, be sure to consult first with an experienced layout consultant or a trade association. Examine trade journals and visit stores carrying your type of merchandise to see their arrangements and judge their effectiveness.

The amount of space to be given to a department often determines its location. Departments composed of a large percentage of bulky items and low unit sales are naturally forced to the rear of the store. Departments made up of high unit sale items come to the front. "Call" merchandise is displayed in the rear. Impulse items, whose sales depend upon display and visual suggestion, should usually be near the entrance to the store.

Keep your premises clean and attractive. Be sure the store entrance is kept free of litter, containers, slippery substances, snow, and puddles. Stairways should be well-lighted and unobstructed, and shelves and display stands sensibly stocked. To eliminate fire hazards, keep the store cleared of excelsior, boxes, rags, paper, flammable liquids, and articles which may ignite from spontaneous combustion. Have heating equipment inspected regularly. Do your part to ensure that the building harbors no rodents or insects.

Giving That Extra Attention

Successful store owners do not run their stores to suit themselves; they generally must cater to the tastes and requirements of customers. This may mean keeping a store open on certain evenings, on holidays, or at other times when competing stores generating potential customer traffic for the store are open.

The small store should answer customer complaints promptly and offer redress whenever possible. Exchange on colors and sizes and service on faulty merchandise should be given willingly. You can create immeasurable goodwill by arranging accommodating payment terms with regular customers on high-priced items. Some storekeepers win customers' loyalty by making unscheduled deliveries for important occasions. Many firms create business by sending reminders, for example, for periodic car servicing, tire replacements, carpeting cleaning, or reupholstering. Be conscientious about your reminders. Do not mail them before the customer's real need is likely to arise. Otherwise, the card will be tossed aside as just another bit of advertising.

Try to develop wide product-and-style knowledge about your merchandise and be generous and honest with your advice to customers. Shoppers will remember the salesperson who recommends a lower-priced fixture because it is better-suited to their particular needs. The extra business honesty brings you will soon compensate for any loss you may suffer on one sale.

Improving Customer Relations

It goes without saying that proper attitudes and behavior on the part of the sales staff will make a shop more attractive to customers. But there's more to customer relations than that!

Do you have service or credit policies that seem oppressive to customers? Be sure to avoid slighting one customer to the benefit of another. Express appreciation for customer purchases and prompt payments of outstanding balances (acknowledgment of the latter is usually appreciated).

Be pleasant to sales and service people who come into your store; customers are always affected by how others are treated in the store while they are there. Never berate store personnel in a customer's presence. Try to have a private, soundproof room available for discussions when controversy may arise and voices may be raised.

If you have lost customers, try to find out why. This is an essential part of marketing research. Were former customers alienated by your selling techniques, service, or credit policy? You need to know. Evaluate your sales staff. Are they able, helpful, and well-informed about your stock? Does your advertising have sales appeal?

When you do find out why you have lost customers, offer restitution promptly and pleasantly if you have been at fault. Even if the complaint seems unjustified, it is usually best to give the customer the benefit of the doubt.

If you are a specialty house—such as an auto-paint distributor or air-conditioning installation and service company—you might consider keeping the names of lost customers on file. Use every opportunity to send letters with a "news flavor"—new items, new policies, new personnel, new services, new floor space, etc. Take steps to build up an impression of progress and improvement. Be as ingenious and original as you please—you have nothing to lose and much to gain.

If the lost customer is a business house, mail sales tips and clippings of articles or news items which should interest the company. At times, a lost account can be picked up again by offering a bargain item from stock too limited for general sales.

Special Promotional Events

Special sales will attract many customers if the values offered are genuine. You may choose to promote a special line of goods which you obtained at bargain rates from your wholesaler. To this, you can add some other items of regular stock. You should, however, check the results of this promotional gimmick. Does it result in reduced patronage after the sale? Does a long-range increase in customers become noticeable? If the answer to the first question is yes, to the second no, think twice before you try another special sale!

Many stores organize attention-attracting events to put their name before the public. Sometimes a contest, fashion show, raffle, celebrity visit, or other popular activity will help stimulate sales. Food and toiletry distributors frequently make use of samples, coupons, and premium offers to gain attention.

Advantages of a Self-Service Store

Self-service stores enjoy lower labor costs and higher sales from open displays of merchandise. Customers can examine items without the pressure of salesclerks. The open displays often lead to impulse buying.

Your savings on wages will be considerable. Customers make their own selections, so clerks are needed only to ring up sales and bag the merchandise. Of course, some clerk assistance is needed in departments where a knowledge of the goods must be supplied by the store or where sizes or fittings are in question. Expensive merchandise must also be tended by a salesperson.

Self-service in the small store requires special display stands for apparel. A service desk, equipped with a cash register, is needed for completing the sale and wrapping the goods. To protect cash more effectively, place registers behind a counter which isolates checkers effectively from customers when sales are rung up.

The Discount Store— Specialty and Department Stores

The specialty discount store usually focuses on one particular line of items or, at most, on several related lines. These might be records and tapes, leather or brass goods, appliances, computers, imported items, or exotic food items. Although shopping centers are often favored locations, the specialty discount space may be able to occupy nearby quarters where occupancy costs are considerably lower than those in the center. Customer services are reduced or provided at an added charge.

The emphasis in the discount store is on fast-moving merchandise. Usually, the inventory turns about 7 or 8 times annually. Some items turn nearly twice that fast. Many discounters are franchised outlets.

The full-line department store has entered discount retailing, and in doing so, has created opportunities for the small-industrial-store operator. If the traffic in a full-line discount department store gives you important advantages—such as a predictable flow of potential customers—you might do well by opening a concession in the store. Rental of space will probably run between 5 and 14 percent of your sales, plus the cost of the fixtures you use. Usually your lessor will wish to control the advertising and limit your maximum margin.

On the other hand, if you buy or build a structure big enough to house merchandise of department-store variety, you might lease out a number of departments to concessionaires and so reduce your own investment and management responsibilities.

Planning a Buying Program

If you run a large store, you will probably have to hire an experienced buyer to formulate buying plans, schedule and make buying trips, check on delivered items, set prices, and plan advertising and promotions. Small-shop owners will have to assume most of the responsibility for these tasks. But even they use some help if they have doubtful tastes in merchandise selection.

Real buying skill comes from practice. As you start out, adopt the price lines most suited to your customers' pocketbooks. You will have to keep abreast of trends in your line of business and subscribe to upcoming styles even when they do not coincide with your taste. Recognize the point at which trends change; timing is especially important in merchandising consumer goods. But the time to change should not be dictated by media reports of new fashions. Customers often resist, or even reject, fads depending on the local culture, social influences, and/or moral values. Let sales trends be one of your guides.

If you do not want to be the trendsetter in your marketing area, obtain ideas about local preferences from watching the displays and advertisements of other stores. And talk to vendor salespeople; they are usually good sources of emerging market likes and dislikes. Listen to and add up the requests of customers.

If you are not a specialty or franchised store, balance your stock between nationally advertised and private brands. Nationally advertised brands attract customers who are constantly reminded through advertising of their quality, durability, and value. They require little selling effort. Because of the manufacturers' promotional costs, these brands usually have to be merchandised at a narrower profit margin.

On the other hand, private brands often offer greater values than comparable nationally known brands. Stores can offer these items at attractive prices while enjoying a bigger profit margin. Sometimes it is possible to obtain exclusive local distribution of a brand. The exclusive right to merchandise, when it is fairly priced and in good taste, often gives the retailer the individuality needed to attract patrons. But when handling national and private brands, avoid selecting merchandise that is too similar in quality and price. Similarity between items slows customer selection.

Intelligent buying requires a knowledge of terms offered by the seller that goes well beyond costs and discounts. You must know how goods are packed by quantity and assortment. Sometimes the manufacturer or wholesaler will prepare well-balanced assortments that sell out completely. However, you must be alert in ordering assortments because often they contain end sizes and less desirable colors and styles.

You must also know the methods of delivery and the delivery time lag. Although the manufacturer's packing of an item is referred to in quantity units, you should always think of merchandise in units of time: a week's, a month's, or a season's supply. Stock of the safe-and-sure volume items on hand and on order should be gauged for a longer time than stock maintained on items needed to add variety, to complete assortments, to build customer interest, or to increase markup.

Before setting up your buying program, study these common practices of manufacturers:

1. Advanced datings are sometimes granted to induce buying prior to actual needs. This alleviates the pressure that sellers experience when goods must be produced and shipped to all buyers at the same time. In such cases, you are not obliged to begin payment until the advance-payment date listed on the invoice.

2. Consignment sales provide for payment after the sale, sometimes at a regular monthly rate. The advantage to consignment buying is that you do not have to invest your own money in the goods you purchase.

3. Job lots, sample lines, and closeouts can be profitable purchases if you know the quality of goods before you buy. Speculative buying is to be indulged in only with money that is not required for the normal operation of a business. It is a dangerous risk for the average merchant with limited funds.

4. A good buyer will make reasonable purchases of untried items. Some will prove highly profitable; others will not. Here again, experienced judgment and sufficient money are needed to contain the risks involved. The payoff is in the learning that follows such purchases.

5. Advance buying in a rising market is standard practice for experienced merchants and of low risk for inexperienced merchants. The merchant who has bought in advance can either mark up the goods on hand to agree with the increasing market prices or, assuming the costs of the advance purchases were less, maintain former prices in an effort to undersell competitors.

Dealing with the Wholesaler

The progressive wholesaler puts as much effort into serving as into selling and can give practical advice and information on many phases of retail selling. Some of the larger wholesalers help their customers select a location. They may even supply or help choose the equipment and give suggestions on financing, record keeping, and store operation. The more aggressive wholesalers may also offer financial assistance in the form of providing the initial store stock on extended credit terms.

Your wholesaler's salesperson can suggest what merchandise you should stock. He or she knows the price ranges that will be profitable for your type of store and particular location and can advise you as to how much money you should invest in inventory, store fixtures, and equipment.

Your wholesaler may be willing to overlook your credit problems for a time. But, remember, your credit rating will be a big factor in your relations with your suppliers during critical times, and to a lesser extent in good times. When goods are scarce, the choicest and most needed merchandise naturally goes to retailers who pay promptly.

Another source of buying is the manufacturers' agents or brokers. Their function is to sell the merchandise but not to warehouse or handle it in any way except for credit and billing. The manufacturer drop ships, that is, ships directly to the buyer. Specified minimum quantities must be purchased. The manufacturer pays the representatives' and brokers' commissions.

Use of Buying Offices

Many proprietors are unable to make frequent trips to the market and affiliate themselves with a buying office. These offices maintain a staff of experienced buyers, each specializing in certain merchandise. The buyer can line up good sources and lines for the retailer and schedule advance showings of goods, enabling the retailer to accomplish perhaps an entire year's buying in a few days' time.

Some buying offices will handle a store's complete buying program. Most of these offices serve only one store in a given area or city, ensuring the retailer an exclusive line of goods. For a certain percentage of your store's most recent annual sales volume, you can get lower merchandise costs, better selections, and increased profit. Generally, you will need to sign a 1-year agreement. Monthly installment payments can usually be arranged.

Some buying offices also supply their clients with advisory and bulletin services dealing with store operations. They might let you know what goods to dispose of and how to do it, which markdowns to take at certain times, and how to operate on a turnover basis.

You may also become affiliated with a *commission office,* which charges the manufacturer, rather than the retailer, a commission percentage for selling. *Listing offices* are another important buying-service setup for some stores. In return for a uniform fee, the retailer receives a catalog listing various types of merchandise with prices, sources of supply, and minimum-order requirements. The merchant places orders directly with the listed factories at the prices quoted in the catalog. These buyers have searched the market for fast-selling merchandise, with values and prices that enable the independent variety store to compete with the large chains.

Usually the listing office or other types of buying services are used along with the services of the regular wholesaler. Most buying offices do not supplant the services of a regular wholesaler.

Working with a buying office makes a lot of sense for small retailers. Even if you can afford the several trips a year and weeks of work that buying entails, you may benefit from the services of a professional buying organization.

How to Price Your Merchandise

Although profitable pricing of merchandise by the retailer is essential to business success, few small retailers do this very well. They tend to price in accordance with so few variables that when they set prices high enough to cover costs, they limit sales volume, and when they set prices low enough to sell in volume, they attract the irregular, one-time, bargain-hunting customer. Poor pricing can quickly put a retailer out of business.

What governs markup? Some stores set prices merely by following the competition. Better sense says decisions on prices must be made on a broader, more-farseeing basis. The following principles embody that basis:

1. Your markup must be large enough to cover your operating expenses.

2. Value is determined by what customers want. Value, therefore, is relative. Whether customers will judge your prices to be fair or out of line depends on the prices on the same items offered by your competition, particularly on easily identified items such as brand goods.

3. The greatest purchasing power available to retail stores falls in the middle range of income. Therefore, in the nonluxury store, have price levels that will appeal to the thrifty segment of the well-to-do,

the large middle-income group, and the upper level of the low-income group.

4. If the store is located in a high-income neighborhood, it is probably advisable to offer credit and delivery. You may assume that customers are willing to pay for these extra services in the form of higher prices.

5. If the store is located in a medium-income neighborhood and offers no special services or types of goods to differentiate itself from its competitors, you'll have to keep your prices close to the general price level of your competitors.

6. If the store is located in a low-income neighborhood where many customers require credit and you provide credit service, you are justified in charging more than your cash-and-carry competitors.

7. Distance from competitors is an important factor in determining the prices that can be charged. If you own a small grocery store, for example, an attempt to compete on a price basis with a supermarket five or six blocks away would be foolish. You will have to content yourself with the fill-in, pick-up, and "off-hour" business. You may legitimately charge higher prices than competitors who do not render these types of service.

In addition to the problems of location and competition, you must consider two other factors in determining selling price: sales volume and selling expenses. If you offer merchandise at a low price, you may enjoy a large sales volume, but perhaps not realize sufficient revenue to cover the costs of selling the merchandise. On the other hand, if you set prices high, your sales volume may be so low that you will be unable to meet your operating costs.

Clearly, the best prices are those which yield the *most* dollars after all costs are subtracted. This does not mean the highest possible markup on each unit or a price that will yield maximum sales. It means that prices should be fixed at the point where markup per unit multiplied by the number of units sold will yield the maximum gross margin over operating expenses.

It is inadvisable to use the same markup percentage for all items of merchandise. The guiding principle should be that the price of each item should cover the costs associated with it plus whatever other contribution it can be expected to make to the general overhead and net profit. If demand for some items is small, an attempt to use an average markup could make matters worse or not change things at all depending on the nature of the product and the demand for it. (For example, if a markup caused the price of an article to rise too high, that could cause a further decline in their sales.) As a result, there will be even fewer dollars of gross margin to contribute toward overhead expenses. On the other hand, some products will sell almost regardless of the prices set for them or because their high prices confer prestige on their purchasers (for example, a Rolls Royce automobile, which is certainly not the best car from the point of view of road handling, acceleration, or fuel economy, or an apartment facing Central Park in New York City, which is neither bigger nor more comfortable than one on the West Side on Ninth Avenue.) Worse, you may establish an image for the business as being a high-priced house, whose image is much harder to get rid of than it is to change prices.

Only experience can teach you the feel of the market. If you are to succeed in making up for merchandise you are forced to sell at low markups or even at cost, you must learn which items you can sell at higher markups.

There are certain special factors to consider in setting your prices.

1. *Leaders and loss leaders.* A leader is an article given a special price, usually below that charged by other merchants, offered as a promotional item to increase store traffic. Leaders can be sold at a profit or at a loss. A loss leader, in its simplest terms, is one that is sold below its cost. It may be priced below its cost plus the estimated expenses involved in handling it. If the invoice cost of an item is 31 cents, and if the expenses are 18 cents and it is sold for anything under 49 cents, it becomes a loss leader. A good leader sells itself; it should need no promotional effort. Items that are in everyday use, that are bought frequently, and that have a well-established value make good leaders. The point of a loss leader, however, should *not* be lost sight of. It is to increase traffic and, thereby, overall profits.

2. *Staples.* Staples have a higher-than-average cost of goods sold because the markups are below the average. They are sold on value and price. Higher-priced lines cost less in proportion to the lower-priced lines. The lower-priced lines sell faster, are in the store a shorter time, and cost less to handle. Low-price lines should give value. People are more likely first to sample low-price lines. If these are found satisfactory, the same persons may later become steady users of both the popular and high-price lines. Staple volume depends on store traffic. Unless there is something distinctive about such merchandise, it does not benefit from promotion.

3. *Novelties.* Novelties that catch on show a good markup at the start and as long as they continue to be popular. Soon, however, other manufacturers come into the field. The price is then reduced, and customers begin to look for new items. To cash in fully during the popular stage, you must anticipate your needs. If you are overstocked on

novelties in the initial period before the price is reduced, your profits will be reduced by the necessary markdowns. If they sell out and must be reordered, the reorder may not arrive until after everyone has purchased them elsewhere.

4. *Extremely fashionable goods.*   These are in the same class as novelties. The fad may involve a color or a design, but its appeal depends on novelty. The markup is high. So are the markdowns at the end of the season.

5. *Fast-selling items.*   These usually carry a lower-than-average markup. This is only fair. Their rapid turnover reduces the handling expense. It is important to have competitive prices on fast-selling items. Customers are familiar with their prices and values and are critical of small price differences on fast-selling, popular goods. Slow-selling merchandise should have a higher-than-average markup, under the presumption that it is normal for the item to sell slowly. If the item is not a normal slow seller, it may have become unattractive to purchasers because of its quality or price. First, check how your competitors are handling the item. They may be causing your slow sales by a more aggressive pricing policy. You may have to lower your markup in response. If the product is not selling normally anywhere, you may have to slash your markup to get rid of it. Consider dropping the item in the future.

6. *Prices fixed by manufacturers.*   Pricing sometimes is not left entirely to the discretion of the merchant. State and federal laws governing retail selling should be checked with your supplier.

Simple Formulas to Find Profitable Markups

To understand the relationships of costs, markups, selling prices, and gross margins, it is necessary to restudy some retailing arithmetic. You may not make constant use of the formulas and calculations which follow, but you should understand them.

1. *Cost of goods.*   Cost of goods is the cost of goods delivered at the store. It is expressed in dollars or as a percentage of sales. The cost divided by the selling price is the cost percentage. Thus, if an item costs $1 and sells for $1.50, the cost percentage would be

$$\frac{\$1.00}{\$1.50} = 67 \text{ percent}$$

2. *Initial markup.* Initial, or original, markup is what is added to the cost to get selling price, or the difference between cost price and selling price. It is expressed as both a percentage of sales price and a percentage of cost. Thus, in the case of a $1 cost and $1.50 selling price, the initial markup would be 50 cents. That is 33⅓ percent of selling price,

$$\frac{\$0.50}{\$1.50} = 33\frac{1}{3} \text{ percent}$$

or 50 percent of cost price,

$$\frac{\$0.50}{\$1.00} = 50 \text{ percent}$$

3. *Retail reductions.* Retail reductions cover all reductions of the original retail price, including markdowns and shrinkage. They are expressed as a percentage of final selling price or as a percentage of cost.

4. *Additional markups.* Occasionally, an item is erroneously under-priced, or an increase in the original price is desirable for some reason. Increases after the original markup has been taken are called additional markups. Downward revisions of the retail price are also common.

5. *Markdowns.* A markdown is a reduction of an original selling price. After a retail price is established on any item (by adding a markup to its cost), the price may have to be reduced for any one or more of the following reasons: For special sales to stimulate volume, to clean out remnants, leftovers, poor assortments, and damaged goods, to get rid of poor buys, or to meet sudden changes in the market price.

Early markdowns are the smallest. The sooner you discover that merchandise is not moving and start making markdowns, the smaller your loss will be. The time to sell is when people want to buy and not at the end of the season after everyone has bought. When you start to mark down, forget all about cost and continue marking down until the goods are sold.

6. *Gross margin.* Gross margin, also called gross profit, is the difference between the costs of the goods sold and the income derived from their sale calculated for a specific period of time. It is expressed in dollar amounts and also as a percentage of sales.

It is easy to determine the selling price if you know the cost and percentage over cost by which you are marking up prices. The formula is

$$\text{Cost} \times \text{markup percentage} = \text{markup}$$

$$\text{Cost} + \text{markup} = \text{selling price}$$

Suppose all the items in the store get marked up 30 percent. According to the formula, an item that costs you $1.50 will be priced at $1.95 (since $1.50 \times 30\% = \$0.45$; $1.50 + \$0.45 = \$1.95$).

Keep in mind that the average markup for a store is made up of different rates of markup for the different goods handled. Some goods have to be sold at a close margin, either because they are competing in price with merchandise in other stores or because they are used as leaders to bring in trade. Other goods will be sold at about the average markup sought. Still other articles will carry a high profit markup. Then there will also be goods that will be sold at different markup rates as their salability comes and goes. A little arithmetic will show how to arrive at the average total store markup under such conditions.

Let us assume for simplicity that there are three items, or three departments, with sales and markups as follows:

Department	Sales	Maintained markup percent
A	$20,000	20
B	10,000	25
C	5,000	35
Total	$35,000	

The gross margins then would be:

Department	Gross margin
A	$4000
B	2500
C	1750
Total gross margin	$8250

$$\text{Average store markup} = \frac{\$8250}{\$35,000} = 23.6 \text{ percent}$$

If the average markup is not sufficient to allow for a net profit after expenses are deducted, you have some serious strategic thinking to do. Expenses must be reduced, some revisions in the lines must be made so that more goods are sold at a higher markup, selling prices must be raised, or sales volume increased to lower the expense percentage. Of these options the hardest to accomplish is to increase margins by arbitrarily raising selling prices.

The next problem is to calculate an initial markup to establish original retail prices, allowing for markdowns and shrinkage, which are known as *retail reductions*. If you price goods at the outset at your desired markup without taking retail reductions into account, you may find that the realized margin is far below the total you had planned on to cover expenses and profit if markdowns and shrinkage occurred.

Retail reductions will apply more to some lines than to others. Some staple lines in steady demand, with little or no spoilage, breakage, or theft and on which no cut-price sales are made, are seldom subject to reductions. The initial markup on such goods may be counted on as a maintained markup.

But on merchandise having a style or use obsolescence on which markdowns must be anticipated, or on goods subject to deterioration, pilferage, or other shrinkage, the initial markup will have to be higher than the planned, maintained, or realized markup.

At the start, you will have to make some rather arbitrary allowances for such anticipated retail reductions. As you gain experience, you will know more precisely what goods will be subject to the reductions and how much the reductions will usually amount to.

One object of good merchandising is to reduce markdowns to a minimum. Accomplishing that involves improvement in practically all phases of the store's operations, but principally in buying, selling, stock care, and pricing.

However, you can plan a markdown when settling the original price; thus, when you mark down the item later, you still end up with the amount of profit you intended. The formula for setting the original markup to take into account a subsequent markdown is as follows. (Note that these percentages are figured on the sales price, not your cost, because a sale advertised to shoppers as "10 percent off" refers to a discount from the sales price.)

$$\text{Markup percentage on sale price}$$

$$= \frac{\text{Percent gross profit desired} + \text{markdown percentage}}{1.00 + \text{markdown percentage}}$$

Example

$$\text{Percent gross profit required} = 40 \text{ percent}$$

$$\text{Markdown percentage} = 5 \text{ percent}$$

The markup percentage on the sale price would be calculated as follows:

$$\frac{0.40 + 0.05}{1.05} = \frac{0.45}{1.05} = 0.4286, \text{ or } 42.86 \text{ percent}$$

If a markup of about 43 percent on the sale price is required, the percentage by which the cost price would have to be increased would be approximately 75 percent; that is,

$$1.00 \text{ (selling price)} - 0.43 \text{ (markup)} = 0.57 \text{ (cost)}$$

$$\frac{0.43}{0.57} = 0.7544, \text{ or } 75.44 \text{ percent markup on cost}$$

Many goods are bought to sell at a designated retail price in accordance with competition and with your analysis of what price lines will sell best. When you are buying goods to advantage so that you can sell at the desired prices, the initial markup is automatically set by the cost price.

Suppose that you want to carry a $1.95 line of toys and that the quality you want will cost $17.40 a dozen, or $1.45 each. The initial markup is set at $1.95 less $1.45, or $0.50. Thus, the initial markup would automatically be 25.6 percent of the selling price. Excessive retail reductions would bring the realized margin dangerously low.

If allowance must be made for markdowns and shrinkage, two questions arise:

- At a given initial markup and an estimated shrinkage, as a percentage of sales, what will the realized gross margin be?
- In order to realize a planned gross margin with a given initial markup, how much can be allowed for retail reductions? See Table 8.1.

The calculation for the first situation is as follows:

Cost of goods × percent retail reductions = cost reduction

Initial markup − cost reduction = maintained or realized markup

Example

Percent initial markup = 40

Percent retail reductions = 5

Table 8-1. Initial Markup to Produce Specified Gross Profit, Allowing for Stated Retail Reductions

Gross profit to be realized, percent	Ratio of retail merchandise reduction to net sales, percent					
	5	6	7	8	9	10
	Gross markup required, percent					
25	28.57	29.25	29.91	30.56	31.19	31.82
26	29.52	30.19	30.84	31.48	32.11	32.73
27	30.48	31.13	31.78	32.41	33.03	33.64
28	31.43	32.08	32.71	33.33	33.94	34.55
29	32.38	33.02	33.64	34.26	34.86	35.45
30	33.33	33.96	34.58	35.19	35.78	36.36
31	34.29	34.91	35.51	36.11	36.70	37.27
32	35.24	35.85	36.45	37.04	37.61	38.18
33	36.19	36.79	37.38	37.96	38.53	39.08
34	37.14	37.74	38.32	38.89	39.45	40.00
35	38.10	38.68	39.25	39.81	40.37	40.91
36	39.05	39.62	40.19	40.74	41.28	41.82
37	40.00	40.57	41.12	41.67	42.20	42.73
38	40.95	41.51	42.06	42.59	43.12	43.64
39	41.90	42.45	42.99	43.52	44.04	44.55
40	42.86	43.40	43.93	44.44	44.95	45.45
41	43.81	44.34	44.86	45.37	45.87	46.36
42	44.76	45.28	45.79	46.30	46.79	47.27
43	45.71	46.23	46.73	47.22	47.71	48.18
44	46.66	47.17	47.66	48.15	48.62	49.09
45	47.62	48.11	48.60	49.07	49.54	50.00

The maintained markup would be calculated as follows:

$$1.00 - 0.40 = 0.60 \text{ (cost of goods)}$$

$$0.60 \times 0.05 = 0.03 \text{ (reductions at cost)}$$

$$0.40 - 0.03 = 0.37 \text{ (maintained markup)}$$

Suppose, in the case of $1.95 toys, that you estimate the retail reductions to be 5 percent. What would the realized margin then be? The calculations follow:

$$1.00 - 0.256 = 0.744 \text{ (cost of goods)}$$

$$0.744 \times 0.05 = 0.0372, \text{ or 3.72 percent reductions at cost}$$

$$0.256 - 0.037 = 0.219, \text{ or 21.9 percent maintained} \\ \text{markup or gross margin}$$

If the 21.9 percent gross profit is lower than you want, just what retail reductions may be taken to leave you the minimum realized margin (say, 23 percent)?

Those calculations to arrive at this answer follow:

Initial markup percent − percent of gross margin desired
$$= \text{percent of reductions at cost}$$

Reductions at cost + cost of goods
$$= \text{percent reductions allowable at retail}$$

Example

$$0.40 - 0.37 = 0.03$$

$$\frac{0.03}{0.06} = 0.05, \text{ or 5 percent allowable retail reductions}$$

Let us apply this calculation to the $1.95 toys where the initial markup is set. You want to know just how heavy a retail reduction they will stand to give you a final stipulated gross profit, in this case 23 percent. You know that the initial markup will be 25.6 percent of sales, and you know the desired gross margin. Let us see in this practical example how far you can go in markdowns and shrinkage reductions.

$$0.256 - 0.230 = 0.026$$

$$\frac{0.026}{1.000 - 0.256} = \frac{0.026}{0.744} = 0.0349, \text{ or 3.49 percent retail reductions}$$

You know that at the cost and selling price of these toys, you can afford to take retail reductions of only 3.49 percent if you want to realize at least 23 percent gross profit.

Stock Control in the Small Store

Your stock control system should keep you aware of the quantity of each kind of merchandise on hand. An effective system will provide a guide for what, when, and how much to buy of each style, color, size, price, and brand. The system will reduce the number of sales lost from being out of stock, identify slow-moving articles, and indicate changes in customer preferences.

The size of your establishment and the number of people employed are determining factors in devising an effective stock control plan. Your accountant should be able to advise you. If you have installed a computer system to handle your accounting (see Chapter 17), it should include software for entering and keeping track of inventory items.

If you do not track inventory by computer, can you keep control by observation? Or should you use "on hand, on order, sold" records, detachable ticket stubs, checklists, or a perpetual inventory?

The observation method, unless you have an unusually alert sense of quantities, usually fails as a check on merchandise depletion. If you record shortages of goods for reorder as the need occurs to you, you'll only reorder when faced with stock outages. Usually, orders will be placed only at the time of the salesperson's or agent's regular visit. These stock outages will result in lost sales while waiting for new goods to arrive.

Detachable stubs on tickets placed on merchandise afford a good means of control. The stubs, marked with information identifying the articles, are removed at the time the items are sold. The accumulated stubs may then be posted regularly to a perpetual inventory.

A simple checklist, often provided by wholesalers, is another effective counting device. The list provides space to record the items carried and the selling price, cost price, and minimum quantity to be ordered for each. It also contains a column in which to note whether stock on hand is sufficient and when to reorder. You might also keep a chart on slow-moving merchandise, listing each brand and item which begins to lag in sales.

Regardless of how effective your stock control system is, much of its value will be lost unless you do your buying on budget. Usually the buying budget covers a 6-month period, but it could be limited to 3 or 4 months. The main consideration should be the peak selling period. After the sales estimate is completed for a given period, you can prepare the buying budget.

Maintaining an Adequate Supply

Until you have experience on which to draw, you may find it difficult to determine how much stock to carry and how many times your stock must turn over yearly to give you a satisfactory return on inventory. Your wholesaler may be able to advise you at first. If your business is in an industry that has an association of members, you may be able to get figures on turnover rates for firms of your size. To find how rapidly your stock has turned over, divide the dollar amount of sales during a given period by the average of the beginning and ending inventories valued at retail prices for that period. You might choose instead to obtain the ratio by dividing cost of goods sold by the average of beginning and ending inventories figured at cost.

Figuring Occupancy Expenses

Labor and maintenance costs rise when goods are held. Money must be spent for rent, heat, and light for storing or displaying them. Therefore, in buying larger-than-normal quantities to secure extra-quantity discounts, weigh your quantity discounts against the additional costs of carrying the goods for a longer period of time. As a rule of thumb an item carried in stock twice the average length of time will be unprofitable unless you can sell it with a higher margin of profit.

Always be sure to order well in advance of the peak season. This gives you an ample supply of goods for large displays at the time when buying interest is intense. Delay in ordering may result in overbuying and late deliveries. Failure to meet demand on time leads to the accumulation of unsold stock.

Take stock once a month to find sales trends. Do not rely upon the physical inventory which you must take at least once a year in order to prepare your profit-and-loss statement. This inventory involves counting the quantity on hand of each item in stock and determining its value. The total represents the value of the entire stock. Strictly speaking, the physical inventory is not a means of controlling stock, but an accounting tool which tells you little about stock movements.

Figuring Profitability

Examination of profit by the average merchant is a fairly simple routine. Assume it is winter and you are selling children's gloves and mittens in navy, brown, and multicolor at $5 a pair. This year, youngsters favor the multicolored gloves and mittens; conservative brown and navy ones move at a moderate rate only. You have been paying $36 a dozen for all styles. This cost is low for the selling price; you could pay more and still realize a profit. Sales volume for dark colors is satisfactory, but you think you could sell more of the favored multicolored gloves and mittens.

Reviewing your overall selling pattern, you decide that you will continue to pay $36 for brown and navy, but for $42 you could get a greater variety in better multicolored gloves and mittens; you will promote this favored seller. You explain your sales strategy to the staff, knowing that the results of the promotion will help you decide what to do next season.

To simplify the example, assume the cash discount equals the freight charges on the gloves. During the previous season, 75 pairs of multicolored gloves and mittens were sold.

$$\$36 \text{ per dozen} = \$3 \text{ per pair}$$

$$\$5 - \$3 = \$2 \text{ markup per pair}$$

$$75 \times \$2 = \$150 \text{ gross margin on multicoloreds}$$

This season, 110 multicolored pairs were sold.

$$\$42 \text{ per dozen} = \$3.50 \text{ per pair}$$

$$\$5 - \$3.50 = \$1.50 \text{ markup per pair}$$

$$110 \times \$1.50 = \$165 \text{ gross margin on multicoloreds}$$

$$\$165 - \$150 = \$15 \text{ increased gross profit}$$

The increase is not startling. New lines often are slow to win acceptance. You will need to weigh all factors before deciding whether to continue buying this higher-priced stock. You might continue with the better gloves and mittens because you think the increase in sales will continue. Or, you might consider the effect of this individual item on the business in general. Increase the sale of any line in the store, and all lines usually benefit. A higher volume of sales raises your expenses at a modest rate in comparison with the added net you will realize.

As your sales volume increases, the profit percentage of each new sales dollar increases. That is because the portion of sales volume that represents fixed costs (rent, insurance, merchandise) is decreasing. Likewise, as sales volume declines, the percentage of your sales volume that represents profit also declines because your fixed expenses cannot be cut.

The increase in profit from a larger sales volume is disproportionately great. The gain in sales volume may be only 3 percent; that difference can produce a hefty gain in profit. Therefore, volume is the name of the game. The more you sell, the more your profit escalates. Fixed costs do not rise as fast or in proportion to rises in volume. It usually takes a sizable increase in sales to cause the costs to rise at all.

The Inventory Trap

Sales volume and turnover time are more important than percentage of gross profit. For example, the owner of a hardware store normally buys 60 heaters every year, each heater costing $50. The heaters sell for $100, thus generating $3000 on the $3000 investment. When sold, this 100 percent gross profit is the same as the store owner makes on all inventory, which the store owner typically turns over once a year.

The supplier offers the hardware store owner a deal: 500 heaters for $7500, a cost per heater of only $15. The hardware store owner can then lower the retail heater price to $90, with the intent of selling 50 percent more heaters, while making a profit of 500 percent.

The hardware store owner should turn down this offer because it will probably tie up cash in unsold heater inventory. For example, if he cannot sell more than, say, 75 heaters a year at $90 each—which is likely since he sold only 60 a year in years past—it will take almost 7 years to sell all the heaters. Total profit on the heaters is $37,500, or about $5350 a year. Had the $7500 been invested in regular inventory, it would have been subject to the hardware store owner's normal 100 percent markup, generating a yearly profit of $7500.

Therefore, it would be a blunder for the hardware store owner to put a lot of money into heaters which would remain in inventory for a long time. Although the percentage of profit would be greater in the special deal, it would only be on those heaters sold in the year of purchase. In the long run the resultant sales volume would be too little and the turnover time too long to make money on the deal. Had the heaters been priced at $40 retail and sold out in the first year, the owner would have profited because the percentage of profit would be greater than normal while the turnover time would not. High sales volume usually does more for profits than bargains which swell the inventory.

Keeping a Record of Customer Sales

Another ingredient necessary for maintaining smooth store-customer relations is good records management. If you have a retail store and do not use a computer system to track sales, you may still be able to keep adequate records without an undue amount of paperwork. Your customers' sales slips, filed vertically, can be used as a sole record of customer accounts. Once a month, you can total these slips, or, if it is more convenient, post each sales total to a monthly statement immediately after it is made. If storage of these records becomes a problem, you can reduce the amount of space needed by microfilming your records. Consult the yellow pages of your telephone directory for the names of agencies from which you can rent one of these devices.

Cutting Delivery Costs

Delivery costs are an item of expense often overlooked by store owners. The costs are seldom broken out and analyzed.

Your delivery service might be limited to employing a youngster on a bicycle carrying office supplies, medical prescriptions, or other small, easily handled items. Some stores use motorbikes. A proprietor might use his or her automobile or station wagon for delivery. On a larger scale, the store may use its own truck, hire a service which delivers for several companies, mail merchandise by parcel post, or a combination of these. Check with delivery services for rate quotations, which are generally computed by weight and time. In some states, rates are regulated. Some delivery services charge a set fee.

Your first job is to compile a factual study of the advantages and disadvantages to your store of the methods of shipping available to you. On the other hand, will your business benefit from having a cash-and-carry policy? If not, should you require a minimum purchase from customers before delivery is made? Perhaps charging a reasonable fee will satisfy them and at the same time enable you to realize an adequate profit on the sale.

9
Profit Pointers for the Wholesaler

Perhaps no class of business has been affected as greatly by changes in business practices in recent years as wholesaling. A trend has arisen between manufacturers-importers and end users to shorten the distribution lines between them and deal with each other as directly as possible in order to stem rising distribution costs and meet intensifying competition. Independent wholesalers have been caught between these two main groups seeking to wring extra margin out of the delivery chain by eliminating them whenever possible.

The independent wholesaler also has an especially intense problem maintaining supplier and customer loyalty. Again, the two groups on either side of the wholesaler have common bonds, bonds which center around the issue of brand loyalty. Original equipment manufacturers, for example, nurture brand loyalty by heavily promoting their products by name. They make heavy demands on any distributor of their products between themselves and end users, and will take their products away from those who do not meet the demands. When that happens, the wholesaler who has lost distributorship of a brand loses many of the customers loyal to the brand.

Building customer loyalty is generally difficult for the wholesaler because independent wholesaling is a price- and service-sensitive industry susceptible to losses of business to:

- Expanding chains that buy directly from the manufacturer
- Newly established distributors that operate on a limited basis out of their home garages or vans
- The withdrawal of customers who feel they were poorly served

To counter these potential sources of loss, wholesalers must diligently exercise the advantages at their command. Error-free management of a wholesale operation is impossible, due to the wide variety of items that most wholesalers handle, and the many imponderables (such as delays in shipments from vendors, unforeseeable spurts in consumer demands, and even the vagaries of weather) that wholesalers are subject to. But all wholesalers have the same problems. What distinguishes successful wholesalers is how well they manage the variables under their control.

Here are suggestions for making a venture in wholesaling satisfying and profitable.

The Starting Place

The thinking of independent wholesalers is prone to be dominated by their biggest single investment, inventory, and its management. Wholesalers certainly should be concerned with having adequate stocks on hand, with keeping turnover high, controlling obsolescence, and so forth. But too often the intensity of those concerns obscures the fact that the business of wholesalers—as it is of all other types of enterprises—is creating transactions which benefit the parties involved, not managing inventory. Wholesalers should always remember that they are in the business of creating profits for their customers and themselves, and managing inventory is only a part of that business.

Creating the transactions benefiting the parties involved is called marketing. Wholesalers tend to think marketing involves only manufacturers and retailers. But, in a world so filled with the glistening teeth of competitive methods taking increasing bites out of the distribution dollar, the independent wholesaler had better put marketing first on the list of priorities if he or she wants to stay in business. Therefore, whether you are just starting up in wholesaling or are an established wholesaler, make sure you have marketing policies and programs which provide services which are unique, superior, and money-makers for both your suppliers and customers. If you cannot formulate such policies and programs, you probably won't or don't have attention-arresting, business-stimulating services, and you will be in real trouble!

Once you establish marketing policies and programs, you will know what is needed in the way of support for them. They will answer a myriad of questions, telling you where to invest, where to cut costs, how to price your merchandise, how large a territory to serve, how to use credit, and what you should ask of your computer or accounting system.

In terms of investment, the research underlying your marketing plan may indicate the value of maintaining a showroom where retailers can come to examine new goods or goods which they do not stock, and, if relevant, to learn how the goods are used or installed. The research may also yield guidelines for handling customers threatened with going out of business. The loss of a retailer causes a wholesaler to suffer in two ways: An outlet is lost for the wholesaler's merchandise, and the wholesaler loses money on the items the merchant has received but not yet paid for. Since you are unlikely to avoid loss if the customer goes under, from a marketing point of view, it might be a sound move to extend the repayment period, ease credit terms, or take other measures to keep the retailer from bankruptcy.

Marketing research will also point you toward opportunities to use the computer as a marketing tool. Computers make selective merchandising by mail economically possible by enabling the wholesaler to direct its promotional pieces, price lists, and other mailings only to the most receptive audiences.

Serving the Retailer

The process of creating transactions of benefit to all parties involved begins with recognizing what you can do that others cannot do for those who may buy from you. Don't bank on tradition for good answers; the world is changing too fast for that. Look at the facts to find out what you as a wholesaler can do better than anyone else for customers.

Hard-nosed answers will tell you, first, who your customers will be, and, second, how you must serve them. The inquiry will also provide you with the framework for erecting the structure of your firm's profitability.

The inquiry will yield these facts:

1. *Wholesalers' customers are mostly small retailers.* Large retailers buy directly from the factory and have their own intermediate warehousing operations.

2. *The value of wholesalers to small retailers lies in their ability to sell retailers' goods at prices which permit them to compete.*   That ability originates in their combining many small orders into large orders to manufacturers. Many manufacturers cannot offer their merchandise directly to retailers because they can't move their goods into retailers' hands as cheaply as wholesalers can.

3. *Retailers can buy small quantities from wholesalers.*   Wholesalers sort and break down large incoming orders into smaller quantities, and offer delivery on them, enabling retailers to keep their inventories low and improve their cash flows.

4. *Wholesalers deliver more quickly.*   The time lags between ordering and receiving goods from other sources is considerably longer than between ordering and receiving goods from wholesalers. Next-day delivery of ordered goods is often possible.

5. *Wholesalers ease retailers' cash problems.*   They do this by extending merchandise credits to the retailer. They also provide financial aid (for example, they may finance the initial inventory of a retailer just starting up). The retailer's financial picture is also improved by the wholesaler taking back inventory that the retailer is having trouble moving in return for credit toward other merchandise.

6. *Progressive wholesalers help retailers anticipate and meet demand.* They cover many outlets in the market and know which items are moving and which are not. When the sale of an item spurts or significantly declines, or a price increase is likely, they tip their customers off, enabling them to order up or down or to order before the price increases.

7. *Wholesalers help retailers price their merchandise.*   Many independent wholesalers have set up a procedure for assisting retailers in pricing their merchandise. They advise customers how to meet competition by varying the markups on individual items and in finding the markup which results in the largest volume of sales yielding the best profit. This is a major task for retailers. Progressive wholesalers know the nature, quantity, and frequency of their customers' orders and send out merchandise prepriced.

8. *Wholesalers help customers merchandise their goods.*   They do this by telling them about the good practices of the efficient merchants among their customers. They get involved in the promotional advertising of products, even advising retailers how to display their products and how to price them. They instruct retailers on good merchandising techniques, and encourage them to enhance their image with attractive storefronts, more effectively designed and illuminated interiors, and attention-arresting advertising campaigns.

9. *Wholesalers help retailers with their buying.* Wholesalers keep their customers posted on price changes, new lines of merchandise, and merchandise being discontinued. This service is valuable to retailers since it eliminates some of their accounting and clerical costs.

10. *Wholesalers offer assistance to customers in running their businesses.* Often, this assistance is not easily available from other sources. For example, wholesalers compose accounting forms for use by the retailer, offer product and sales training for customer employees, provide purchasing and inventory maintenance services, assist their customers in computerizing their systems, and establish computer-to-computer systems for access to wholesale and retail prices, stock replenishment, and accounting assistance. Because the astute wholesaler recognizes that his or her business depends on the success of the retailer, the range of assistance offered is wide.

These factors indicate why, even in the face of increasing competition from manufacturers and the growing number of national chains, independent wholesalers have an assured place in business and the resources with which to prosper.

The key resource is their lower cost of purchases; the size of a wholesaler's order entitles it to discounts not extended by manufacturers to retailers. In computing discounts manufacturers also consider the savings in shipping costs resulting from sending a large amount of goods at one time to one place. But this resource is a vulnerable one. Wholesalers can only profit if the addition of their overhead expenses to the cost of merchandise still permits them to charge the retailer a lower price than the retailer could have gotten directly from the manufacturer. The ability to do that depends entirely on meeting customers' needs with *high efficiency*. Failure to meet such needs efficiently is the leading cause of wholesaler failure.

Price is not the sole factor considered by retailers in choosing suppliers. They also take into account the services wholesalers perform and are inclined to go to and stick with those who help them prosper in their businesses. It is the wholesalers who do not offer additional services that have the lowest prices and thinnest margins in their markets. The only reason customers buy from these wholesalers is to get the prices. But living on such purchases is a risky business for a wholesaler!

Planning Operations

The key to understanding what to plan for in operations is to recognize that wholesalers survive by providing services to enterprises which cannot be as well provided by anyone else. If you accept that fact, then you will also recognize the necessity for providing those services at the lowest cost compatible with excellence of service. It is the difference between your purchasing costs and cost of service that keep you alive. The difference between the two is too small to permit much inefficiency.

In order, your two greatest costs are, of course, order processing (including order entry) and the warehouse. Let's look at each, beginning with order processing.

Order processing is the heart of the delivery system. The quality of order processing controls relations between the wholesaler and his or her customers; a wholesaler who cannot respond quickly and accurately to customer inquiries and orders cannot generate or keep customer loyalty. Between inquiries, order entry, order fulfillment, and invoicing, there are boundless opportunities to make errors.

Order processing is a prime area for systems development. Because they must handle a vast amount of data in conducting their affairs, wholesalers are "naturals" for computerization. Computer terminals can be particularly helpful in order processing. They can speed up order taking and eliminate errors. With some systems all the order-taker has to do is type the caller's name or "customer number" into a computer to automatically retrieve a file noting the customer's address, phone number, and other ordering information. That saves time and reduces the number of mistakes. An on-line computer system can help eliminate one of the most common problems of distributors, exhausting the stock of a particular item. With a computer system the order-taker can tell whether the company can immediately ship the item or not and, if not, when (if at all), and inform the customer accordingly. Once the order is entered, the system can also print out order-picking documents and customer invoices.

Although order processing is one reason to computerize, there are others. For example, a wholesaler who runs a computerized operation can help a retailer maintain inventory. A wholesaler might use pressure-sensitive labels with bar codes on products; on making a sale, the retailer strips off that label and pastes it on a card. The wholesaler receives a batch of cards, runs them through a reader, and the computer ascertains the retailer's requirements in terms of profitable merchandise.

An area of cooperation that helps both the wholesaler and retailer is in retail pricing of the goods. Retailers with a sound feel for current retail pricing can help lower wholesalers' operating expenses by creating prepriced labels for volume purchases.

Your second largest operational cost is your warehouse. This is where the retailer draws goods when needed and in the quantities required. To enable the retailer to do that with profit to you requires that you understand the prime factors which bear on warehouse efficiency and manage the warehouse accordingly. The factors are:

1. The layout of goods
2. The degree of automation employed
3. The quality of training of warehouse personnel
4. Monitoring of operations
5. Knowledge of costs

Let's look at these factors.

Layout is critical to cost-effective warehouse operations, for example, to the work content of receiving, stocking, order picking, order assembly, shipping, and inventory control. What kind of shelving is used, how inventory is distributed and stocked (bins, shelving, pallets), what mechanization is employed (for example, forklift trucks, conveyor belts), and the width of the aisles, depends upon the goods handled, the equipment used, and the quarters occupied. But all well-laid-out warehouses have these things in common:

1. Rational organization of stocks
2. Proper shelving (bins, etc.)
3. Freely negotiable aisles
4. Good lighting

Rational organization of stocks means assigning space locations to merchandise with respect to the economics of storage, replenishing, locating, and retrieving them. Although the analysis necessary to decide where and how high to store items is by no means simple, it is critical to the control of costs. The analysis should extend to the other factors of shelving, aisle width, and lighting. You may want to look into interruptible light sources, such as photocell and infrared controls.

Automation of warehouse process is also a profitability factor. The merchandise carried by some high-volume wholesalers is such that a high degree of automation is economically justified. Although automated order picking and conveying is beyond the means of most wholesalers, don't overlook the possibilities of replacing labor with mechanization, because these possibilities are constantly expanding.

Training of personnel is essential to efficient warehouse operations. You may have to bear extra expenses to train personnel if you must locate in an area (such as an inner-city area) where turnover of personnel is high and uncontrollable.

Monitoring of operations is also essential to attaining and maintaining efficient warehouse operations. To achieve low warehouse costs, you must know what your costs by unit activities are (to pick a line, number of lines picked per hour, etc.). You'll also need to know what the average, low, and high costs for the industry are; you can get these figures from your industry association. When you know those costs, you can decide whether or not you need to change your costs. You should have the costs monitored on a regular monthly basis.

Choosing Your Territory

Manage your territory. If you extend it too widely, you will probably increase your operating cost out of proportion to the volume you can hope to obtain and will spend money to serve areas which earn less for you than your core territory. On the other hand, if you do not extend enough, you may forfeit desirable trade. How do you determine the dimensions of the territory you may profitably serve?

You can approximate the boundaries by determining the acceptable costs of serving customers and expanding it outward. Since all costs, other than selling and delivery, can be charged to outgoing merchandise on an equal basis regardless of destination, you can determine the profitability of a given area by adding selling and delivery costs. Then compare the result with the gross profit which the area yields.

Before opening a new territory, scout your direct competition to see whether other companies have built up a big following on their own brands. Is there a retail-owned wholesale house in the territory? At what price is your type of merchandise selling in that territory?

Do not refrain from entering a new territory just because competition is there already. An established market may be able to accommodate you as well. If it appears that you have reached agreement with another wholesaler to respect each other's markets, you may both be prosecuted for violating antitrust law. Also illegal are arrangements with manufacturers or distributors to fix prices or to prevent customers from buying an item unless they also purchase other goods.

If you wish to expand your territory by opening up a new branch, plan the location with an eye toward minimizing your transportation costs. You may also look into cooperative warehousing. Some wholesalers combine to share distribution centers, thus reducing the expenses of opening a new branch.

Expanding Sales Volume
with Cash-and-Carry Outlets

Many wholesalers find it profitable to have a cash-and-carry branch. Select your location carefully. Be sure it is outside the area covered by your own sales force. After all, you wish to draw your trade from competitors, not from your own sales force. When a branch is opened, send circulars to every prospective customer in the area. List the staple merchandise they can obtain from your outlet at low prices. Later, send a second circular to the retailers in the vicinity who are not patronizing the branch.

To be most effective, the outlet should be geared to handle only fast-moving items which can be stocked in a small area and readily assembled for customers. Do not stock it with every item carried by the primary distributor. If you find a profitable location in an area covered by sales agents, be sure the outlet does not carry the long-margin items for which you have the exclusive agency and on which you rely for much of your profit. Prices should be high enough to cover all cost plus a fair profit. Close any branch which constantly shows a loss.

When possible, have the manufacturer drop-ship merchandise to the branch. That eliminates several handlings and greatly reduces cost.

Should you decide to open a cash-and-carry branch, recognize the importance of establishing marketing policies consistent with your overall marketing objectives. For example, whether to sell to anyone who comes in or not.

How Mail-Order Sales
Increase Profits

You might consider extending your market by using mail-order wholesaling to reach locations outside your convenient delivery area. In these transactions, your customer should pay delivery costs. If feasible, terms should be net, cash in advance.

The price sheet is your only contact with the mail-order customer. It should contain all items offered and all terms, allowances, and discounts. Every price on the sheet should remain in effect until either an amendment or a new sheet is mailed out. Note that it is illegal to quote different prices to different customers without some adequate economic justification.

Be sure that your mailing list does not include customers who are contacted by your sales personnel. Again, you should be sure to establish appropriate marketing practices, such as not mailing price sheets to customers in direct competition with your own good customers.

Begin your mail-order program by sending price sheets to prospective customers. To those from whom you get no response within 3 months, send a friendly letter reminding them of the range of your services and products. If no business results within a reasonable period (such as 3 months), strike their names from the list.

Controlling Costs

Because of narrowing gross margins, rising expense levels, and increased merchandising of controlled brands, you will need an effective system of cost control to operate profitably.

To keep your prices competitive, take steps to limit transportation costs. One way is to seek alternatives to operating your own trucks: railway freight, air delivery, and contract trucking. Small local distributors that find these alternatives impractical have to find other ways to cut costs. One answer may be to schedule deliveries rigorously. Although your customers prefer delivery at their convenience, they will understand if you plan the deliveries so as to cut fuel costs while serving all of your customers. If you establish and keep to schedules of sales calls and deliveries, your organization will establish a reputation for reliability that customers will appreciate.

Regularly review the performance of your sales force by conducting sales and margin analysis. Ask for reports on sales volume by each salesperson and the volume of each product, class, or brand. Check the dollar gross margin of each salesperson, minus his or her direct expenses, as a means of finding the salesperson's effectiveness. Evaluate the records of sales to each customer in total or by department. Keep close control over the credit-granting powers and collection activities of salespeople, using records to disclose current conditions in the outstanding accounts of each salesperson's customers. These policies, combined with more stringent credit standards, can speed your collections and reduce your bad-debt losses.

What method should you use in compensating your sales force? Many wholesalers pay commissions on dollar gross margin. That way, the salesperson is motivated to sell high-profit lines. But commission compensation may not be in the best interests of the company if, for example, it does not provide sufficient incentive to fulfill marketing objectives. You might institute a bonus program that rewards the attainment of the marketing objectives (for example, moving out obsolete merchandise, introducing new merchandise, or increasing the sales of new merchandise). You might also try giving bonuses for expense reductions. But if you go to a bonus program, don't be stingy. No one responds to picayune payouts.

Watch net profits which are a result of two variables: *dollar gross margins* and *dollar operating expenses.* Net profits may be changed by your shifting either or both of the variables. You can get an increase in net profits by eliminating unprofitable customers, even though such a move reduces the total sales volume. Your savings in operating expenses will exceed the loss in dollar gross margin.

Try to increase the profitability to you of accounts by creating inducements for your customers to increase their order sizes. Larger sizes cut selling, delivery, and credit costs.

Look beyond the dollar gross margin by determining the relative profitability of different brand groups. Be sure to weigh the actual dollar contribution each brand group makes to the operating profits of the business. For example, one brand may carry a high gross-margin rate, but because of small sales volume contributes little to the dollar gross margin of your business. Another brand may have a low gross-margin rate, but because of high sales volume contributes a large part of your dollar gross margin.

Good Accounting Needed for Control Systems

Successful wholesalers manage their financial position on a current basis. Effective control demands that the manager be guided by detailed records and reports on daily, weekly, and monthly operations.

You will require a sales and gross-margin analysis to determine your most profitable commodities, customers, and brands from the standpoint of dollar gross margin. Your inquiries will disclose slow-moving and duplicate items and brands which should be eliminated. With careful daily or weekly analysis, you can find the gross-margin rates on individual items needed to obtain a satisfactory average gross margin for the business as a whole. Your salespeople are an integral part of the effort to control finances. They will be kept alert if their sales and gross-margin attainments by commodity, departments, customers, and brands are regularly reported.

How do you proceed with your analysis? Find the cost of goods and gross margins by items or by totals on each invoice. Classify by departments, sales personnel, or customers. Your totals should aid you in making policy decisions.

A simple way to arrive at your figure is by columnar or computer spreadsheet analysis of invoices, yielding volume of sales, cost of goods sold, and gross margins of individual commodities or departments. Enter the current cost of each item on the office copy of the invoice and extend it to obtain the cost of goods sold. Then subtract this from the extended selling price to obtain the gross margin for each item.

Some wholesalers enter only the cost extensions on the invoices. Then they total the sales price figures and the cost figures of the items listed and deduct the cost total from the sales price total to get the gross margin only for the invoice as a whole, disregarding sales and gross-margin analyses for each commodity, but making such analyses for the sales force and for the entire business.

Where the wholesaler's only interest is in total sales gross margins for the house and for each salesperson, the invoices are first sorted according to salespeople. If figures for sales and margins are needed by individual commodity departments, the invoice items can be resorted by commodity departments.

To proceed with the columnar-analysis method, prepare an analysis with a column for each department and post the amounts of the invoice lines into appropriate columns. If you have a computer, install the analysis in a spreadsheet program. Add these columns daily, semi-weekly, or weekly, and transfer the totals to summary sheets. If you want a departmental analysis by salespeople, sort their invoices and use a separate columnar sheet for each salesperson. Total all these to secure house totals.

Finding the profit and loss by customers, commodities, brands, departments, and territories is as important as gross-margin analysis. To do this you must allocate all expenses of operations.

You may be able to locate weaknesses in your profit structure by making comparisons with the costs and revenues reported by sample segments of the wholesaling field. Use the methods developed by the U.S. Department of Commerce for allocating unit costs to individual customers and to commodity departments or lines. Your accountant can readily install these for you with the aid of the booklets issued by the Commerce Department.

Many wholesaler groups have very strong, active industry associations which do helpful work. In addition to providing education, industry associations often promote open forums with manufacturers to resolve mutual problems, governmental lobbying, and financial and operating statistics which can be used to measure the quality of the results you are achieving.

Working for Good Inventory Control

Inventory represents a large proportion of your capital. Your success largely depends on your instincts for maintaining a suitable quantity of each item you sell. Data provided by your inventory-control system should call attention to the need to reorder when an item approaches its predetermined minimum stock level (order point). Avoid an over-supply of any item, whether staple or seasonal, and thus increase the rate of turnover (order quantity). A good inventory control system discloses slow-moving items, thus permitting you to reduce purchase quantities and set minimum stocks at lower levels in a timely fashion.

Today, the management of inventory in most wholesale firms is computerized. As a small, independent wholesaler, you may not want to be bothered with the complexities of the computer. But, computers offer the most satisfactory system of inventory control for your business. They have become so low in cost and have so many software packages available that it is almost mandatory that you explore them for applications to your business.

Inventory control systems fall into three classes: (1) observation methods, (2) periodic stock-count methods, and (3) perpetual inventory control.

The ideal inventory-control system measures the actual amount of stock on hand of each item and its value at any time. It also shows the rate of movements, or sales, of each item.

The *observation method* is simplest and least expensive. But it is generally the least satisfactory because heavy reliance is placed on judgment and memory. It gives you no record of the rate of movement or quantity on hand of any given item. There is no information on which to base minimum and maximum stock points, ordering points, and economical purchase quantities. It is not really an inventory control.

The *stock-count method* is an improvement. A regular periodic count gives you some indication of the rate of movement, as well as of the quantity on hand. It also furnishes a written record of your experience with any item. Its principal disadvantages are opportunity for error, lack of data between counts, and concealed errors in the calculated rate of movement.

The *perpetual inventory-control method* furnishes the most complete information, although it involves a greater investment of time and money. But the cost is moderate in view of the controls it gives. Under this system, you record complete data on every item of merchandise. Enter each purchase, receipt, sales, and return on this record. This procedure eliminates the necessity of taking a physical count. You will have the previous inventory balance, plus receipts, minus sales, to equal the quantity on hand. Occasionally you will want to take a physical inventory to check the *actual* count against the *book* count.

On small items, you might consider the use of a container as a reorder reminder. With this system, you fix a point at which your supply will need replenishing, allowing for gaps in ordering and delivering time. This "cushion" amount is placed in a separate container. When the regular source is exhausted, it is time to reorder.

To gain a true perspective on your merchandise, you might keep a file box containing cards for every item in stock. List the number sold annually, cost per unit, and total expected value. Arrange all cards in the file box from highest to lowest according to sales quantity. This enables you to evaluate the relative profitability of each item in stock and decide which should be culled from your lists.

A similar system of inventory control can be set up on a small business computer. However, there can be problems in computer-assisted inventory control using automatic reorder points. The correct timing of inventory purchases often hinges upon complex variables not programmable into the computer. For instance, when a manufacturer offers special deals, you have to be able to alter your inventory purchase pattern to get a good buy. An automatic reorder may also fail to take into account a revised sales forecast for the next period. If a new product is altering customers' needs for other products (for example, a new engine with less need for lubricating oils), you want flexibility on reorders while you determine what the pattern of new customer demand will be. Finally, automatic reorders will not benefit customers who expect a great deal of personal service.

The computer is most valuable for rapid sorting. It can scan your items to pick out those not in stock. A computer can quickly point out all the items furnished by one of your suppliers. It can also automatically inform you when your goods fall below the reorder point. Traditional methods will do the same but can never equal computer speed.

A good perpetual inventory-control system will reduce the amount of goods you need to carry in stock, thereby increasing your turnover. Purchasing fast-moving merchandise in diminishing quantities to achieve a high turnover may merely result in increased buying, receiving, and other expenses. It may give you a higher cost of goods and an increased risk of out-of-stocks, without compensating advantages. By reducing inventory, you can often reduce financial charges on your investment (interest, insurance, taxes) as well as space costs. If you have space to fill, try eliminating slow-moving items and replacing them with goods having a higher turnover rate. Your investment costs will be the same, but the increase in total dollar gross margin should leave larger net profits.

Another recourse is to increase sales volume without a proportionate increase in inventory. This results in a larger dollar gross margin without increasing the finance and storage expenses of inventory.

10

Service Firm Management

Service firms require minimal capital and entail little risk. The principal capital of a service firm is the owner's skills. Moreover, there is scarcely an area of the country without a demand for reliable services of some kind. If you have the requisite technical and managerial skills, a service firm may prove to be a profitable investment of time and money.

Opportunities for Entering the Service Field

Technological advances, such as electronic document transmission, and social changes, such as the increase in the aging population, have driven the development of new business sectors, many requiring minimal capital.

Besides the traditional service areas such as plumbing and heating, custom carpentry, auto repairs, "home" laundry, and appliance repair, new sectors calling for entrepreneurial solutions have opened in recent years and are continuing to open up. A list of some of these areas follows.

- Specialized repair and maintenance (such as computers)
- Specialized construction (such as skylights, sun rooms, and energy-efficient windows)

- Leisure enhancement (such as tours and sports training)
- Home and health services (such as child care providers, part-time companions, housekeepers, and cleaners)
- Training and retraining (as in computer instruction and plant openings, particularly in rural areas)
- Tool rental (for do-it-yourselfers and small companies)
- Modernization (of kitchens, bathrooms, etc.)
- Financial advisory services (such as investment counselors and tax advisory services)
- Novelty items (such as gem polishing and supply, fossil shops, and glass cutting)
- Specialized laundry services (for industrial and contaminated garments)
- Specialized pickup and delivery (such as local chauffeur services)
- Highly specialized products and services (such as a car customizing or restoration shop, sporting goods repair, and security systems)
- Technical consulting (such as asbestos treatment or removal in buildings and contaminated material disposal)

In all of these opportunities, it is what you do rather than the articles you sell that generates income. Furthermore, you do not need large investments in machinery or large inventories to conduct your business. Examples of enterprises that have these characteristics and have become popular in recent years are child care centers and specialized automobile repair shops. Examples of enterprises that have these characteristics which continue to hold their appeal are service stations, dry cleaning, hair styling, and beauty shops. We'll discuss each one in this chapter.

Enrollments in private child care centers now outnumber public preschool enrollments manyfold. The growth of the private preschool industry is primarily due to the increasing number of families with two working parents. The federal tax credit given for dependent-care expenses is also contributing to the growth of the nursery school industry.

One of the attractions of the field is that the knowledge requirements are not formidable. Those interested in opening child care facilities are usually interested because their natural gifts incline them to the work. Many people have acquired expertise in handling small children through their own experiences as parents and grandparents. Others have received training as franchisees.

Another attraction to some entrepreneurs is that child care centers require little in the way of operating expenses. Some people get started in the business to supplement their income by caring for other people's children at the same time they watch their own. Others, with more of an investment, have become franchisees of Montessori and similar franchisors.

The vehicular service market is still big. Although franchise organizations are becoming even more influential, this market continues to appeal to the entrepreneur who wishes to work entirely alone. Today, skilled automobile mechanics no longer look to invest in service stations; they open up repair shops instead, usually specializing in the more complex operations such as electrical problems diagnosis and repair, engine rebuilding, or diesel engine service. Mechanics with the highest skills open up foreign car repair shops. The time-consuming pumping gas detracts from more profitable major repair jobs. Mechanics who open service stations now desire the money earned on emergency repairs and small jobs such as tune-ups, tire repairs, and brake adjustments to supplement the income from gasoline sales.

Dry cleaning is another enterprise that continues to attract entrepreneurs because of the prevalent demand and the fact that the market continues to be best served by small firms. Dry cleaning also is attractive because it does not impose the horrendous hours imposed on owners of establishments such as restaurants and convenience stores, and because it is almost all cash and carry. Except for its service to a few firms, dry cleaning establishments don't carry accounts receivable. Further, the market is appealing because it is somewhat fluid. For example, location and access to the shop are such vital factors to dry cleaning stores that advantages can often be gained through them over longer-established competitors who have not moved while the neighborhood around them did.

A hair salon venture may offer profitable prospects. The first step is to decide your specialty. A salon may specialize in women's hair, men's hair, or unisex styling. Do you want to attract a well-to-do clientele interested in the height of fashion, a trendy crowd desiring the latest styles, or a more conservative clientele seeking a perpetuation of the look to which they have become accustomed? Will the market area of your shop be sufficiently populated with your target customers to provide you with enough clients? You must first decide your specialty before you can pick the location best fitting the market.

You might consider buying a franchise in a chain of beauty shops. Your franchisor will help you select the location of your shop, design the salon for the location, help find your staff, and work with you to formulate a realistic budget of expenses. The franchisor will continue to provide advice and consultation as styles change. The franchise fee varies depending on the particular franchise and the type of industry; for example, certain top franchise names can easily cost you thousands of dollars. In addition, a percentage of your yearly gross income must be paid to the franchisor. Not only must you invest in equipment and fixtures for your location but keep in mind that your initial outlay also must cover the cost of licensing, insurance, advertising, phones, security, equipment, initial salaries, and rents.

Select Carefully

There are risks in service work as in any other type of small business. The market that a service firm serves can change because of changes in neighborhood demographics, general economic conditions, technological developments, or unexpected governmental edict. If the market declines or disappears, the firm may have to move or shut its doors. Here are some examples. A neighborhood becoming industrialized may lose its need for a sporting goods store; a recession may reduce the revenues of a gourmet store below those needed to sustain it; the development of new clothing fabrics in the distant future may make dry cleaning obsolete. An example of thriving businesses hard hit by change are the lawn companies put out of business because of the lawn chemical scare. But risks to service businesses are no greater than those faced by business generally. And they are considerably less for the individual service company owner than for individual employees whose income from salaries cease altogether when they are laid off by their firms because of hard times. The knowledgeable and adaptable self-employed service company owner has the advantage of often being able to find other ways of serving the same needs, new needs to cater to, or survive on reduced income until the demand for the company's services rises again.

As part of the research you do before entering a business, identify the risks entailed, be honest and objective about them, weigh them carefully, and have a contingency plan for dealing with them should they materialize. And don't forget that not every crisis that can affect a new service enterprise will necessarily prove fatal. For example, a recession would reduce the amount of disposable income available, but may not hurt your sales if you are in the reupholstery business. When money is tight and people delay the purchase of new furniture, the skills of a good upholsterer are more in demand to keep older pieces in service. The same is true of the vehicle repair industry. When money is tight, companies and individuals usually invest to keep their trucks and cars going longer, rather than buying new vehicles.

The do-it-yourself trend was once thought of as a threat to service company sales. However, that did not prove to be the case. The do-it-yourself project often leads to complications which drive the amateur to the repair shop for solutions. Therefore, if you are serving a market with do-it-yourselfers in it, you can limit your risks of losing business to them by freely offering advice to those trying to cope with plumbing, carpentry, mechanical, or similar problems. Sooner or later you may be paid to finish the job that proved too complicated for the amateur to do.

While you're researching the field you wish to enter, look for trends in taste or usage which may affect it. Some businesses are profoundly affected by changes in aesthetic attitudes. Using furniture again as an example, period furniture is appealing increasingly to homemakers and that shift augurs well for upholsterers and furniture restorers. But a shift in one direction only indicates the plasticity of taste.

A major risk factor you should look into concerns how your characteristics and those of the business you want to enter match. If you want to start or buy a service business, start with taking an inventory of your skills and personal characteristics (a service business has little room for impatience or brusqueness). Then search for the service area closest to those skills and your experience. Don't enter a business without possessing the skills required or preparing to possess them.

Suppose you are considering entering the dry cleaning field. There is a good deal to know before you can safely engage in this business. The dry cleaner needs four types of knowledge: mechanical, electrical, industrial, and power plant. This knowledge can be acquired by studying dry cleaning in a technical or trade school, taking a correspondence course, or working in a dry cleaning plant first to gain experience.

Some owners plan on succeeding by employing someone who has the training or background in the trade. That is a big handicap, and it can be fatal. Depending upon the knowledge and skills of others is risky. If you're an amateur yourself, you're in no position to judge the competence of a prospective employee. Learning the trade involved as you go is also a big handicap to overcome.

In looking at the acquisition of a going service business, chase down all the common facts. Before investing (for example, in a service station), find out why the former lessee or owner gave up. The station might be located too far from the beaten path, too close to another station selling an equivalent brand of gas, may not have the repair revenue necessary to make it a going proposition, or may have been so poorly run that it has a lasting black eye. In some cases, changes in an oil company's policies drove the operator out of business (for example, revised gasoline allocations or increases in the wholesale price of gas).

Next, carefully assess the financial requirements of going into the business of your choice to determine whether it is a tolerable investment. For example, the capital requirements for entering the dry cleaning field are considerable. Up-to-date machines are required if the business is to be competitive, such as the latest pressing machines, sorters, dryers, and conveyor systems which transport the clothes between the steps in the automation process and retrieve them when the customer calls for them. But, while the machines eliminate the need for costly labor, they require a sizable capital investment.

Expertise and enthusiasm may give you a successful start in the service business. But don't bank on it. Many service businesses have "partners" in the form of the various government agencies. To get your business safely under way, you will need to know the numerous regulations that you must meet.

Check state and local regulations that control your activities. Investigate zoning restrictions and the licenses you will need to operate special equipment. For example, if you enter the dry cleaning business, some states insist that your cleaners, spotters, and finishers be certified as qualified technicians. Most states also require licenses for the various trades, such as plumbing and electrical work. You may need additional certification to expand your basic business to services such as saunas, exercises, massages, and facials. Some states, for example, have laws forbidding female cosmetologists from working on male clients. Consult with city hall, your attorney, and any applicable state boards before acting.

Many federal regulations impinge on the conduct of smaller businesses: safety and hazard control, minimum wages, pension rights, etc. Even your job application forms must comply with federal antidiscrimination laws and the fair employment practice laws of your state. Add investigation of these to your list of items to research and discuss with your attorney.

When conducting your research, contact your district's Small Business Administration (SBA) office. It can assist you in assessing your opportunities and finding the areas of service in which a business person might make a successful livelihood. The SBA publishes a series of pamphlets which give many important details on operating various types of service firms. Read all the available literature before you make a decision.

Organizing the Operation

Many service firms suffer from poor management, stemming from inexperience, inadequate training, or, more usually, the lack of patience and attention to detail. Fine trade skills alone do not suffice. Many an excellent artisan has failed in the service business because he or she couldn't *manage* to show up on time or get the work done at the estimated cost.

Sloppy bookkeeping is often the leading expression of the deficiency and the least defensible one. If you can't manage to keep your books in order, don't go into business for yourself. You'll run into disaster, not merely because you'll lose track of who owes what to whom, but also because you'll have no basis for identifying the problems you need to work on or, better yet, how to develop business growth. Inventory control of materials and supplies is another chronic weakness. Although the inventory may be fairly simple, a service company needs to pay particular attention to orderly storekeeping procedures. After all, when a sales organization is out of an item, it loses the profit from the sale of that item only. But when a service firm is prevented from working because an item is lacking, it loses the profit from the sale of that item and the service that went with it. Don't make the mistake of thinking that you will make up the profit when you obtain the item and do the job later. Profit lost during the time you could have done a job is *profit lost forever*. Then there's the matter of the residual effect on your business of stock outages. Customers become irritated when their goods can be located only after an extensive search or when the work they want done is held up because of outages of regular stock. If this situation becomes too common, customers will stop coming to you with work.

An identification system for work in progress is also essential. Have you ever gone into a lawn mower repair facility and had to wait a half hour while a search was conducted for the mower of the customer before you and then for yours? Such bumbling is not merely irritating, it also creates room for doubt about the operator's technical competence.

Part of organizing to do business is to consider and establish the policies governing how the enterprise is going to run. The place to start is with marketing. You should first identify the character of your market and then the segment of that market you will serve. This process has two aspects, geography and sector. Some service firms thrive by directing their appeal to the general population in a small geographical area or to specific potential customers in a large geographical area, or to many other combinations of the two factors. Examples of firms that serve segments of the total market are service stations catering exclusively to taxis or trucks; employment agencies specializing in placing engineers, office help, domestics, factory help (possibly in a given industry, such as the garment industry); laundries emphasizing the cleaning of household items such as curtains, slipcovers, and rugs, or attracting the singles trade with advertisements of special care for shirts and blouses.

Also, before opening your doors, figure out your *initial* pricing strategies. We say initial because pricing is relative and is not something that, once set, is set for life. For example, to focus attention on the opening of the enterprise you will probably put promotional prices on your services and/or wares. Once the opening is past, you will want to review your situation and price for profitability. Thereafter, you will probably want to price for growth.

Keep in mind the fact that the pricing of services does not respond to all the factors pricing of hard goods responds to and few of the factors pricing of brand-name consumer goods responds to.

With careful planning beforehand, even if you decide to set up in a community which already has established service firms, you may be able to distinguish your firm above the others.

Opening the Business

What steps can you take to attract customers when you are opening your firm? Getting a good start can be critical to the success of the business; poor starts can prevent a business from generating enough income to see it through the first year or two.

The first step, of course, is to make it known that you're opening for business. An announcement of that fact alone will stir little interest. You will have to couple it with some motivating factor such as the opportunity to save money, learn something, get something free, or a combination of these.

Of the three incentives, the first two (the opportunity to save money or to learn something) are the best. Everyone responds to appropriate invitations to save money, especially your target customers in their area of interest (such as motorists saving on lubricating oil). But an opportunity to learn something is as much or even more powerful, depending on the customer group. Hobbyists and do-it-yourself mechanics are particularly interested in acquiring new skills or advancing their existing skills. Free gifts are both the least motivating and the most costly to the entrepreneur. Unless a gift is deemed worthy in the receiver's eye—in which case it will probably be a very costly strategy—it may lead to the perception of the firm as "chintzy," of having a low appreciation for quality.

Advertising your opening in the local paper is almost a must. Advertising, combined with some kind of special offer, can make the community quickly aware of your presence. In smaller communities it is not difficult to get the newspaper to include a circular in the paper at a reasonable cost. The newspaper is also likely to be willing to carry a brief article about you and your shop.

But don't limit your opening advertisements to the newspaper. If not distributed with the local newspaper, circulars announcing the opening of your enterprise (and the philosophy governing its operations) and, perhaps, opening specials can be delivered by hand to residences. A mailing program can reach commercial and industrial firms within your marketing area.

Another possibility in publicizing your new business is the use of posters and public notices. Many firms that will be doing business with you may be willing to put posters notifying customers and passersby of your opening on their windows or waiting rooms. The possibilities are endless and deserving of investigation.

One of the first steps you will take upon opening up is to get into the yellow pages of your telephone book. That will help keep the town aware of your location and services although it will not bring your opening to their attention.

Building the Business

Once the business has opened and stabilized, it is time to consider growth strategies. If you don't move positively toward growth, you'll only invite intensified competition.

Once you have some experience with the pulling power of your advertisements, set a standard for future placements. Keep the style simple, clear, and consistent. Your makeup style should be easily recognizable. Do not alter it from entry to entry.

Once you've gotten started, you can continue developing your business by selectively seeking out prospective customers. You may be able to identify potential customers from news stories about newlyweds, newcomers to the community, purchasers of houses, births, job promotions, and purchased lists readily available from list makers. Computers have allowed list makers to become sophisticated in providing the names and addresses of potential customers ranked by age, income, sex, housing, and geographic area.

You can make your shop noteworthy by contributing money or personal effort to community activities. You might lend some item of equipment to a parade or fair or, if in a central location, devote space in your front window to worthy causes. Usually credit is given, either verbally or by program, to merchants who aid in community drives.

But all of such efforts are subordinate to the strongest promotional element of all—word of mouth, one person telling another they should buy from you. The foundations of word-of-mouth rests in two sources—honesty of dealings and quality of work.

Honesty with customers is the first rule of the service business. Be open and truthful with your customers. For example, if an appliance can be repaired at reasonable cost, tell the customer so and don't try to pressure the customer into buying a replacement. High-pressure tactics betray themselves quickly, and your reputation suffers. If you run a repair shop, try to keep your customers informed on the status of their appliances. Will the repair take longer than you forecasted? Is the bill going to be significantly higher? Let your customer know before proceeding with the work. For example, an automobile repair shop should tell a customer that the radiator which seemed repairable cannot be fixed and needs to be replaced. Obtain a phone number so that you can keep your customer posted. If you can supply a substitute while an item is being repaired, you will win customer loyalty.

Quality work at a reasonable price is part of the success formula for the service firm. Your reputation with satisfied customers will bring others to you. From the start, make it clear that you stand behind your work. Customers' memories are long.

If there are any industry codes of ethics and standards, post them in your shop along with your own which show your intention to exceed the norm. For example, you may offer a longer warranty period than your competitors and service repairs for a greater range of problems. A more liberal credit policy or acceptance of credit cards may be sufficient to attract customers from your competitors. Can you offer something extra for services which run over a certain amount of money? Some service stations, for example, offer a free car wash after repairs over a stated amount. Some service businesses tie in premiums of their merchandise with the scales of purchases made. The recommendations of satisfied customers are the greatest force in expanding a clientele.

If you run a general repair shop, demonstrate your overall expertise when discussing your services so the customer will be aware that you can deal with other problems besides the one you are attending to. For example, when the customer picks up repaired storm windows in February, you or your helpers can point out that a lawn mower or hedge trimmer may need overhauling by spring. A motel operator can inform departing guests of special attractions in the coming off-season. A locksmith might also discuss the need for a burglar alarm. Quality work is the best way to build sales, but it can be enhanced by added inducements.

11

A Basic Guide to Franchise Operation

Franchise operations are everywhere. In every town and city, you have seen, and at some time have used, the services of a franchised operation. In 1992, it was estimated that there were over 540,000 franchised units accounting for more than 35 percent of total retail sales in the United States. There were also more than 3000 companies offering franchises. Leading the pack were restaurant franchises, followed by nonfood retailers, hotels, motels, campgrounds, business services, auto products and services, and convenience stores. The names of leading franchisors indicate the range of services offered: McDonalds, Subway Sandwiches, TCBY, and Domino's Pizza (food), Radio Shack (electronics), Midas (car service), Blockbuster Entertainment (video rentals), and Alpha Graphics (printing services).

Some people predict that within the decade more than 50 percent of U.S. business will be franchised operations. There are certainly success stories to be related, and new franchising opportunities—one of which it may be your good fortune to find and develop—abound. However, it is important in approaching franchises to be less optimistic than the franchise promoters. There have been many failures and cases of fraud and misrepresentation. The franchise field is relatively new; its great growth occurred only in the 1980s, and the legal rules regulating franchises have not been fully developed; gaps in the law favor franchisors.

Franchising is a business system of marketing and distributing goods and/or services of a franchisor by a franchisee. The franchisor grants the purchaser (franchisee) a license to market a product and/or service through a system developed by the franchisor. The franchisor provides the product, a marketing plan or format, management and marketing support, and training. The franchisee finances and manages the franchise location, expecting to minimize risks by taking advantage of public awareness of the franchisor's trademark and products and utilizing the franchisor's training, supervision, and assistance. However, the potential jumpstart to success may be offset by a loss of independence: the franchisee is dependent upon the franchisor's ability to promote and continue public recognition of products and services and maintain quality standards. This "dependent" status distinguishes franchisees from other independent businesspersons and generates problems unique to franchising arrangements. At the same time, franchising does not relieve the franchisee from usual business problems. A franchised operation is a business like any other business. The franchisee must deal with employees and customers and keep account of business transactions. The success in many individual franchised operations requires long hours of work and supervision. This has especially been true in the case of franchised food operations. There is no easy ride.

Can You Operate as a Franchisee?

Despite their attraction, franchises are not for everyone who wants to be in business. They attract people who want to reduce the risks of being in business by themselves and who want the advice and direction of experienced businesspersons.

Analyze yourself as well as each franchisor to determine the match between your personal characteristics and those required to be successful by the franchise. Evaluate your aims, strengths, and interests. If you delight in gourmet cooking, can you be happy preparing and selling hamburgers? Determine what kind of work you enjoy first, then look for a franchised business that offers that kind of work.

Do you have the personal qualifications called for in the particular type of franchising that interests you (for example, does cooking interest you, do you like to deal with retail customers)? Can you work within the system (for example, do you take instruction well, are you uncomfortable with ambiguity, do you prefer a structured environment to an open-ended one)?

Your own self-examination will help you identify the types of franchise suited to your personality and abilities. The examination will be helped by your asking yourself questions such as the following, and being tough about answering them (performing the exercise on paper will help even further).

1. *Do you work well under supervision?* Since the success of a franchise depends on its being the same everywhere and on being recognized as such by the consumer, the best franchisors keep a tight rein on their franchises. If the franchisor changes the formula, both franchisor and franchisee lose the benefit of the system. Hence, a franchise is not a good business for those who don't like to be told what to do. That leads to a caveat: Beware the franchisor who allows franchisees to do whatever they wish. There will be little help to you in running the business from such a franchisor; and the area advisor supposedly available to you will manage to be conspicuous by his or her absence. The question then will be can you go it alone, if need be? If the answer is yes, then you should ask yourself why you need a franchise at all?

2. *What is your business experience?* Next comes the matter of your exposure to business activities and what you learned from it. Franchise operations is no field for a neophyte. Some franchisors advertise "no experience necessary" and imply that raw energy and intelligence are enough. They sometimes are, but liberal application of both can often create troubles as well as benefits. Even if the franchisor offers an extensive training program, you should still thoroughly evaluate the total background you can bring into any enterprise. Can you handle personnel? Have you experience in buying, selling, and accounting? Can you cope with government paperwork? While some individuals have succeeded in totally unfamiliar lines, knowledge of the business you propose to enter could be a lifesaver.

A franchise may not be suitable for a person whose business experience was gained in a large corporation. Franchisors have tried to lure former corporate executives who lost positions during the recession into investing in franchises. However, the experience of a corporate executive may not be the "right stuff" for making a go of a franchise. A corporate executive can rely on the company structure for support and to delegate authority, but a franchise owner generally has to make and execute many business decisions which may require an expertise beyond his or her experience. Furthermore, the hours of work will often be long and demanding, and the initial income return small in comparison to that earned in a large corporation.

3. *Are you genuinely enthusiastic about the franchised line you are contemplating?* Lukewarm interest is unlikely to generate profits or help you through difficult days. Enthusiasm is needed to carry you

through the very long hours of hard work most franchise owners have to put in. There's nothing new about that, of course; owners of independently owned firms also have to put in long hours. But, remember, you are buying into somebody else's business. The total entrepreneur has his or her own business, and that helps sustain interest. An individual small business owner holds the reins on his or her investment, does not have to adhere to the rules, and procedures imposed by others, and shares no part of the profit in the form of royalties or other ongoing fees with others—and in that there can be great satisfaction. The person with a strong sense of identity and many ideas to be put into action may be too restricted in a franchise.

Obtaining Information on Franchises

Select a field you are interested in and gather all the information about it you can. Pay particular attention to market demand, projected growth rates, local demographic data, and where the product or service is in its life cycle. Hesitate to enter a field with no growth potential. Franchise opportunities appear in the business sections of such newspapers as *The New York Times, The Wall Street Journal,* and *USA Today.* Also, franchise brokers provide information and offer choices of different franchise investments. If a national franchise that interests you is not advertised among the current openings, write to the main office of the company to inquire about new franchises.

The book *Franchise Opportunities Handbook* (available from Superintendent of Documents, U.S. Government Printing Office, P.O. Box 371954, Pittsburgh, PA 15250-7954) alphabetically lists various types of franchised operations, companies doing business under those categories, and general information. If you are interested in, say, fast-food operations, you can look up a number of companies and check what equity capital is required; what, if any, financial assistance, managerial assistance, and training are provided; how many franchises are in the operation; and how long the company has been in business. In addition, this valuable government booklet offers useful guidance to the potential franchisee and sources of further information.

You can obtain further information from the International Franchising Association, 1350 New York Avenue N.W., Washington, DC 20005. Also available are the *Directory of Franchising Organizations* from Pilot Books, 347 Fifth Avenue, New York, NY 10016, and the *Franchise Annual* from Info Press, 736 Center Street, Lewiston, NY 10942.

You should be alert to current articles and news items on franchising in business magazines and newspapers; they report on franchise successes and failures. Your public library can assist you in looking up publications and in guiding you to books on the subject.

You should also attend a franchise show. Here, you can talk with representatives of franchises and pick up their pamphlets and, perhaps, sample copies of their contracts. But beware of pressure tactics to sign up at once and any "this is your last chance for this profitable location" deals. Gathering information is your present objective; getting caught for a heavy financial commitment before you can assess the situation is not.

Franchisors are required to give the names and addresses of at least 10 franchisees whose locations are closest to your planned site. Spend the most time with people who have been with the company the longest and ask them what they think of the training they received, the kind of support the franchisor now gives, the quality and prices of the products purchased from the franchisor (if the franchisor provides such products), and the many other questions that can be asked to determine the comfort level of the relationship.

When your interest has narrowed to one or two franchisors and to establishing yourself in a certain location, you can launch inquiries about the franchisors at a better business bureau, the chamber of commerce, and the local bank. In that way, you may learn of any negative factors about them and whether there is an overload of similar businesses in the area.

Legal Considerations

As franchising is a relatively new method of doing business, the law spelling out the legal relationships and responsibilities of franchisors and franchisees is in a state of development.

There are no federal laws directly regulating franchises. Furthermore, only one-third of the states have specific laws affecting franchises, and these laws vary from state to state. However, due to complaints of abuses, Congress has begun to take action in this area. For example, when this book went to press, legislation was being considered that would increase franchisors' disclosures to prospective franchisees and prohibit abuses of certain contractual clauses. The Federal Trade Commission was also considering stricter disclosure requirements. Thus, in light of the current legal flux, the most important cornerstone of your relationship with a franchisor will be the contract that you negotiate and sign. Here, unfortunately, the franchisor is generally in the driver's seat.

The franchisor not only has a financial advantage but also has access to information and legal advice unavailable to you, the franchisee. As a result, an unequal bargaining relationship may be created which frequently results in one-sided franchise agreements that are offered, and generally accepted on a take-it-or-leave-it basis. There is generally little opportunity to negotiate or alter contract terms, particularly for first-time franchisees. Most franchise agreements are highly standardized and incorporate a number of potentially disadvantageous provisions in the contract. Be on the lookout for the following: (1) a unilateral right of termination without cause; (2) a right to refuse to renew a franchise agreement for any reason; (3) a requirement of prior approval by the franchisor of the sale or transfer of a franchise and the right to withhold such approval for any reason; (4) a right of the franchisor to recover a franchise, or the property, supplies, and equipment associated with the franchise, in the event of termination or nonrenewal; and (5) a requirement that upon termination, a franchisee may not compete in a similar business within a 50-mile radius for a 2-year period.

In the absence of federal legislation (although Congress may decide to step in) there has been an increasing body of state "fairness legislation" that has sought to intervene in franchise relationships to moderate the one-sided nature of franchise agreements. For example, some states prevent arbitrary terminations and nonrenewals of franchises or provide compensation for terminated franchises.

Thus, when considering franchise opportunities, before you sign a contract, review every clause with an attorney who is experienced in this area of the law. Analyze each commitment and the possible repercussions. Determine if the franchisor will amend objectionable contractual terms, and if not, determine what you can live with. Essential points to consider are as follows:

1. *Franchise fees, royalties, payments for equipment, etc.*   Determine whether the franchise fee is a one-time or recurring payment. What are you getting for it? You may also have to pay royalties in a specified amount or as a percentage of gross sales. Will you gain certain financial advantages as a franchisee to help balance any such constant payment? Your investment may cover such items as inventory, licenses, and permits. Establish just what it does cover and what you need in addition. Do you have to buy trucks, fixtures, or equipment? Must you buy such essential items from the franchisor? Could you buy elsewhere for less?

2. *Sales and prices.*   You may have to fulfill a certain quota within a specified period. What happens if you fail to meet the requirement? Failure may allow the franchisor to terminate the contract. Prices may be set by the franchisor. Will this limit you in meeting competition?

The franchisor may stipulate a limit to the amount you can withdraw as your personal management fee. If so, is this a reasonable and businesslike arrangement?

3. *Financial details, accounting, and banking.* Franchisors may prescribe all details of bookkeeping and banking and may stipulate their own access to financial details. Are you willing to go along with all their requirements?

4. *Advertising and promotions.* Some contracts call for the franchisee to make a specified contribution to national advertising and to follow company directions on local advertising and promotions. To what extent will you benefit from this advertising? Will it provide some of the fanfare for your opening? Must your advertising be approved?

5. *Business premises and repairs.* The franchisor may demand final say in the building or alteration of your premises, require certain standards of maintenance, set time limits on painting and repairs which are done at your expense, and be free to send supervisors and inspectors at any time. Are the stated terms reasonable? Could you be put out of business if you fail to fulfill any of them?

6. *Employees.* The franchisor may want final say on hiring and firing, employee uniforms, company-sponsored training courses, and wages and fringe benefits. Check that you, as the employer, are satisfied with the conditions.

7. *Insurance.* The insurance company may be picked by the franchisor, who decides on the coverage for which you must pay. Do you have alternative plans you think should be considered?

8. *Products, inventory, and supplies.* Clauses in the contract relating to these matters are vital. The franchisor may attempt to curtail your right to add lines to your inventory, insist you carry all, or only, franchise products, or require that only certain suppliers provide the ingredients for your line. The courts have ruled favorably in a number of cases where franchisees have shown that they could obtain supplies at better prices from other sources. The Federal Trade Commission has also forced companies to rewrite contracts so that any suggestion that franchisees are compelled to purchase from specified suppliers is eliminated. Review your contract to see if unwarranted limitations are being placed upon you. However, the franchisor may legitimately demand that the standard of the franchise product be maintained.

9. *Hours, pricing, and conduct of business.* The contract may set your opening and closing hours, set prices, and require conformity to all company policies and regulations in the conduct of business. Can you accept this standardization?

10. *Territory and location.*   A clear definition of your territory, or a map showing it, should be part of your contract. Has the company reserved any rights to curtail your territory? In some circumstances, a company may need freedom to change, expand, or meet new demands. Your area might be able to take more franchises without undercutting your business. The location of your store or service should be entirely to your satisfaction because inferior location may spell failure even to the best-run business. Large franchisors usually have experts investigate a location before a new outlet is opened and, because they can pull some weight, obtain sites not available to the small business owner alone. Conduct your own survey of the location; you may want to retain the right to turn down a spot allocated to you. Return on your investment hinges on the right location.

11. *Termination, transfer, or renewal of contract.*   Your failure to fulfill any one of the conditions of the contract may be cause for cancellation. You and your lawyer must review each clause specifically to see where the company has retained revocation rights. The threat of termination might hang over, say, the failure to fulfill a sales quota. Or, in the event of the franchisee's death or disability, the family might be ousted from the business with less than just recompense. Some franchisors eventually want to take over highly profitable stores or eventually want services to be company-owned and run. The contract may provide an option for the company to repurchase the business. Has the means of establishing a fair market value been set in the agreement? Sometimes a provision is included which states that the repurchase price should not exceed the amount originally paid for the franchise. In consequence, the franchisee stands to lose the results of many years of building up the business. Check also provisions relating to transfer, renewal, or sale of the franchise. The franchisor may demand to approve a buyer proposing to take over your franchise. Your right to sell and make a profit may not be questioned, but the company wishes to keep a control on selection of its franchisees—and perhaps to make sure that some competitor is not trying to take over through an intermediary.

Federal Trade Commission Disclosure Requirements

The Federal Trade Commission has rules requiring disclosures. These disclosure requirements apply to an arrangement that has these three characteristics:

1. The franchisee distributes products or services associated with the franchisor's trademark or identifying symbol.

2. The franchisor provides significant assistance and/or significant control over the franchisee's method of operation.

3. The franchisee is required to pay at least $500 to the franchisor during the first 6 months of the operation of the franchise.

The FTC requires franchisors (and franchise brokers) to provide prospective franchisees with a basic disclosure statement. The franchisor must also provide the investor with a copy of the actual franchise agreement at least 5 days before the agreement is to be executed. Then the seller must provide the potential buyer with an earnings claim document anytime the franchisor makes a statement, written or oral, as to what sort of return a buyer might expect on his or her investment.

The earnings claims document must be updated every 90 days by the franchisor to reflect the latest income statistics. The data in the report must be based on actual results, not estimates.

These documents give the investor a lot to study, but even if they make the franchise appear to be a good investment, don't sign the contract until the terms have been reviewed by a lawyer familiar with franchising. Statements as to the legitimacy of the business often fail to indicate crucial restrictions in the operation. Although the various statements provide more information than you would normally receive from the seller of a small business, the financial viability of the setup might be designed for an area with a different cost of living or where people have different spending habits.

The basic disclosure document has 20 categories of information:

1. It must provide the name under which the franchise does business, its trademark, and the name and address of the parent company.

2. It should identify the directors of the franchise and the franchise's chief executives for marketing, service, operations, and training by name, and it should reveal their business experience and previous employment during the last 5 years.

3. The operators should state the length of time they have been selling the franchise. If the parent company has been selling other franchises, the names of these franchises and the length of time they have been sold must also be revealed.

4. The franchise owner must reveal and describe the history and settlement of any court actions for felony convictions, embezzlement, restraint of trade, injunctions, and civil actions that have been

made against any of the franchise operations or any of the franchise owners.

5. The disclosure statement must reveal the bankruptcy history of any of the franchise directors, officers, or executors, including reorganization due to insolvency.

6. The franchise business, the product line, and the probable market for the product must be fully described.

7. There must be a listing of the initial funds required to be paid to the franchise or its affiliates, such as down payments, rents, inventory costs, and other fees.

8. The periodic payments the investor must make to the franchise owners should be fully listed, such as leases and rentals. If some of these fees are expressed as percentages of the outlet's volume, estimates must be provided as to what the percentage fees may amount to.

9. The purchaser must be provided with a list of persons with whom the operation will be required to do business and the affiliation these people have with the franchise.

10. If the purchaser is required to do business with certain people, the disclosure statement must give a basis for calculating what revenue the franchise receives from these people (thus disclosing rebates and kickbacks).

11. The purchaser must be given a list of materials he or she is required to lease or purchase. If the materials must be purchased from a specific person (including the franchisor), the names and addresses must be provided.

12. Financing arrangements provided directly or indirectly by the franchise must be disclosed, including the names of lenders, amounts to be lent, percentages charged, collateral necessary, and the default provisions.

13. The franchisor must state any limits as to what products may be sold, whom they may be sold to, where they may be sold, and what sales territory is protected.

14. If personal participation in the franchise is required of the investor, a description must be provided of the duties he or she is expected to perform. This may indicate that silent investors are not wanted.

15. The disclosure statement must spell out the terms by which either the purchaser or the franchisor can terminate, cancel, or renew the contract to run the franchise. Also to be revealed are any obliga-

tions that might exist after termination or expiration: whether the investor is allowed to sell the operation; what the rights of the purchaser's heirs are; and, should the purchaser leave the franchise, what would be the nature of a covenant not to compete.

16. The disclosure statement must include statistics as to the number of franchise operations, the number voluntarily terminated, the number terminated by the franchisor, the number for which renewal was refused, and the number of operations canceled by the franchise in the middle of the agreement. The franchisor must also provide the owners' names and addresses of the 10 franchised locations nearest to the one being purchased.

17. It must be stated whether the franchisor must approve the location of the site of the purchaser's operations. If so, the statement must specify the range of time between the signing of the franchise agreement and the site selection, and the usual length of time between the signing of the franchise agreement and the opening date for a purchaser's location.

18. The minimum amount of training required of a franchise operator must be indicated as well as the type and cost of training offered by the company.

19. If a public figure is involved in the promotion of the franchise, the statement must reveal that person's investment in the franchise, his or her remuneration, and what the celebrity's obligations to the franchise are.

20. The franchisor must provide the investor with a balance sheet and income statement for each of the last 3 years.

The disclosure requirements are in a state of flux. In response to disclosure rule violations and continuing complaints concerning inadequacy of the rules, the FTC was moving to toughen disclosure requirements as this book went to press. There were also renewed calls in Congress for direct legislation that would not only increase the franchisor's disclosure responsibilities but also specifically govern the relationship between franchisor and franchisee.

Investigating the Franchisor

You should evaluate both the information you have received and the company's willingness to provide it to you. There are certain facts you need to know.

1. *What do present franchisees say about the organization?* From a list of franchisees in your prospective area, arrange to interview these people and find out how they rate the company. Can they get advice when needed? Are they too heavily supervised? Have they any financial grievances? Do they have complaints about the contract? Are advertising arrangements satisfactory? How is business? Is profit measuring up to expectations? Did the franchisor quote reasonably accurate figures on the costs of setting up operations, on actual operating expenses, and on profits? Be observant while on the franchisee's premises; if possible, spend a day at a franchise. When possible, also see franchisees whose names were not supplied by the company. You want to make sure you are talking freely with unbiased people.

2. *How is the franchisor faring? Is it making a substantial profit?* It is important with a relatively new company to check the source of the franchisor's income. Has it been from the sale of new franchises or is it operating income? A franchisor earning substantial income from royalties is showing a better current position than one relying on the sale of new franchises.

3. *Are you pressured to sign a contract?* A bad sign is the overeager approach on the part of the franchisor. The legitimate company wants to check out potential franchisees and will urge that the franchisee have a lawyer go over the contract and other details of a commitment. The franchisor who evades investigation is to be avoided.

By mail or in person, there are some questions you should ask a franchisor:

1. *What training and assistance are given to franchisees?* You want specifics on the type of training you get from your franchise, for how long, at whose expense, and whether it would be sufficient to prepare you for owner-management. The training provided by some franchises has proved to be totally inadequate. Is there an area supervisor or troubleshooter regularly available? What kind of help does he or she provide? Is that person (or team) designated solely to work with franchisees? Some area personnel are actually salespeople for franchises and render little help to those who have already bought.

2. *How are differences between company and franchisees settled?* Find out if the contract calls for arbitration of disputes and if both parties are bound to accept.

3. *What is the extent of territory protection?* Your company or its subsidiaries might set up other franchisees in the same or a similar line too near for your profit. Find out what restraints are operative.

4. *What is the potential profitability for the franchisee?* You and your accountant need a precise breakdown of figures involved in a particular enterprise. Quite apart from the difference between going into business as a dry cleaner and running a motel, there may be many financial variations within a particular franchise organization; for example, costs differ from one location to another and in a new enterprise against one taken over from another owner-manager.

The costs should be spelled out in the disclosure statement. Match costs with income projections to determine how long it will take to reach a cash flow breakeven point. Until this point is reached, a franchise will drain your finances just as any other small business would.

Franchises that are profitable almost immediately command the highest prices. Some of the more famous can cost as much as $1 million to start.

Should You Be a "Silent Investor"?

Thus far, discussion has been mainly directed to the interests of franchise owner-managers. But some owners are not managers. Some franchises are geared toward the investor who has no intention of personally managing the business and can afford to hire a manager to run it. A lot of money has been made that way; a lot more has been lost.

A franchise is not a license to make money! Silent investors who profit from franchise ownership do not simply invest their money and turn their backs on the business. They do not just drop in from time to time to see how things are going. They control the business as carefully as a full-time operator, inspecting operations and the books as frequently as necessary to keep tabs on trends and results.

People with money to spare for investing and little time of their own to spend on a business can find franchises available where a reasonable profit can be attained even though a manager must be employed. Silent investors do not need the specific experience needed to run a franchise business successfully, but they must have both the general business knowledge and the time to see that the business is run properly.

Franchising Your Own Ideas

Franchising your own business idea has this attraction: You can broaden your business with the help of the funds and labor of others. You may have developed a catchy and attractive way of merchandising a product or service. You have been successful and feel able to package and service the concept for others to use. However, a good idea is not enough. Organizing a franchise business requires considerable planning and research. You are licensing a name and business system in return for fees and a percent of sales. You must not only develop the business concept and the means of executing it, but you also must meet Federal Trade Commission rules for disclosure documents. You must then market your franchise and interest prospective investors, and once they have started a franchise, you must supervise their operations and monitor their financial responsibility.

If you believe you have a good concept, service, and/or product, study the experience of others. Sources of franchising information have been discussed earlier in this chapter. If you decide to go ahead, also consider hiring the services of a consultant experienced in marketing franchises.

Tax Considerations

If you are considering a "silent" investor status, review the passive activity tax restrictions which (1) defer the deduction of losses until you have income from the activity on sell out and (2) treat your income from the "silent" activity as passive income. Whether you should be a silent or active participant depends on your other income-producing sources and whether the investment will produce income or loss.

If you have passive activity losses from other activities, you will probably want to be a silent investor. The reason: If the franchise income is passive, you can offset that income by your losses from the other passive activities, such as a rental investment. On the other hand, if the activity operates at a loss, and you do not have passive income from other sources, you will want to be treated as an active participant in order to claim immediate loss deductions. There are technical tax rules that are applied to determine active or silent status. For example, working for more than 500 hours in the business will make you an active participant.

The passive activity tax rules are complicated and should be reviewed with your tax adviser.

12

Mail-Order Business

Buying by mail fascinates consumers now as much as it did a century ago. Despite changes in their buying habits, Americans continue to enjoy perusing and sending for items from catalogs. You can order through catalogs almost any movable item, from a bar of soap to a prefabricated house.

The current popularity and future prospects of mail order attract many entrepreneurs to the business. There are spectacular success stories as well as failures. Where money can be made quickly, the opportunities to lose it also abound. That aphorism applies in spades to mail order.

Let us now examine how to go about getting into the business.

Choosing a Product

The decision whether to go into mail order or not should begin with answers to these three questions: Is the product unique? Is it already being sold through any medium? What is the market for the product like?

If the product is unique, the questions to be resolved are: Can the product be sold at all and, if so, can it be sold by mail? Don't be misled by the dogma that having a unique product to sell is the key to the market. The plain truth is that the marketing of unique products presents problems wherever and however it is done. Loyalty to existing products is always an obstacle; familiarity does have its affections. And then there's the fear of newness; fads are more sponsored by sameness than by difference. The recent craze for Spanish wine is an example. A liquor store selling the wine has done well selling recognized brands or vintages. But none have prospered selling Spanish wine made from berries or weeds, or with totally unfamiliar labels. Even when loyalty and opposition to change do not have to be overcome, there is the matter of the marketability of the product itself. For example, before the onset of the cholesterol scare and calorie-counting, Teflon could not be sold as a utensil coating. Its color and texture ran counter to every culinary rubric.

Once you've established through appropriate tests that your unique product can be sold, you must confront the fact that not all products are suited to mail order, however salable they may be through other sales media. For example, fresh tomatoes—which have as close to a universal market as any product can have—cannot be sold through the mail because of their spoilage rate and their need to be seen and felt before they can appeal to the purchaser. Pears and grapefruit, on the other hand, can be sold through the mail because their ripening rates are such that by the time they reach the customer they are at their peak of appearance and flavor. Can your product survive in the mail? Aside from the question of survivability in physical terms, there is the matter of taste. Few products which can be successfully sold through mail order demand much in the way of imagination and judgment of their purchasers (otherwise, they wouldn't get sold). But unique products don't afford consumers the opportunity to base their selection on prior experience.

After you have determined that a product is suited to sell through the mail, you must then deal with the collateral question: In what volume can it be sold? Not every product that can be sold by mail will sell enough to justify the costs of selling it that way. Printing and mailing catalogs is enormously expensive, even on a limited scale. Direct-mail advertising, while less expensive, can only cover an item or two, and the cheapest alternative, newspaper advertising, is seldom rewarding on less than a programmed basis (that is, recurrent advertising on a carefully scheduled basis). Getting a fix on volume will tell you which form of mail order you can afford to enter.

If the product is not unique, the question to be answered is: Is it already being sold successfully by mail? If it is, the next question is: What kinds of advantages must be created for my product to be successful? You need not bother asking: Is the market big enough for a similar product? That another product has been brought to the market first should not deter you. Piggybacking is a strategy that works! The other product having arrived first may have created the opportunity for your product.

Pioneers in a marketplace often have a lot of proselytizing to do. As a follower, you will not have to do that. On the other hand, you will have to create in potential buyers the recognition that purchasing your product will confer special benefits of some kind—notably in performance, price, or prestige.

Having discovered that the product is marketable, the last question to be asked is: What is the nature of the market? Is it national, regional, or local? Is it universal or segmented? That is, will the products appeal to the general population or to only a portion?

Most successful mail-order ventures promote and sell commonly used items. Kitchen appliances are an example. As marketed by mail order, the appliances appeal to the vast number of people who feel overwhelmed by the gadgetry offered in their local stores (and pressured or ignored by the salesperson). The mail-order ad explains the function of a formerly mystifying gadget, usually with a picture of the item actually operating in a domestic setting. A good catalog explains in great detail everything the customer would need or want to know about the item. A reader made aware of the item's appealing qualities may be tempted to send away for it.

Mail-order businesses have been founded by individuals for the marketing of items that they themselves have made. If you or perhaps a friend, has a special skill—in candlemaking, leathercraft, ceramics, or woodenware, for example—you might test your possible success with a tastefully produced magazine advertisement, a simple brochure, or a postcard. Rare or sometimes (by modern standards) eccentric acquisitions often attract readers' attention. For example, recent energy and fuel shortages and expenses have led to the marketing of a plethora of heating devices, from foot warmers to old-fashioned potbellied stoves, which have renewed appeal to the frugal homemaker. Often these items are not readily available in department stores or are not conspicuously displayed. Your advertisement can awaken the interest of a customer who had previously never given a single thought to the item you are advertising.

If you are looking for something out of the ordinary to sell by mail, look through foreign magazines for items sold abroad that have not yet reached this country or visit foreign trade shows. A similar technique is to read decades-old magazines, looking for items that could be coming into fashion once again or that might now be marketed on their quaint or chic appeal. When supply is a problem, you might be able to find a manufacturer who could develop your product.

In choosing a product, beware of advertisements that purport to offer you the secret of a successful mail-order venture. These promotions claim to provide you with a marketable mail-order product and advice as to how to sell it. They ask you to invest in certain business tools necessary to make, market, or mail the product. It is very unlikely that such an investment will lead to your enrichment. If the product were marketable, the company would be selling it directly instead of trying to sell it to you. Publications dealing with the mail-order industry will acquaint you with product selection strategies and techniques at a lower cost than you would pay for a "magic success formula."

If the item(s) you have selected prove successful, expect competition. Most mail-order businesses shift from product to product as the demand for an item tapers off. They milk the maximum from a product and then come up with a new one to sell. Businesses can stay with a single item only when they are fortunate enough to control the source. When you buy the item you sell from a manufacturer, you must accept the fact that you will probably be able to sell it profitably for only a short period of time before competition enters the market. Few manufacturers are in a position to give exclusive rights to the marketing of their products.

Mailing Your Letters and Products

The customer programs division of your post office can provide you with booklets of information about the postal rates, regulations, and requirements which might affect your mail-order business. If your local post office has no booklets, write to the Customer Programs Division, U.S. Postal Service, Washington, DC 20260. The amount of presorting you do to the mail (grouping it in bundles of similar zip codes) can lower your postage rates. Business-reply cards and envelopes must be approved by your postmaster. Permits for bulk rates (a fraction of the cost of first-class mail) must be applied for with the appropriate postal form and the payment of annual fees. Postage meters allow you to prepare mail in the office and earn you reduced rates because the post office can process the mail more quickly.

Postal rates are not cheap. Always compare the fees for parcel post and express mail with those charged by competing delivery firms, such as United Parcel Service. There is now keen competition between the U.S. Postal Service and private shipping and mail firms.

Your product must not be so bulky that it cannot be sold easily through the mail. Fragile products may encounter problems as well, and returned broken products decrease your profits. Good packers and shippers are worth their weight in gold. If you anticipate having problems with the mail, consult with your postal authorities and with competing shippers about packaging, parcel insurance, and other aspects of special handling.

In addition to postal problems, your product may be subject to other restrictions that reduce the effectiveness of a mail-order campaign. Foods may perish on shipment. Drugs may lose their potency between the time they are bottled and the time they are shipped, if they are stored for significant periods of time. Items such as toys that must be shipped disassembled might prove difficult for consumers to reassemble. Such problems can get your business in trouble with the Federal Trade Commission, the Food and Drug Administration, the Better Business Bureau, or postal authorities.

You can consult with a lawyer as to your responsibilities to the purchaser. If you also manufacture your product, you may want to investigate product liability insurance. There are also organizations that will, for a fee, aid mail-order businesses. For example, the Direct Marketing Association, Inc., (6 East 43d Street, New York, NY 10017 or 11 West 42d Street, New York, NY 10036-8096) will sell you a book summarizing current legal responsibilities.

Working with Your Suppliers

If you do not make your own mail-order product, then you must find a supplier who manufactures items which interest you. Many manufacturers are wholesalers and will not sell their products in small amounts, but many do—depending upon how much they want to be a part of your "wonderful" catalog. You may need to find an intermediary who will obtain the quantity you need. Or, more simply, you may be able to obtain the items you need by examining mail-order directories at a library. These will tell you where you can obtain a wide selection of suitable items.

For the best possible profit, purchase your goods from primary sources. Secondary sources will need to tack an extra margin onto the manufactured price in order to realize their profit. If you can buy direct, you can avoid paying that margin, but you can also complicate your life at the buying end. Reordering in a hurry can be a real hassle if the item takes off. Secondary sources usually can assure a manufacturer much more volume than can a single purchaser and, therefore, usually have a stronger call on the manufacturer's output.

You do not need to mail the product yourself. You can have the supplier drop-ship the product to your customer. This means that you accept the customer's order with payment and then send a payment to your supplier with a mailing label for the customer; the supplier then sends the product directly to the customer. This eliminates your need for storage quarters but puts you at the mercy of the drop-shipper's mailing practices and business ethics. It is a wise practice to obtain from your suppliers a written agreement that they will not copy your customers' names for their own future solicitation. Your customer list is one of your principal assets, particularly if it has been qualified over time.

Be certain the products you advertise fill all the claims you and their manufacturers make of them. You will be held legally responsible for any misleading or false information about the merchandise offered in your advertisements.

Selling Your Mail-Order Product

Daily newspapers often carry mail-order advertising, but their appeal is, in general, too broad to claim maximum customer attention. If newspapers do suit your product, the regularity with which you can present your advertisement may prove an advantage over monthly publication advertising. The Sunday magazine or classified section of a newspaper often provides an excellent opportunity for mail-order advertising. Customers interested in mail order have made it a practice to peruse these pages for new and interesting offerings.

Monthly, bimonthly, quarterly, and biannual publications still may be productive outlets for mail-order advertising. You can direct your appeal to a specific readership—homeowners, hobbyists, gardeners, car owners, etc. The readers of the publications you choose should be the logical customers for your merchandise. Do not necessarily be deterred by high advertising rates. The return per dollar on your advertisements determines their profitability.

Your advertisement may contain a complete description of the merchandise and include an order blank. The more information you offer at first, the better chance you have for the sale. But for high-priced items, it is customary to give a few particulars about the products and ask interested readers to send for complete details.

Schedule your advertising strategically. Nonseasonal items sell best from advertisements placed in magazine issues in fall, winter, and early spring. Items which may be purchased as Christmas gifts should usually be advertised no later than September (people tend to shop early). The length of time it takes to get results varies from one type of publication to another. From newspaper advertising, you will receive about 70 percent of your orders within a week. Items placed in the magazine section of newspapers usually pull about 40 percent in the first week. With monthly magazines you can expect to get only 10 percent of your orders in the week after the issue reaches the stands. During the following 2 to 6 months, you will get the full flow of orders.

Composing the Advertisement

Your advertisement should convey clearly all the pertinent information about your product: what it is, how it is constructed, what it does, and how it does it. What are its exclusive qualities and advantages over other makes of the same type of item? Where can the customer order it? You may get good results by offering your merchandise on installment terms, with a discount provided for all customers who make payment in full on receipt of the merchandise.

The actual design of the advertisement is usually left to advertising agencies and their commercial artists and typographers. Tests have shown that illustrated sales copy is read by more people and produces more orders or inquiries than purely verbal advertisements. A photograph of the product will prove more valuable than a drawing, since readers may question the accuracy of the drawing.

An aid to help the reader respond, such as a coupon, will increase the response to an advertisement. A direct mailer can increase responses by enclosing a business-reply card or envelope. A toll-free 800 phone number will also increase responses.

Direct-Mail Selling

Direct mail is selling your product through the mails by means of specifically addressed advertising. You work from mailing lists of likely customers for your product. If buyers have already responded to your advertising in publications, you have the names of these customers for a direct approach in selling new merchandise. You may wish to continue advertising in various publications at the same time you begin direct mail. The list of names you build up can profitably be rented or exchanged.

A typical mail-order package for your direct-mail list consists of a sales letter, a descriptive circular, an order form, and a business-reply envelope. Experienced firms have found that they will get 15 to 20 orders from each 1000 mailings. At times, second and third mailings will get additional results. Experimentation will show you the possible gains in repeated mailings.

Even if you get your customers from classified advertisements, you will want to prepare a direct-mail campaign to alert known buyers to your next offering. Repeat business opportunities cannot be ignored. The most valuable mailing list you will have is the carefully maintained list of your former customers.

Other Media

Your advertisement can be placed upon billboards, passenger buses, placemats, or in programs for cultural or sporting events. Matchbook advertising can be effective depending on how much you are willing to spend to reach a wide audience. (Consult the Atlas Match Corporation, 1801 South Airport Circle, Euless, TX 76040.) Television and radio are also effective forums for a mail-order campaign. While the TV viewer or radio listener may have difficulty writing down the particulars, the use of a toll-free 800-area-code phone number can overcome this hurdle. The potential customer, by noting one phone number, can get in touch with your sales personnel. The cost to you per hour of use varies depending upon the area being served. If your sales personnel talk to 20 customers an hour, 3 minutes for each, the cost per sale can be very low.

Some Marketing Hints

1. October is generally recognized as an excellent month for a mail-order advertisement, but holiday catalogs should go out at the end of August.

2. Some publications make editorial mentions of new products. Prepare a publicity release of an innovative product, and send it to a publication whose readership would be appreciative, 3 to 4 months in advance.

3. Direct-mail campaigns are better than classified advertisements when you want to shield your product from potential competitors.

4. The most important single word in your classified advertisement may be *guaranteed*.

5. Your initial classified advertisements should provide a relatively complete description of a product so that the consumer's lack of

information will not retard your sales. Once you have determined that the product can be marketed successfully by mail, you can modify your ads to target your audience more closely.

6. It is all right to experience a slight loss in entering the marketplace if the prospects look good for running a profit on the repeat business you generate. Everyone should expect to lose at the beginning.

7. If your product cannot be easily sold by mail, use classified advertising to establish contacts. Then have sales personnel visit the prospective customer to try and close the sale. The sales personnel can demonstrate the item being sold and deal with the customer's questions. The sales agents have a better chance of making a sale to the respondent of a classified advertisement than to a potential customer solicited out of the blue. This combination of mail order and sales agent is employed by many businesses, the sellers of vacuum cleaners, encyclopedias, and insurance policies, for example.

Obtaining Mailing Lists

Any published directory is an obvious source of lists of names. Some examples are city directories, telephone directories, voting and tax lists, and users-of-utilities lists. Another source is trade associations and societies.

Some firms, such as list brokers, specialize in the compiling of lists of names, which the mail-order company may purchase at a price per 1000 names. The price will vary upon the degree of selectivity needed. The Small Business Administration can provide you with a list of mailing list houses. The classified pages of the telephone directory may also be a valuable source of special-list names.

Usually a mail-order business rents a list of names through a broker on a one-time basis. Sometimes the firm which provides the lists will prepare the mailing and send the advertisements for you. Lists are usually sold by the thousands. Often a minimum of 5000 names is required if a one-time test sample advertisement is being mailed.

It is common for magazine publishers to rent out lists of their subscribers. The lists can be highly segmented depending on the nature of the publication. For example, they can point you toward a group of homemakers, world travelers, sports fans, theatergoers, hunters, or boat owners. But nothing beats a good customer mailing list of your own. A list of satisfied customers has far more potential for your business than rented lists, however selective they may be. It constitutes another asset, as well, because you are in a position to rent your list to other businesses or to a list broker. The broker's commission is 20 percent of the fee charged to renters of the list. Very often competitors will exchange mailing lists, saving the money they would have spent had they bought each other's lists through the services of the list broker.

Be sure the list of mail-order customers you receive is kept up to date. It has been estimated that 200 to 300 addresses in every 1000 mailings become inaccurate in a year's time. Mailing lists should be verified at least twice a year. One method of checking addresses is putting a "return requested" label on each envelope so that those that are undeliverable will be returned to you. When the postmaster returns a mailing piece to you, you can cross that particular address off your list.

The post office will correct a list of names, submitted on cards, at a charge of 25 cents per name. Each name and address must be presented on a separate card, about the size of a postcard. Carriers will verify names and addresses for you, though they cannot guarantee correct name spelling and titles. Such names imprinted by stencil can be sent third or fourth class depending on the weight, but handwritten or typed cards will require first-class postage. First-class mailings may be address-corrected by the post office at no charge.

Employing an Advertising Agency

Most mail-order houses work with advertising agencies which specialize in this type of business. Some agencies handle both mail order and direct mail; others handle one or the other. Watch the competition. Your chosen agency should not be handling another client whose product is similar to your own.

If you operate from a small town, you may have to find a mail-order advertising agency in a nearby city. While not so convenient as a local agency, a medium-sized-city agency can serve you very well through mail and telephone contact and an occasional conference. The volume of advertising would have to be considerable to make it worthwhile for the agency to work with you on a commission basis. A fee basis is more likely.

Printing Your Literature

In mail order, you will need various types of advertising circulars, catalogs, brochures, letters, and perhaps printed or copied instruction sheets for your customers. In direct mail, the need for attractive print-ed material is vital since it has to sell your goods.

Offset is generally cheaper than letterpress, but since you may need both types of work, you should seek a printer who can provide both. Your printer will supply the paper and advise you on the size and quality needed for the job. Select a firm with which you can work sat-isfactorily. You may require a company that can handle more than a print job. Addressing and mailing services are offered by some. If you launch your business on a small scale which does not include the use of an advertising agency, your printer may be able to help you in such matters as design.

You can give your printed sales letter a hand-typed quality through the use of a photographic reproduction procedure. In direct mail, addressing the reader as a member of an elite group may be an effec-tive approach—for example, "Dear Art Lover," or less elite, "Dear Car Owner." Concerns employing mail-order increasingly are using com-puterized mailing so that potential customers are addressed by their own names, e.g., "Dear Mr. Goldman."

The direct-mail business owner who has developed a worthwhile enterprise should check into the costs of installing a small photo-offset printing machine on the premises. With a camera, such as a platemak-er by Itek or 3M, plates can be produced at a reasonable cost for run-ning on offset machines.

Mail-Order Techniques

Usually, the printing of descriptive direct mail can be done more cheaply by hiring out the task to a professional printer. This is espe-cially preferable during the formative period of the mail-order endeav-or when failure would leave you with a large investment in printing and mailing machinery. Your company will have to become quite large to afford that investment.

The advantages of having printing machinery in your own shop are, of course, better quality control over the printed product and a greater ability to ensure that the material goes out on time. The larger the business gets, the more sense it makes to set up your own printing facilities. The overhead cost will become a relatively small part of the cost of the goods sold. Other machinery that will pay for itself once the business gets off the ground is electronic letter openers and automatic letter inserters.

Your responses to customers should also become "mechanical" through the use of form letters. Business-reply cards are a sort of form letter. Form letters used to respond to customers' complaints enable you to be consistent in both civility and legality.

Experimenting with Your Mailing Lists

To find your most profitable market, you might try sending out literature to names taken from three separate mailing lists. Mail to at least 1000 names from each list. Send all advertisements on the same day to allow for psychological differences that might result from day-of-the-week delivery. (Are customers more susceptible to sales pitches at the busy beginning of the week or at the end, when they anticipate a day or so of relaxation?)

The successful mail-order firm is constantly testing to ascertain its most favorable products, selling techniques, and locations. Should you decide to conduct such a test, allow only one variable per mailing. If you permit several variables, you will not be able to discern which was responsible for the difference in buying patterns.

Maintaining Good Customer Relations

Slow mail deliveries often impede the mail-order firm's early progress. If merchandise is late in arriving, many customers, fearing they have been duped, appeal to government agencies for restitution. Your best response is to quickly send another shipment to the same customer, requesting return of the original shipment when it arrives some time later. Notify the post office of the missing package. Thus, you will give satisfaction to your customer before your firm becomes the victim of unfair publicity.

Always replace damaged goods immediately after the package is returned, and never carry on a long-distance quarrel with a customer over a product which does not satisfy him or her. Make a refund as soon as a refused item comes back. The time you waste in justifying your product can be spent far more profitably seeking other sales. Reluctance to refund payment to dissatisfied customers can give your firm a bad name.

The Federal Trade Commission, a state attorney general's office, or city authorities may investigate a company which fails to fulfill orders and may put it out of business. The operation might have started as an honest enterprise, but demand may have outpaced staff and facilities, or suppliers may have failed to meet time schedules. For the reputation and stability of your company, see that orders are filled promptly. When a wait is necessary, notify the customer—and see that the order is kept under the close attention of your staff. The customer may demand a refund or substitution of other goods in cases of prolonged nondelivery of an order. Be aware that the Federal Trade Commission has ruled that a customer has the right to cancel any order not received through the mail within 30 days of order.

Misleading "free offers" and order forms, substitutions of shipments without customer authorization, and failure to offer refunds, as well as dubious collection practices, have been condemned by the Federal Trade Commission. The Federal Trade Commission is in a position to issue cease-and-desist orders against offending mail-order firms.

Some consideration should be given to the reception your merchandise will receive from the customer. It must meet the customer's expectations or you will be plagued with return problems. Even if your advertising is not meant to be misleading (such as selling children's toy kites under the name "Ben Franklin Electrical Unit"), the reader of the advertisement may indeed get the wrong impression. Dissatisfaction with the product or a poorly conducted return program can cause enough bad will to ruin your business reputation or simply destroy your profit margin by the extra postage and handling charges involved.

Know the effect your product will have on its users. Will cosmetics cause rashes on some customers? Can clothing be expected to fit? Will auto parts be effective when installed in any car? Will toys break almost immediately under the normal stress provided by a 5-year-old user? Questioning your own product and being guided by the answers can save you a lot of money in the mail-order business.

Combining Retail and Mail Order

Many retailers conduct mail-order campaigns to supplement store sales. One retailer recently found that his store operations returned 12 percent profit while his mail-order campaign yielded about 21 percent.

Mail-order customers have greater confidence in doing business with a firm that also maintains a retail outlet. Some of the eventual mail-order sales are generated by walk-in traffic. A customer sees an item in the store, perhaps even handles it or tries it on, and later makes the decision to purchase the item by mail. Mail-order customers also feel more secure when they know they can return an item in person.

The reputation of the retail outlet serves to attract mail-order business; well-known specialty shops routinely list the procedures for ordering by mail in their magazine and newspaper advertising. Many retailers find that computers ease the problems in adding a mail-order line. If the store uses a small computer to handle its regular inventory control, the computer can handle the mail-order inventory as well. The computer is also useful in updating mailing lists and processing orders.

A retail store must make a large investment to present its goods for sale. A mail-order business is the same, only the means of presentation are different. The store must have a building and a sales staff, while the mail-order firm must have appropriate printed materials and/or TV and radio time—both expensive. These are two different ways of selling, but the cost of getting the consumers to buy is similarly large for both.

13
How to Operate an Efficient Plant

Of itself, no book can give you competence in running a factory. That comes with experience. However, a book can be useful by pointing out the aspects of factory management which the inexperienced should pay particular attention to. Attention to the right things in the beginning leads more quickly to efficient and safe plant operations than comes from relying solely on learning from experience.

Rent, Buy, or Build

In acquiring space in which to conduct factory operations, you have several options. You can:

- Rent
- Buy
- Build

Each has its benefits, each its downside.

Renting, of course, has the virtue of obviating a large capital outlay. On the other hand, a rented property hardly ever conforms entirely to manufacturing requirements and usually has to be modified to do that. That in itself can be costly.

Buying a plant has the virtue of giving fast response to space requirements. In some parts of the country, buying may be cheaper than renting or building new space, depending on locale, interest rates, and construction costs. Buying has the potential disadvantage of locking you into high occupancy costs which can hurt during economic slumps.

Building has the advantage of giving you the space and arrangements which meet your needs, providing you know specifically and objectively what the needs are. The obvious disadvantages are the delay in occupancy while land acquisition, design work, and building are going on, and the cost of overruns and mistakes caused by forecasting errors and planning oversights. Construction and leaseback is currently a good way of obtaining space built to your specifications without the need for a large outlay of capital. The drawback, however, is that you most likely will be locked into a long-term lease. For a growing company this is not likely to hurt much in boom times, but it will in a recession.

Designing the Layout of Your Plant

However you acquire the space you will occupy, you should detail your space requirements carefully and be guided by them when selecting facilities. A schematic depicting the entire material flow for the plant from the unloading of supplies to the shipping of the finished product will help accomplish that.

Keep the plan as clear-cut and uncluttered as possible. Ideally, the plan will show the raw materials entering your plant at one end and the finished product emerging at the other. The flow need not be a straight line. Parallel flows, U-shaped patterns, or even a zig-zag that ends up with the finished product back at the shipping and receiving bays can be functional. However, backtracking is to be avoided in whatever pattern is chosen. When parts and materials move against or across the overall flow, personnel and paperwork become confused, parts become lost, and the attainment of coordination becomes complicated.

Investigate using conveyor belts, cranes, hoists, and industrial trucks to keep materials moving. It can be less costly to have materials moved by machine than to lose time by having employees do it (the opposite may also be true). If you decide in favor of such equipment, make sure that your building plan allows sufficient aisle space or ceiling height to accommodate the means of conveyance. It is not uncommon to lose the benefits of mechanization because of space limitations.

One objective of a processing plan is to reduce the need for machinery by improving handling or coordination. Having employees perform related tasks near each other minimizes the distances materials have to be moved.

All traffic lanes should have wide aisles. Their width should match the size of the biggest of the equipment that will travel them, the size of the loads, and the frequency of trips. Take care to provide aisle room for machine replacement and maintenance. Room is needed when dismantling machines and equipment. The aisles should be wide enough not to impede the removal of shafts, headstocks, etc., and to allow equipment needed to lift heavy pieces such as machine pedestals to be brought in.

If your factory will need a shop for maintenance and repair activities, put it where it will interfere as little as possible with manufacturing. Keep in mind that maintenance and repair work is an "out of sight, out of mind" activity. Because it is visible only when it is needed, it is seldom adequately provided for in terms of equipment, facilities, or management, despite its importance in many manufacturing operations.

After construction is complete and machinery and equipment is in place, identify the danger points along the aisles. Shafts, housings, pillars, braces, and other dangerous projections which extend into the aisle space should be painted in attention-compelling colors. Yellow and black bands painted on them will help prevent collisions. Use yellow striping to mark the edges of openings in the floor, such as pits and elevator wells. Reduce the possibilities of accidents by placing potentially dangerous structures and machinery away from the flow of employee or visitor traffic.

Be generous in allocating space for receiving and shipping. While space does tend to fill itself up, receiving and shipping rarely get enough space for the work to be done effectively. Entrances should be adequately sized. In many cases it pays to have bays with entrances large enough to allow the largest trucks used by your suppliers to be driven inside for unloading. Loading ramps and platforms attached to the outside of the building can ease the handling of materials. Try to minimize the hand labor required to unload heavy machinery or materials by having overhead or wheeled lifting equipment appropriate to the facilities and the tasks at hand. For security, economic, and convenience reasons, have a small door separate from the delivery door by which people can enter and leave the area.

Inside the building, storage facilities should take advantage of all the vertical space available. On the higher shelves place items that are used infrequently (and are light enough), such as parts needed to keep your machinery going. Skids and pallets can be used to increase storage space. When laying out your storage area, compile a parts list. The list will help you know what storage to provide for. Keep the list up to date thereafter; it will help locate the items when needed. Incidentally, while making up the list, you should also note the sources, costs, and specifications of each item on the list. The notes will be invaluable on certain occasions, as when an item out of stock must be obtained quickly from a supplier in order to keep the plant going.

Next, take a look at your need for inspection space. Almost any production item requires some sort of inspection before it is ready for customers. If you cannot perform the inspection as part of the manufacturing process—and every effort should be expended to do so—give careful consideration to where it should be performed. Inspection can be virtually eliminated by use of statistical process control. Better outgoing quality can be achieved at less cost by "doing it right the first time" and making operators responsible for their own quality output. Prevention is more effective than correction (100 percent inspection is only about 80 percent effective anyway) and less costly. But, if inspection cannot be avoided, you must set aside space for the workers and equipment needed. If sensitive equipment is involved, you may need to perform your inspection in a clean, vibrationless room.

The same is true of research and testing operations. If a laboratory is needed for such purposes, isolate it from the heavy work load area.

Another room that may have to be isolated from work areas is the lobby for your building. It is commonplace these days to provide a place for customers, salespeople, and others to wait. But if you are going to go to the expense of providing a waiting room, make sure it is useful to your business. Make the room comfortable and the correct size for the maximum number of people you expect at any time, and decorate the room to create an informative and selling environment.

A lounge for employees is a good idea especially if the building is away from stores and fast-food shops and the operations area is noisy or cold. But do not put it close to the reception area. As a security issue, employees should not mix with customers, and they will if the two are close. On the other hand, lounges should be furnished for the use of both salaried and hourly employees. This can foster information exchanges useful to both parties and, therefore, promote teamwork.

The days when employees were separated by class have passed. Open parking, open dining, open offices, etc., break down barriers and create an atmosphere of equality in which everyone is more productive. Therefore, you should take this goal into account while laying out your building.

The building should be laid out so as to keep traffic and the need to communicate to the minimum. For example, your purchasing and sales offices should be located near the reception room since the majority of visitors are vendor salespeople and purchasing needs close contact with sales and vice versa. Accounting and bookkeeping offices should be situated near the executive offices so that original records are easily available. With the advent of computerization and terminals, it is no longer necessary to have accounting and bookkeeping close to sales offices for general-information availability.

If production control and timekeeping are important to your operation, locate these offices close to the production area so that production personnel will not have to travel through other offices to do their work. A window opening between the production and control areas will also serve as a step saver and, if your product creates dust or grime, will help keep offices cleaner.

Even the location of lavatories should be carefully planned. One manufacturer thought to save money by designing one large lavatory to be used by the entire work force. Later the manufacturer realized that the extra expense of building two small lavatories instead would have paid for itself in short order by reducing the extra time involved for travel to one main lavatory.

Space for and the location of the computer installation—when there is one, or when one is expected—must also be planned, especially if the computer will be used for process and inventory control. Too often the provision for computer equipment and personnel are improvised, resulting in poor security, protection, and usage. On the other hand, don't go overboard on the facilities. Computers are rapidly down-scaling in size and cost, and very few installations these days last more than 5 years before they are replaced. You'll want to locate your computers in a clean, cool environment.

In planning your building, don't overlook your possible needs for space in the future. If growth is indicated, leave some room for expansion either inside the existing plant or through a feasible addition to the existing structure.

Lighting the Plant

Light and productivity are two variables inextricably wound together. Poor lighting can mean low output, while good lighting can help increase output. Try to produce as much lighting as you can!

Start with natural light. In your initial planning, do not stint on sources of natural lighting. As artificial lighting became more efficient and cheaper, plants increasingly were designed to rely upon artificial sources of light. Today, because of rising energy costs, windows are once more recognized as being important in an industrial structure. To provide sufficient daylight, your windows and skylight areas must take up at least the equivalent of 30 percent of the floor area. Be sure that windows are located handily for cleaning. Windows become less-efficient light sources as grime accumulates.

When all the plant equipment is installed, you will be able to see what the effects of natural lighting are. You and your lighting specialist (or the local power company) can then plan the supplemental lighting that will be necessary during the daytime and at night. A badly lighted workplace may save on utility bills, but production will suffer for it. However, you can see to it that no more lighting is used than necessary by gradually turning on more lights as conditions grow darker. The adjustments can be made automatically by using a sensor to detect the natural light available at any given moment.

By choosing the right combination of lighting—mercury, vapor, or fluorescent—you should be able to avoid glare and provide for optimal working conditions. Recent research has shown that the closer artificial light approximates actual sunlight, the healthier and more efficient workers are. On that score, sodium-vapor lighting rates high and costs about 50 percent less to operate.

Paint—its color and cleanliness—is an important lighting factor. A light-colored paint on ceilings and upper walls helps to reflect the light to working spaces in addition to making the entire shop look more efficient and well-planned. Contrasting colors on machinery facilitate perception and the correct placement and movement of parts and material being worked on in addition to making the work safer.

Heating and Ventilation

After you've engineered the plant's lighting and painting, you should formalize the plant's heating and cooling. The lighting and colors used in a plant have some bearing upon its temperature and humidity control needs. Consider the following in deciding how to heat and ventilate your plant:

- Temperatures for efficient working conditions are approximately as follows: machine shop 60°F (16°C); welding shop 50 to 60°F (10 to 16°C); and office 65°F (18°C).

- Circulation of air is needed both in summer and winter. Ventilation cannot safely be left to chance, especially where noxious fumes are produced.

- In places where combustion takes place, such as engine and boiler rooms, the air has to be changed every few minutes. In the average shop, about 1200 cubic feet of air per person per hour is needed to provide proper air sanitation.

- Installation of a hood and blower to eliminate dust and fumes at their source may provide sufficient air turnover for the whole shop.

- Humidity is best maintained at 50 percent, but can range safely from 35 to 80 percent in ordinary shops.

- All heating and cooling equipment should be thoroughly inspected and cleaned at the end of the season of use and needed repairs made before the next season. Keep dampers closed in the off-season.

If you content yourself with poor ventilation in order to "save money," you lose the price of good ventilation many times over in lessened output by your employees and increased amounts of spoiled work and scrap. Natural ventilation through doors, windows, and skylights is usually not dependable. In the absence of a full-fledged airconditioning system, ventilation should be enhanced by the addition of exhaust fans and, if necessary, of ducts which reach the bad spots.

There are many moves you can take at low cost to maintain good working temperatures. For example, spraying water on the factory roof after exposure to a hot sun often gives considerable relief. Air conditioning can often be attained simply through the use of exhaust fans to remove bad air and intake fans to draw in fresh air. In some situations, normal air currents, aided by windows, louvers, and ducts, will suffice. If your process requires controlled air conditions, study the problem with the manufacturers of the equipment needed. They can supply full information about the temperature-control systems available.

In finding the cheapest methods of heating, start with exploring ways to reduce the need for heating. The following is a sample of the ideas you can look into:

- If different departments have their own storage facilities, see if you can combine them into one storage area that need not be heated.

- The use of skylights, windows, and southern exposures to make maximum use of natural heat.

- Using the ventilation system to move air made overly warm by machinery to heat other parts of the plant.

Consider passive-solar construction when designing the facility. It will save a lot on heating and cooling. It will make a difference in the construction, insulation, and design of heating and air-conditioning systems whether the plant is in the north latitudes or in the Sun-belt. Also, depending on the product that is to be produced, Occupational Safety and Health Administration (OSHA) requirements may be a consideration.

Organizational Efficiency

Personnel, machines, supplies, work in progress, finished products, and deliveries must all be coordinated if your plant is to be successful. Production effects must be judged by time, cost, quantity, and quality.

An efficiently run plant will keep employees and machines constantly busy, and busy doing the right things. There will be a steady flow of materials between and good coordination among departments. Provisions will have been made to accommodate rush orders. Inspection ratios will be examined daily for any serious and costly discrepancies.

Regardless of your plant's capacity, you should be guided by customer orders. Production schedules should be geared to sales forecasts and actual sales. When the two begin to be exceeded by production, it is time to scale back. Continuous production is no advantage if it means you will have to store large amounts of merchandise. To cover periods of low production, have a plan which identifies other tasks to which the labor force can apply themselves. Layoffs are extremely costly to the firm that has to hire workers back when production picks up. They should be avoided whenever possible. To avoid them successfully takes planning, and planning takes organization. Your organization itself should be as carefully planned as any other aspect of your business—finance, plant layout, production.

The starting point is establishing an organization chart with the fewest number of levels possible which shows the relationships of positions (by title) and functions: management, sales, purchasing, manufacturing, and shipping. Keep the size of your departments balanced; otherwise, you will have excess costs when one department may be very busy while another is idle. Prepare job descriptions which define each function thoroughly, and which minimize the overlap of duties and authority.

Watch the span of control. Too narrow a span leads to waste of effort, underdevelopment of employees, poor morale, and the loss of the best employees; too wide a span leads to poor work quality, excessive communicating, and lower productivity. Generally, a single supervisor should not have to oversee more than 6 positions, if those positions require a lot of supervision and support. As many as 30 easily learned jobs, requiring little support and control, can be overseen by the same supervisor.

As to the need for a different supervisor for each function, that will depend on the size and character of your operation. In a small plant where precision is not a concern, a manager will have to wear more than one hat, serving, for example, as supervisor, receiving agent, and maintenance engineer. But in a larger plant or in one where specifications are abnormally tight, these responsibilities will have to be managed by different people.

While writing the job description—which need not be elaborate, by the way—give a lot of thought to the responsibilities that you delegate. On the one hand, don't be afraid to delegate authority; quite the opposite, fear not giving enough authority. Withhold the power to make decisions, to initiate action, to reverse decisions, to create, and you'll end up with stunted employees (those who stay with you) and, possibly, a heart attack. The best managers demand a lot of their people, and a prime tool for getting it is delegation! It is also the key to making business a lot of fun. On the other hand, it could be fatal to give authority liberally without the controls needed to enable the firm to recover from misuse of the authority.

Other Helpful Charts

Sketching organization charts is a favorite pastime of many managers. Doing so can help you feel creative and masterful. But drawing them as singular charting exercises is delusory. They should be drawn *after* other charts, such as flowcharts of operations, have been sketched out.

An operations flowchart will depict all the steps in any process and will clearly point out the logistics involved, the time lags, and the conditions of the products it delivers. A Gantt chart, named after one of the pioneer industrial engineers in America's industrial revolution, breaks down each step in an assembly operation to give the time required to perform it. That helps in scheduling employees and supplies. Machines and activities can be microscheduled by seconds, and minutes, and macroscheduled by hours, days, and weeks. Each machine can be graphed separately, and the need for parts and materials planned before the work is performed. A project evaluation and review technique (PERT) chart can plot a series of interconnected production activities which mesh to complete a common goal. Efficiency, productivity, and quality control are stated as probabilities, giving the plant manager a realistic appraisal for determining output and production time. Some indicators of customer satisfaction and competitive assessment will keep the employees informed of what it takes to stay in business and be competitive and thus further their job security.

Industrial Research and Quality Control

To keep their products competitive, small plants must make some provision for research and quality control. Larger concerns experiment constantly to find more economical ways to create their products and to make them better. Owners of smaller firms cannot do that, and when they address research and quality control, they usually have to get outside help. They often go to university research bureaus or hire private research firms. Your trade association may have a research program that will aid you. You may also hire a member of a university faculty as a consultant.

Though you are small, do not ignore the need for quality-control investigations. If you want to stay in business for long, your product must stand tests to prove that raw materials, intermediate items, or finished products are up to specifications. Very often, this testing can be handled adequately when done honestly by your production manager. It usually doesn't take much time. Quality-control investigations may involve something as simple as a sifting apparatus to sort out units which are undersized or oversized. On the other hand, it may require very specialized viewing equipment and a qualified technician to observe units under specific temperature and stress conditions. Unless you can keep such equipment and the technician fully occupied, you probably should engage the services of an outside laboratory.

Using Automation

Automation, the replacement of human effort by machine, is today a competitive element. Handwork has its value, but only where individuality has value. That value is almost entirely limited to the world of art or wherever taste is the prime discriminating agent. Even so, many different appearances cover products with a high automation content (who wants a unique watch that doesn't keep time?).

Automation is a flexible tool; it can be designed into a plant from the beginning or brought into a plant after design and gradually integrated. Progressive automation may include feeding mechanisms, such as rotating hoppers and vibration bowls that sort and feed small parts into a process, or loader and unloader conveyors that transport components from one workbench to another. The former are not very costly; the latter can be.

A pick-and-place robot, controlled electronically, ranges in price from $5000 to $30,000. Robots can be designed for specific assembly jobs. They can be computerized to have artificial sensing abilities. They have been developed to the point where they can be programmed to memorize almost any sequence of movements.

Before you invest in automation, however, do careful financial analysis of any investment in it. Look at the leasibility of automation equipment on a payback basis. Be sure to include in your calculations the costs of training workers and running two work systems in parallel until the equipment is in full operation. After decades of the automation revolution, we have learned the high cost of irrevocable commitment to sophisticated equipment. The backup for automation should be manual except where a manual operation cannot do the job, is too costly, or manually impossible, such as in nuclear fission.

Having backup systems available and ready to go into action quickly is also essential if you are to keep production going when automated equipment breaks down. Also, repairs on automated equipment are almost always expensive and time-consuming. Therefore, before you purchase the equipment have your lawyer check to see if the contract clearly stipulates the vendor's responsibilities for repairs. You might also look into business interruption insurance so that your business is not hurt by production delays. But the insurance can be very expensive, depending on the nature of your business.

Using the Right Materials

Glass in industrial and business buildings is a hazard, and more glass than is economically justified leads to more accidents. Be sure that only safety glass is used in areas of danger where glass is necessary. And be liberal in defining what an "area of danger" is.

For floors, concrete is satisfactory in most industrial structures. Wooden floors, whether of planks or blocks, are not as strong, durable, stable, or level. Although wood is softer and less tiring to the feet, it is likely to become oil-soaked and flammable. Nevertheless, wooden floors still have a place where economic factors (as in second floors) are operative and safety is not an issue.

If you are buying a building, check the thickness of the concrete floor. You can drill a hole if it can't be measured in any other manner. Check for patches which may be different in composition or thickness from the original floor. Do not trust loads on the floor which exceed its margin of strength.

There are alternatives to concrete floors today, but the product and the process carried out in the plant should dictate the material. Assembly operations use concrete because it is easy to keep clean. Foundry or forge operations find concrete hazardous; dropping and turning heavy dies on concrete is not good for the floor or the dies. Consult with a construction engineer to find the ratio of thickness to weight needed for a given load. Choose a ground-floor location if possible. It gives better foundation for machinery and is more accessible for shipping purposes. Level, nonsagging floors, rarely found in upper stories except in steel or concrete buildings, are needed for maintenance of close tolerances for welding heavy assemblies.

If the ceiling has exposed steel beams, you may find them useful for mounting a chain block or hoist. A hoist can facilitate the unloading of equipment. It should hang from a beam strong enough to carry safely any load it will be called upon to support.

Buying Your Materials and Supplies

Your relationship with suppliers can be a decisive factor in your business. Small firms are frequently at a disadvantage in dealing with their suppliers. In periods of shortages manufacturers are apt to favor larger customers who can, with one order, buy out an entire stock. Thus, the small firm must exert special efforts to maintain its relationship with suppliers.

If you can achieve a cooperative relationship with your suppliers, you will find them a valuable source of information and advice. Suppliers may be able to provide repair services on their product, expand credit terms, and apprise you quickly of discount offers. However, if you do not make the effort to get close to your suppliers, they may not think of you when they have deals to offer. Replace suppliers you cannot get close to with those you can.

Also make use of salespeople who call upon you. Usually you will find that they make calls at fairly regular and predictable intervals. Establishing cooperation with them will work to mutual advantage. They can often advise you on the status of competition, trends in product quality and pricing, and developments in the industry. They can also be very useful in expediting delivery from their employer or the firms.

Suppliers and salespersons can also help you achieve a rapid turnover of stock. Slow-moving material may rob your business of the capital needed to acquire the fast-moving items which support your shop. If space is limited, it sometimes pays to patronize a firm which makes frequent deliveries and has fairly complete stock even if its prices are not the lowest. But, do not forget customer service in pursuit of high turnover. Customers hate surprises, and if you are going to specialize in high turnover goods, you'd better let them know that!

Should you rely on one supplier or divide your purchases among many? A dealer may try to convince you that he or she is able to fill all your needs, but dependence on a single supplier can be hazardous—as when a supplier is shut down by a strike or a materials shortage. In addition, it prevents the shopping around which helps you find bargains. Ordering materials from many suppliers, however, will prevent you from winning the allegiance of any of them. Your goal is to decrease costs; a supplier's is to increase sales. Cementing a mutual relationship can benefit both of you by earning you volume discounts made possible by the increased business given to the supplier. The supplier furnishing you the greatest share of your requirements will understand your business situation better and may well extend you privileges such as payment extensions. However, if you are starting a new firm, you may be able to get more credit at first by spreading your purchases.

Be certain that the materials delivered by your suppliers are up to the standard of quality your product requires. Prompt inspection should uncover any flaws or shortages. Check on newly delivered parts by observing their use in production. If you have a complaint, make it promptly, giving supporting evidence.

To earn the respect and cooperation of suppliers use the words *rush* and *emergency* sparingly. Mark orders *rush* only when the need is critical. If you use emergency terminology constantly, your orders will only get routine treatment, however pressing the need may be.

Buying for the Small Plant

How do you locate sources of essential raw materials and components? Obtain all available handbooks or data books issued by business papers and selling companies which contain information on stocks carried by industrial supply houses, wholesale houses, manufacturers who sell direct, and retail stores. You may also advertise for bids.

Industrial-supply houses cater to factories and carry a complete line of materials. Since they sell in large volume, they buy stock at the most favorable prices and terms and can sell to factories at or near ordinary wholesale prices. The types of stock carried by industrial-supply houses are determined to a great extent by the principal class of customer served and so may differ from city to city or even within a single large industrial district. Conversations with the salespeople who call on you will soon inform you which of these houses can be of most service.

Many *wholesale houses* give discounts to factory accounts. In certain areas, the wholesale hardware house and the industrial-supply house compete with each other. Where they do, a buyer can sometimes get discounts for which the shop would not otherwise qualify.

In some instances, the neighborhood retail store can provide some of the supplies required by small plants and a lot quicker than a supply house or wholesaler can. If the plant provides the dealer sufficient business, the dealer may allow credit while supply houses demand cash.

Direct purchasing from manufacturers will give you the lowest costs, but it may require you to place larger orders than you may be accustomed to. Smaller orders will incur heavy express charges. However, it generally does not pay to pad an order beyond probable needs merely to take advantage of a lower price or to avoid high freight rates.

To circumvent the entire range of problems created by supplier dependency, you may decide to make your own components. There are instances when a company must produce its own parts to fit specifications which cannot be duplicated at acceptable costs by another manufacturer. In that case, you will have to purchase the parts and assemble them or make the entire item from raw materials. This means a substantial outlay for machinery and equipment which might more profitably be used in expanding your product lines. The beginning factory usually fares best with purchased parts, if they are available.

Inventory Control

Inventory bears heavily on the cost picture of most plants. The plant layout should be designed to accommodate a minimum of inventory, including raw materials and in-process and finished products, since whatever space is provided is just about certain to be filled up. Kanban, the "just-in-time delivery of materials and/or parts to the production line" system, should be considered for inclusion in the layout to create a "pull" system of production as opposed to the old "push" system. Election of the Kanban system will have profound effects upon the layout of the truck docks, receiving and shipping areas, "materials delivery to the point of use" system, the aisle sizes, and the extent of storage facilities in the plant.

As for repair parts and nonproduct inventory, there are profitable ways of letting someone else keep the inventory and still cover your needs. An example of this is the bearing business; no one keeps an inventory of bearings in their plant anymore. Contracts for a 1- to 2-hour response to a phone request are not uncommon. The costs are higher, but so is your overall profitability.

It is best not to rely on annual or semiannual inventory-taking for control—particularly where the inventory is made up of many items, many of which are small, and some of which have general uses. Consider employing regular random samplings instead. Once a week select 10 items from a table of random numbers, take physical count of the items, and match the count against the record. Few inventories are so large that items worth keeping track of can't be counted at least twice a year (an ideal average).

Your perpetual inventory card should contain a description of material that will be entered on an order blank. Include data on the length of time it takes a shipment to arrive. Show the actual balance on hand, recording each receipt or withdrawal of material. When material has been allocated to a job scheduled for the near future, note the reserve on the card so the reorder point can be stepped up, if necessary, to avoid stockouts.

Keep supplies of small items in stock even though they are obtainable quickly. Metal screws, wood screws, studs, bolts, and nuts, will not tie up much money in stock and having them on hand saves a good deal of running around and loss of time. An occasional glance at the floor sweepings will show whether they are being used carefully.

Bar Coding

The familiar bar codes used at merchandise checkout counters at supermarkets are finding increasing use in manufacturing operations. Wand devices hooked up to computers can speedily and accurately "read" a set of printed bars. They replace time cards as a way of keeping track of workers' performance on specific assignments, maintaining inventory records, and keeping track of material moving through a plant.

Bar coding eliminates writing, loose slips of paper, and reading errors. The wand "reads" the bars, transmits the information to the computer, and the computer locks the information in place. No more "lost" merchandise, no more errors in picking items from inventory, no more production of the wrong items or the wrong quantities. The devices will check what is picked and let the picker know when an error is being made. And the computer will know where the error was made.

By establishing "gates" or steps in the production of your products, your PC will know what is being manufactured within one "gate" and alert the "wand" at the next gate to what is expected and when. When the product passes through the gate, the PC will know it; when the product does not pass through, it immediately creates an exception display or report, informing the supervisor that things are not occurring as planned.

Your PC can print bar codes on any paper: work orders, purchase orders, picking tickets, self-adhesive labels. Self-sticking labels have many uses. For example, you could send the labels to your vendor to stick on items being sent to you. When the material arrives at the dock, the receiving wand reads the bar codes on the purchase order and the items, and the computer will know what has arrived, in what quantity, and against which purchase order.

The possibilities for instant knowledge, control, and cost savings are tremendous. You must seriously consider using bar codes, or sooner or later be at a competitive disadvantage.

Reducing Employee Accidents

The cost of accidents in any plant is high enough to demand programs for their reduction. But they can be the ruination of a small company. Big companies have safety departments that do such work routinely. But in small companies it is up to their managers to see that unsafe and hazardous situations are identified and protected against. Furthermore, the Occupational Safety and Health Administration (OSHA) of the U.S. Department of Labor requires that you maintain safe facilities and operational practices; otherwise, you will be subject to penalties.

Many managers believe that insurance alone will cover the total cost of accidents. However, as a rule, there will be about 4 additional dollars of indirect costs for each dollar of compensation paid by your insurance policy. An accident will lead to lost time by injured employees, lost time of fellow workers who halt operations to help them, and lost time of supervisors and managers who must select and train new employees while the injured workers are recuperating. Damage to machines is a frequent by-product of accidents, leading to lost production, destruction of materials, and other general lapses in output.

In recent years, many small plants, with the assistance of safety organizations, have developed successful safety programs without undue expense or additional personnel. Each of the programs calls for the application of the following basic principles:

- Learn how to recognize hazards of all kinds, especially those that are not self-evident, and learn how to remove them or safeguard employees against them. The following are some factors to consider:

  Plant construction, layout, and arrangement

  Machine safeguards

  Unsafe practices of employees, including those involved in housekeeping of plant and machines, maintenance, use of hand tools, lifting, carrying, and working on scaffolds, ladders, or other elevated places

  Possibility of fire, explosion, or electrical shocks

  Special occupational hazards

- Acquaint yourself thoroughly with the process and equipment you employ so that you can pinpoint the most vulnerable areas in the plant and the machines and tools that might become involved in accidents.

- Ask for assistance from the nearest office of your state department of labor, insurance company, or trade association. They can help you analyze your accident problem and assist you in planning a safety program that will reduce unnecessary risks, generally without charge. They can provide information and guidance on employee instruction, keeping accident records, methods of safety inspection, developing a safety committee, and controlling mechanical hazards.

Sell the idea of safety to all employees. This is the most important and the most difficult phase of accident prevention. It cannot be done overnight. Encourage, demonstrate, and insist upon safety every day until each person has formed safe working habits. The following are some of the ways of selling safety to employees:

- Recognize that, since safety is a management responsibility, it should be planned as a part of plant operation.

- Organize, guide, and encourage safety committees, and delegate responsibility through them and through supervisors.

- Have the committees investigate each accident and publicize the results.

- Publicize the problem, the program, and its results through group meetings, talks, posters, and bulletin boards.

- Supply safety information and knowledge through committees, meetings, talks, posters, written instructions, sound-and-slide presentations, and movies.

New employees, inadequately trained or not yet comfortable with their machines, are safety hazards in themselves. On-the-job instruction can reduce this danger. But try not to assign a new employee to a job that tests his or her capabilities, when doing the job may lead to an accident. Supervise new workers until they are completely familiar with the operation.

Keep records of accidents. The records will serve a number of purposes, such as the following:

- Providing information for studies of the causes and frequencies of accidents.

- Estimating the total cost of accidents and determining their impact on profits.

- Identifying workers who are accident prone.

- Indicating the success of the safety program.

One of the best ways in which to gain workers' interest in safety is by eliminating those hazards over which you have control. The realization that you are doing your part in providing safe working conditions will make employees more receptive to a safety program, thus providing a basis for employee cooperation. They will be more willing to do their part in maintaining safe working conditions and to support the entire safety program. Commence work in the following areas.

Inspection

Accompanied by some key workers, make an *initial safety inspection* of the plant. Even though you may not have had safety training, you can recognize many situations as being dangerous if you study them closely.

Some hazards that may not be found by such inspections may be discovered by *safety engineers* or *inspectors* who can be brought in from state labor departments or insurance companies. They often are asked by safety-minded managers to analyze safety conditions in the plant, make detailed safety inspections, and recommend corrective action.

Once hazards are recognized, *corrective action* may be taken to eliminate them. It is sound business practice to do so since safety and efficiency always go together.

This process of inspection and elimination of hazards is a continuous one, since new hazards may be created by a change in operation or old hazards may reappear.

Plan

Next, plan or replan your layout and arrangement. Proper planning of the original plant layout and adequate control of operations theoretically would eliminate all accidents. Many firms have come very close to that goal. At the time the plant is built, safe working conditions can be provided without additional difficulties or expense, since the most efficient operations are usually the safest.

Changes in layout or operations of existing plants are indicated for reasons of safety and efficiency when materials pile up at certain points, when the paths of materials in process cross each other, when employees do not have adequate working space, or when similar conditions become apparent. These changes, particularly if they are major rearrangements in plant layout or operations, cost so much that another change is not practical for some time. This emphasizes the importance of planning all changes carefully so that other dangerous conditions are not created by the change.

Poor lighting of buildings, rooms, and passageways is responsible, directly or indirectly, for many accidents. Where conditions do not permit constructive improvements, liberal use of white paint or frequent application of whitewash will be of much value. Light-reflecting wall surfaces help the diffusion of available light, whether natural or artificial.

Plant housekeeping—cleanliness and orderliness—is fundamental to good management. It removes many causes of accidents. In a well-kept plant, there are no loose objects on stairs, floors, and platforms, no articles that can fall from overhead, no wet or greasy floors, no projecting objects in aisles, and no projecting nails or sharp pieces of metal to tear the workers' hands.

In plants with good accident records, managers have paid attention to maintenance of plant, equipment, and machinery in the following ways:

- Floors are kept in good condition, without holes or splinters that might cause slipping, tripping, falling, or handling injuries.

- All portable equipment on which workers stand, such as ladders, steps, horses, or scaffold planks, are maintained in proper condition.

- Chisels, portable grinders, and drills are kept free of defects or are replaced. Machine guards are properly made, installed, and maintained, and workers are instructed in their proper use.

- Machines themselves, as well as pressure vessels, electric wiring, and other equipment, are kept in proper condition for both production and safety.

- Operations and methods are planned to eliminate hazardous situations and ensure adequate control at all times.

- Mechanical handling is substituted for manual handling; often it is cheaper and faster as well as safer.

- Workers are carefully trained and adequately supervised to see that all supplies, products, and other materials are moved, carried, and stored in a safe manner as well as in an efficient one.

- Workers are protected from electrical hazards.

- Protective clothing and equipment, such as safety shoes, goggles, and gloves, are worn by workers on jobs where needed; management usually supplies these items and insists on their use.

- All electric circuits and lines are installed and maintained in conformance with safety standards.

Whether a worker wears suitable or unsuitable clothing is a matter largely within the control of the employer. Keep watch on this matter. A ragged sleeve, a flowing necktie, or a loose coat or jumper jacket can do incalculable harm if caught in a moving machine. Workers should be required to confine their hair or wear adequate head protection when engaged in machine operations. For certain jobs special clothing (hand and arm protectors, shoulder capes, hats, caps, welders' aprons, coats, overalls, leggings, shoes, etc.) is necessary for all operators. In the selection of such special clothing, four essentials should be considered:

- The garment should be reasonably comfortable when worn under the conditions for which it was designed.

- It should fit snugly and not interfere unduly with the movements of the wearer.

- It should offer adequate protection against the hazard for which it was designed.

- It should be durable under the conditions for which it is used.

Safeguarding of mechanical apparatus is of prime importance. You must convince workers that guards should be installed on machines and used at all times. Those who have become accustomed to working on machines without guards often resent their installation and will remove them whenever possible. They must be convinced that the guards are necessary for their protection.

Workers who have been trained on guarded machines prefer them. It has been proved that the correct kind of guards invariably increases production through enabling machines to be operated more steadily, or faster, or both.

You should emphatically maintain discipline in the interest of safety—particularly with workers who smoke when smoking is properly prohibited, who drink liquor at any time on company premises or report for work under the influence of liquor, or who tamper with safety protective devices. You need to be tough with those who disregard safety rules—particularly those operating without full use of safety equipment or without authority. Post notices conspicuously, describing the following:

- How to start, operate, and stop equipment.
- What switches and controls must never be touched.
- Where fire-fighting apparatus is accessible and how to use it.
- How aisles are to be kept free for use in case of fire.
- How waste is to be kept out of corners to avoid fire.

Every shop should have a system for furnishing first aid to the injured. The effects of an accident may be intensified by lack of immediate and proper care of the injury; unskilled handling may do further harm, in addition to causing unnecessary pain. Where it is not possible to have a thoroughly equipped emergency room, there should be first-aid supplies available all over the plant. See that locations are known to all and that personnel are trained to render first aid, including CPR (cardiopulmonary resuscitation). Names, addresses, and telephone numbers of physicians and local hospitals should be conspicuously posted.

While managing the costs of safety and accidents is a corporate responsibility, employees will never be safe until they take a personal interest in keeping themselves from getting hurt. They must keep track of what is happening around them and not put themselves in dangerous situations. The only good safety processes are those which stress personal responsibility for safety and train workers accordingly. Most accidents do not happen to young, inexperienced operators. Statistics bear out that older employees become complacent and get hurt more often and more severely than young employees.

Make safety a joint effort involving everyone in the firm. Don't try to get on top of safety by directing *your* attention to the problem. Get your employees to direct *their* attention to the problem. Listen to them, and correct the hazards they point out immediately. Set up a safety committee with a representative constituency and give it appropriate spending authority.

OSHA requirements should be designed into your original plant design. It will be less expensive to do that up front both in capital outlay and compensation for injury and lost time. Management has the responsibility to provide safety equipment and protective implements, such as gloves, and has the right to demand that they be used.

Maintenance Procedures

Small business frequently neglect housekeeping, and this disregard is reflected in their production records.

To get the most out of your machines, follow an inspection procedure that adheres to a definite schedule. If you do not have an employee capable of handling the inspection, get regular inspection service from a local, qualified service. You can do the same thing with maintenance and repair work shown to be needed by inspection or as scheduled.

From your inspection reports and cost records you should be able to detect unwarranted maintenance expenses and adopt corrective measures. Sometimes the problem will be solved simply by the adjustment of a machine. Vigilance against machine malfunction and misuse will save money.

You may find some of the following maintenance tips helpful:

- See that contacts on the fuse block are good and that the right kind of fuse is being used for the circuit.

- If a motor or generator becomes wet, dry it out thoroughly with portable infrared lamps. Temperature should not be raised above 195°F (90°C). The stator may be dried out in an oven.

- Be sure the frames of all arc welding equipment are grounded to avoid shock. When relocating welding equipment, ensure that ventilation is good, otherwise overheating may result, shortening the life of the insulation.

- Have an expert go over your oil-burning system annually.

- To keep firehoses in top operating condition, run water through them at least twice a year. If they should freeze, thaw them out before bending them.

- Get the manufacturers' data on setting saws, care of files, and proper usage. Stretch the life of your tools by using them properly.

- Inspect and test all emergency equipment safety, limitation, and shut-off controls at reasonable intervals.

- Mount safety or relief valves as closely as possible to the equipment.
- Be sure the pressure gauges with which valves are set are correct, usually at about 4 percent blowdown and not less than 3 percent.
- Immediately investigate all undue vibrations in machinery.
- Keep working parts free of harmful waste, shavings, and other extraneous materials.
- Inspect working parts and couplings on a scheduled basis.
- Establish a lubrication routine that prevents unnecessary wear and rust.
- Post fuse requirements in all fuse boxes and wherever fuses are used. Over fusing causes equipment damage and accidents.
- Replace blown fuses only after finding and correcting the cause of their blowing first. It might be a stiff belt, tight bearings, unclean commutator, motor being brought to full speed too quickly, damaged motor, or worn bearings.

14

Doing Business with the Federal Government

The United States government buys huge quantities of machinery, equipment, supplies, and services. It also purchases military hardware and research and development in both the physical and life sciences, data collection and entry, software development, and consulting services. For many companies the government is their biggest potential customer. Many firms, even foreign ones, compete for government business. To succeed, they must:

- Offer a good product at a highly competitive price.
- Produce the goods or services in the time required.
- Follow government purchasing office procedures.
- Represent their firm as well as its products favorably to government purchasers.
- Present a proposal and bid that is responsive to the government's contractual specifications.

This chapter will tell you how the government buys, how to find out which agencies buy your products, how to compete for contracts, and how the Small Business Administration can help you sell your products to the government.

Filling Government Contracts

Before making your bid, you should be certain that you can profitably manufacture the item which the government wants under the strict terms of the contract. If specifications are not precisely met, the government can reject your product. The government also has the right to terminate a contract at any time while production is under way. This takes place when a business fails to live up to specific regulations. Cancellations also occur because of changes in the government's needs. However, when such cancellations occur, the government must pay for work performed.

Specifications for government purchases are very rigid. The quality, grade, size, and other characteristics of components are precisely detailed. This makes government items more expensive to produce than typical civilian products. You will find the specifications listed in *The Index of Federal Specifications and Standards* available from the Superintendent of Documents, U.S. Government Printing Office, P.O. Box 371954, Pittsburgh, PA 15250-7954. The use and development of the standards and specifications are discussed in *The Guide to Federal Specifications and Standards of the Federal Government* available at General Services Administration (GSA) business service centers and field offices of the Department of Commerce and the Small Business Administration. Reproductions of federal specifications and standards are available from Federal Supply Service Bureau, Specifications Section, 470 East L'Enfant Plaza S.W., Suite 8100, Washington, DC 20407, as well as from GSA business service centers. Copies of military specifications and standards can be obtained only from the Naval Publications and Forms Center, 5801 Tabor Ave., Philadelphia, PA 19120. Government contracts often incorporate the various standards by reference. Be sure you know what they contain.

If you wish to sell the government a new or improved product that exceeds existing specifications or eliminates the need for old products, you must go through channels in seeking to interest the government in contracting with your company. File Form 1171, the Application for Presenting New or Improved Articles, with the GSA. If you have a unique product, you can market it directly to the government agencies. Agencies are not required to follow federal specifications and standards when investigating unique products.

The government prefers to enter into contracts on a fixed-price basis. This means you must plan for the effects of inflation over the life of the contract and the costs of the difficulties which might arise in fulfilling the contract. In some instances variations can be written into the contract providing for price redetermination and escalations.

Bidding for Contracts

Contracts calling for payment of the contractor's costs in addition to a fixed profit are used only when the nature of the work makes a fixed-profit contract impractical or reduces the number and capabilities of bidders. When circumstances require the government to act quickly, it will sometimes allow work to begin with only a letter of intent from the contracting officer.

In government contracts that are not outright purchases, the contracting agency appoints one or more contracting offices technical representatives (COTRs). These individuals are responsible for attesting to the contracting officer as to the quality of the work done in compliance with the contract. Often they draft the scope of work and selected standards and specifications. In brief, the COTR calls the shots.

When you know which agencies buy the type of products you make or can make, apply to be put on their list of bidders by filing standard Form 129, the Bidder's Mailing List Application form. The local office of the Small Business Administration can help you find out which agencies normally buy your product. The Department of Commerce publishes the *Commerce Business Daily,* which lists most projects open to private contractors as soon as they are put out for bid. Also listed are sales of surplus property from various government agencies, foreign business opportunities, subcontracting possibilities, and the winning bidders on previously announced contracts. To subscribe to this important information source, write the Superintendent of Documents, U.S. Government Printing Office, P.O. Box 371954, Pittsburgh, PA 15250-7954. You should also check with your local member of Congress or senator for opportunities to do business with the government. They can be of great assistance in putting your firm in touch with government officials and agencies. Another way is to explore having a manufacturer's representative present your capabilities.

When awarding a contract, the government considers not only the size of the bid, but also the responsibility of the bidding company. The government wants assurances that your company is capable of performing within the terms of the contract. If your company has no experience in the field of the bid project, you are unlikely to be awarded the contract because an inexperienced company is more likely to have performance difficulties. Therefore, to assure a government agency that you can meet contract terms, send a complete résumé on your usual production, your plant capacity and equipment, number of workers, background of engineering and management personnel, and your firm's financial position. The agency may also send you a questionnaire to fill out so that it can gain a clearer picture of your suitability for government contracting. Much of this information is required in the Request for Proposal (RFP). Be sure to present your firm's capabilities in such a manner as to instill confidence.

Errors in the preparation of your bids can result in financial loss and also cast doubt on your ability to fulfill contracts. The government is ever watchful of firms trying to buy a contract, and once acquired, striving to sell work modifications and engineering changes to recover financial loss. There is little benefit in cutting all your estimates to the minimum. You may win the contract but fail to make a profit or suffer a loss in completing it.

Businesses performing work under government contracts operate under restrictions which may raise the cost of doing business:

- The components of products you supply are required to be of American origin (if possible) by the Buy American Act.

- The Walsh-Healy Public Contracts Act requires employers on government contracts to pay overtime to employees working more than 8 hours a day or 40 hours a week.

- The Davis-Brown Act prevents a contractor working on a government project from paying workers less than the prevailing local wage and fringe benefits.

- Items produced for the Department of Defense that are on the qualified products list must be tested at the contractor's expense before they are delivered.

If you are sending in a bid on an item for the first time, ask for a copy of specifications and drawings. Instructions accompanying the invitation to bid will tell you whether you can bid on part of the total or on the total amount, your delivery date, and the deadline for withdrawal. It will also give particulars on packaging and shipping requirements.

After the bids are opened in public at the appointed time and read aloud, the lower bids are designated for further evaluation. As price is only one of the factors considered, the lowest bid is not always chosen, unless one firm is "responsive" to the RFP as the lowest cost chosen. The government agency is sometimes influenced by its opinion of your financial stability and your ability to meet delivery and specifications.

At times, the government buys by negotiation rather than by advertising for bids. Using its list of bidders, a procurement office may ask several suppliers for proposals or quotations on the items to be purchased. Those submitting the best proposals are called in for further negotiation, during which government buyers try to get the best deal possible. This procedure is formalized in a bidder's conference to assure all parties have equal access to the technical representative or the government agency's staff.

If you wish to bid on a Department of Defense contract, be sure to first familiarize yourself with the armed services procurement regulations which govern the contracts. The military procurement procedures are explained in the brochure *Selling to the Military*, available from the Superintendent of Documents, U.S. Government Printing Office, P.O. Box 371954, Pittsburgh, PA 15250-7954. Each of the armed services, in turn, has its own set of regulations. But there is considerable standardization through military requirements and specifications. Assess the costs such requirements impose because military standards (MIL STUs) are tough. When you deal with an agency, be sure you receive all your instructions from the contracting officer, who may be a civilian or in the military. The contracting officer, or his or her authorized representative, is the only person qualified to administer the contract and authorize changes. Again remember, the COTR is responsible to the contracting officer, and most often the COTR calls the tune.

Should you invent an item while under government contract, you will face the problem of patenting rights. Some agencies, such as the Department of Defense and the National Aeronautics and Space Administration, have flexible policies on patenting rights. Others, such as the Atomic Energy Commission and the Department of Agriculture, are required by law to take title to inventions and patents which are the product of a contract let by them.

Sources of Procurement Information

In addition to the *Commerce Business Daily*, government projects put out to bid by private industry appear in other sources. Construction projects soliciting bidders are noted in area newspapers, pertinent trade journals, and in industry technical publications.

The business service centers of the GSA are responsible for issuing the invitations for bids in their regions. Business service centers are located in Boston, New York, Washington, DC, Philadelphia, Atlanta, Chicago, Kansas City, Fort Worth, Houston, Denver, San Francisco, Los Angeles, and Seattle. GSA specialists work out of these centers to provide assistance to the business person in securing government contracts.

Defense Department contracts are sometimes issued separately through the Defense Logistics Agency. Interested businesses should send their Form 129, Bidder's Mailing List Application, to one of the Defense Logistic Agency supply centers, located in Columbus and

Dayton, Ohio, Alexandria and Richmond, Virginia, and Philadelphia, Pennsylvania. Subcontractors should send their mailing list application to one of the regional offices of the Defense Contract Administration Services, located in Boston, Chicago, Cleveland, Dallas, Los Angeles, New York, Philadelphia, St. Louis, and Marietta, Georgia. However, your local office of the Small Business Administration should be able to assist you in obtaining Department of Defense contracts.

Difficulties with Government Contracts

At times, economic conditions make it advisable for the government to cancel a contract. When this is necessary, the contractor usually recovers all allowable expenditures made up to the time of the termination. The contractor also will be awarded a reasonable profit on the investment of time and facilities, provided that records indicate a profit would have been made on the contract. If, instead, a loss is indicated, less than 100 percent of expenditures would be recovered. For this reason, it is essential to keep well-documented accounts on all transactions. Additionally, the government reserves the right to audit all contracts.

Most contracts contain a "dispute" clause which permits the contractor to petition the Board of Contract Appeals on any disagreement with the contracting officer. *Your appeal must be made within 30 days of the contracting officer's decision.* While the board processes your appeal, you are obliged to continue filling the contract's requirements. If any disagreement occurs, be sure to contact your lawyer for aid in seeking redress.

Subcontracting of Government Contracts

In competing for government contracts, the small enterprise is frequently hampered by the lack of facilities for mass production. At times, with the assistance of the Small Business Administration, groups of firms band together to bid on government contracts. Frequently, small businesses have received subcontracts from prime contractors who deal with the government. You can build up a good volume of subcontracting if you develop good relations with a number of prime contractors who can use your production facilities.

Before you approach a prime contractor, decide on the type of product you can make and the price you will charge. You will find end products and components bought by the military displayed at the SBA regional or branch offices. Get the specifications on items you think you can manufacture. Then after a close examination of your costs, ask the SBA for the names of suitable prime manufacturers.

Initial contact with the prime contractor might be made by a letter including the same kind of information as is requested on the Bidder's Mailing List Application form (standard Form 129). Military security clearance for work on classified materials should be arranged through your prime contractor. Be sure to be specific about the service or product you are offering. Remember, whenever security matters are involved, your facilities and personnel will be subject to checks and regulations in protecting public secrets.

Subcontracting for government contracts has bolstered production levels for many firms during business declines. You may be able to rent idle government-owned machine tools if your prime contractor sponsors you. Subcontracting also qualifies you for financial assistance from the SBA.

If you should obtain a contract from a prime contractor, be sure to familiarize yourself with the government's terms. Many of the regulations may not apply to you. Your requirements on patent and data rights, financing, disputes, and appeals will also be different from those of the prime contractor.

Subcontracting carries its disadvantages. If you allow defense work subcontracts to absorb the largest part of your volume of production and neglect sources of civilian work, you may find yourself idle when defense work slackens. You might also be left with specialized equipment which you do not need for your civilian work. Remember, military production requires close tolerances and a precision on which you will have to pass inspection from the prime contractor as well as from the government. You are also open to termination of subcontracts during periods when the prime contractor's business slows down and it does the work which was formerly subcontracted.

Government Bidding Considerations

Bidding for a government contract requires high standards of accuracy. Make sure your bid is in line with these considerations:

- Government packaging requirements may call for expensive materials, labor, and machinery not necessary for your civilian product.

- Make an allowance in your profit computations for delivery costs, increases in labor costs, and fluctuations in the prices of raw materials.

- Have a design which complies completely with the specifications and standards of the invitation to bid.

- Furnish the required information in your application. Government questionnaires and applications must be fully completed.

- Demonstrate your responsibility and ability to perform the contract at your bid price.

Above all, if you don't understand the procedures, the rules, or the specifications or scope of work, ask for more information. Despite stories of $100 hammers, most public contracts are competitive, and any required specifications and standards are in the contract because the COTR has convinced the contracting office that they are needed.

15
Hiring and Managing Personnel

Each company has a personal style of doing business which is reflected in the work and attitude of its employees. On a daily basis, you are in contact with the employees of some company: a clerk in the local supermarket, a telephone operator, a receptionist, a bank teller, a manager, or a chief executive. The way he or she handles your business may encourage you to continue to do business with the firm or swear never to set foot on the premises again.

What you expect from the personnel of other companies, people will also expect from the employees of your firm. In setting the tone for your personnel, your attitude is crucial—not only must you be able to hire competent people, you must also have the necessary style of leadership that encourages employees to give their best efforts and loyalty. It is not an easy task. Business pressures place strains on human relationships, and it is often difficult to find and keep the most desirable type of personnel. Compromises sometimes have to be made.

Moreover, employers must be aware of and keep abreast of current labor law restrictions, their application to your industry, regulations on minimum wages, maximum hours, overtime pay, child labor, and details of keeping the payroll records needed for government purposes. Maintaining an efficient staff can be a major and continuous management problem of every business.

Determining Your Requirements

The nature of your operations will fix the number of employees which you must hire. If you are planning to use 10 machines to produce a product which requires an operator and helper per machine, you of course need at least 20 employees for this part of your operation. In other areas, determining the number of people you need is not that straightforward. Only after a period of experience will you be able to determine how many employees you need. Sometimes, the relative ability of the available employees may determine the number of employees required for a particular job. If you are fortunate, you may have an employee whose ability and efficiency makes him or her the equivalent of several employees.

In determining your requirements, prepare a description for every job in your company and the type of employee needed for that job, including education, skills, and experience. It is important when defining a job to distinguish between those things an applicant *must* have or be able to do, versus those things that you would *prefer* the applicant to have or be able to do. This also helps in structuring the "knock out" questions in the interview so that you do not waste time with the unqualified applicant. It is also important when you hire a person, that he or she has challenging and continuous work with which to be occupied. There is nothing as detrimental to an employee and a company as hiring an employee for a position that does not demand his or her full time and energy.

Recruiting Help

You may utilize various sources and agencies to contact applicants. You can advertise in newspapers, call personnel agencies or offices operated by commercial firms, trade associations, schools, unions, and the state, or use referrals from business contacts and customers.

Whatever source you use, make sure that you adequately describe your job requirements. You do not want to waste time interviewing people who do not qualify. Before accepting applicants for interviews, request their résumés of experience or similar records to determine whether their basic qualifications meet your objectives.

When you do interview a person, there are various steps to follow.

1. *Have the applicant fill out an application form.* This should elicit enough information to allow you to judge whether the applicant can do a particular job with minimum training and whether he or she will fit into your company.

2. *Interview the applicant in private, and put the applicant at ease with a few general remarks about the business and the job.* Plan the interview so that you have the résumé and application before you, and take some time to absorb some of the important information. Ask open-ended questions, good self-assessment questions on likes and dislikes, satisfactions and dissatisfactions. Have the applicant work on a project assignment which would provide insight into how he or she goes about solving a problem and the level of resourcefulness that is used. Have the applicant evaluate his or her abilities against the job description that has been developed. Anything the applicant can describe very specifically is a strong indication that he or she has skills in those areas.

3. *Provide some test of the applicant's job skill.* For example, if you are hiring a typist, the applicant should be tested for proficiency and speed. If a technical skill is required, you may have to give some written test which can reveal the extent of the applicant's ability. Any tests that are given need to be validated as well as uniformly applied to all candidates in order to maintain legal compliance. After interviewing and testing applicants, check their references before making the final choice. Because of the legal environment today, reference checking has become more difficult. To provide protection for those that will be referenced, have the applicant sign an authorization to check those references as well as to hold those references harmless for anything they might reveal during the check. This serves to protect the employer making the reference and the individual providing the reference information.

4. *Verify whether the applicant has the skills the job requires or is capable of learning them in a short time.* This is the only criterion necessary, unless the applicant has given you reason to suspect his or her trustworthiness or willingness to work (for example, consistent absenteeism with previous employers). It is illegal to discriminate against an applicant because of the person's race, religion, sex, or handicap. If a person can do the job, he or she must be seriously considered. In many positions, the disadvantaged will perform far more conscientiously and skillfully than the average worker. In most instances, you will have a choice of many applicants who can do the job. You will be able to concentrate on selecting the one most qualified.

Hiring an Employee

For certain classes of employees, you may wish to establish an introductory orientation period. This can serve as an opportunity for both the employee and the employer to get acquainted with one another and through actual hands-on experience be able to determine whether they will be able to work together in a longer-term relationship.

Many companies give physical examinations before hiring a person. This is necessary if the work imposes any physical strain. It also helps you to comply with worker's compensation laws by giving you a record of an employee's health. Should a physical disability occur, you are protected by your written record of the worker's condition at the time of hiring.

Training the New Employee

How you choose to train a new employee depends upon the job being taught, the personnel to be used for training, and how many new employees are being instructed at one time. Unless your company is large enough to have specialized training personnel, the responsibility of instructing the new employee will fall on the person who will be his or her supervisor on the job. The employee must be able to work with the supervisor and meet the supervisor's standards.

Actual methods of instruction vary with the skills and procedures required by the job. More complicated functions may require seminar-type conferences and lectures for large groups of trainees, on-the-job training, and role playing. Lectures and conferences are effective ways to present a mass of background information that the trainee must study and commit to memory. As most background information is usually available in reference materials, it is more important to know where to look things up than to trust one's memory for the information. Have the trainee report on what was learned, how the material could be applied to the job, and then in the course of discussion, make it the trainee's responsibility to apply what was learned on the job and make it part of the performance appraisal as an area to be followed up and evaluated. Background information for a salesperson, for example, is not as important as his or her ability to deal with people.

Role playing also allows the trainee to see things from the other side (that of the customer, for example), thus giving the trainee valuable insight into how to deal with sales problems. Role playing also gives both the instructor and trainee an idea of how much the trainee must still master.

On-the-job training provides real experience, and mistakes can be corrected by the supervisor before they get out of hand. For many jobs, such as those requiring machine skills or cashiers, on-the-job training is the only effective method. Follow these four steps in on-the-job training when no other teaching method has been used:

1. *Teach.* Find out what your employee knows. Take nothing for granted, even if the employee declared on the job application that he

or she had similar experience. Then teach what is not known, keeping in mind that it is better to repeat some of what is already known than to have the employee waste time and material later.

2. *Demonstrate.* Following the job breakdown sheet, show the trainee how to do the job. Proceed slowly, asking questions which make the trainee think of why each step is taken in the demonstrated manner. Then demonstrate at normal speed.

3. *Let the trainee perform.* After the demonstration, let the employee perform the job alone. Your attitude at this point should be one of encouragement. Avoid looking over shoulders. Demonstrate again, if a mistake is made.

4. *Inspect.* You or a supervisor should then check the trainee's work. Point out satisfactory progress, or explain what he or she is doing wrong and why.

For extremely specialized or intensive training, it may be worthwhile for your company to pay the employee to enroll at a local school of higher education. Your industry association may also sponsor educational gatherings such as conferences or symposia. Your employees can be given the incentive to advance their skills on their own if the company normally promotes people from within the company.

Compensating Personnel

From your experience and contacts, you can readily discover the going rate of pay. Depending on your needs and the pool of available prospects, you may be able to offer more or less than the going rate. Here again your actual experience will be your guide. For an important position, you may leave the exact amount open to bargaining within certain bounds.

The level of pay needed to attract talent will depend on your industry, the size of your company, your geographic location, and the responsibilities of the job. If your company shows promise of rapid growth, you may find a capable manager who is willing to start at a lower salary with expectations of a bonus for getting results. Straight-salary income may not be sufficient to attract personnel. You may have to provide added pay benefits: a profit-sharing plan, a possible part ownership of the business, educational benefits, and other fringe benefits. For example, homemakers can be attracted by convenient day-care facilities or a subsidy paid by your company to a day-care facility.

Be aware that the Equal Pay Act of 1963 forbids wage discrimination on the basis of sex. As long as men and women are doing substantially equal work, they must be paid equally. Male and female telephone repairers were ruled to be doing substantially equal jobs, even though the males occasionally carried heavier equipment. Male and female bank tellers handling different kinds of accounts would also call for equal pay as the difference between their duties is minor. Even if an agreement between union and management calls for different wage rates, the pay must be the same if the difference between the jobs is insignificant. Pay surveys are generally available from trade associations, state or federal labor departments, employment agencies, and through consulting firms specializing in compensation.

Providing Fringe Benefits to Employees

Fringe benefits is a term that describes pay benefits other than wage or salary income. Benefits may be provided to employees through group life insurance protection, discounts on company products, educational assistance, health and accident benefits, no-interest loans, and retirement benefits. Fringe benefits to some employees may be more important than a salary increase because a fringe benefit may be received partially or wholly tax-free.

Retirement Benefits

The federal government, through the tax law, encourages the creation of private pension and profit-sharing plans by allowing (1) an employer to deduct contributions on behalf of an employee, (2) an employee to avoid current tax on the contributions made to his or her account, and (3) tax-free accumulation of income earned on funds invested in the plan. Tax is not incurred until the employee begins to collect benefits. If certain rules are met, this tax is generally lower than the tax otherwise due on similar amounts.

These tax benefits apply only to plans which meet technical rules that generally are aimed at preventing owners from discriminating in their own favor. When a plan is approved by the IRS, it is called a *qualified plan*. A qualified plan may not discriminate in favor of officers or other highly compensated personnel.

Types of qualifying retirement plans are discussed further in Chapter 7.

Vacations, Holidays, and Sick Pay

Vacation pay practices vary with each company, but many companies give 2 weeks after a year's service and 3 weeks or more after an additional period of time.

Paid holidays are generally granted for the following 6 days: New Year's Day, Memorial Day, Independence Day, Labor Day, Thanksgiving Day, and Christmas. Additional holidays are often granted in some communities or industries. Other holidays which may or may not be observed in your type of business are Washington's Birthday, Lincoln's Birthday, Columbus Day, Martin Luther King's Birthday, the day after Thanksgiving, and National Election Day. Federal legislation now ensures that 4 out of 11 holidays are celebrated on Mondays, giving many workers 3-day weekends.

Also inform new employees of company policy on paid religious holidays. Ensure that all your workers are treated equally in paid time off.

Sick leave practices vary. A certain number of days may be granted for the year. In some companies, a few days may be allowed under self-care, but above that a doctor's note is required. As for maternity leave, it is handled as any other sick leave. Employers who maintain health and disability plans are required by federal law to provide coverage for pregnancy and childbirth.

The Family and Medical Leave Act of 1993 (effective August 1993) requires private-sector employers with 50 or more workers to provide up to 12 weeks of unpaid, job-protected leave to eligible employees for one of the following reasons:

- Care of employee's newborn or newly placed adopted child or foster child
- Care of employee's spouse, son or daughter, or parent who has a serious health condition
- Inability to perform the job because of a serious health condition

In addition, employers must maintain health insurance coverage during the period of the leave.

As more single parents and working couples join the work force, employers must face the problem of how to treat leave for caring for sick children. Most companies require employees to use vacation time, rather than sick leave, in order to remain home and care for their sick children. You may want to maintain a more liberal policy depending upon how valuable the contribution of such parents are to your business.

An Employee's Handbook

A well-written employee's handbook can provide the new employee with an introduction to your company and its policies. It may tell the history of the organization, with possible attention to its financial status—past, present, and projected. It should list working hours, policy on use of the time clock and other sign-in procedures, rules on rest periods and coffee breaks, as well as the rules for absences from work, the length of the pay period, and the company's safety and accident-prevention programs. You might also economize and prevent future bitterness if you list restrictions on the use of telephones.

Your booklet can also elaborate on such company benefits as the following:

- Vacations and holidays
- Medical hospital and surgical benefits
- Pensions, profit-sharing plans, and bonuses
- Group insurance
- Training programs
- Parking rules
- Service awards
- Credit unions
- Company cafeteria location and fare
- Bowling and baseball teams and tournaments
- Monthly or weekly magazine or newssheet

You may also want to indicate company policy on jury duty and military leave, and state employees' rights to unemployment compensation.

Make sure that the handbook has language that indicates that the material which it contains does not constitute an employment contract. Have a labor attorney review it before it is implemented. An employee may claim ignorance, particularly where he or she has a responsibility to do something, so make sure the handbook is kept current and supply a card with it, to be signed by the employee after he or she has received and read it.

Employing Disabled Persons

The Americans with Disabilities Act of 1990 (ADA) prohibits employers from discriminating against disabled persons who, despite their impediment, are able to perform a particular job. As an employer, you are subject to the provisions of the law if before July 26, 1994, you employ 25 of more employees or if, after that date, you employ 15 or more. A job candidate or employee who claims that you violated ADA provisions may sue you for damages.

Under the law, you may not screen out individuals with disabilities or conduct preemployment medical screening, with the exception of drug screening, or make preemployment inquiries into the nature of an applicant's disability. Furthermore, you may have to take reasonable steps to accommodate the special needs of disabled employees.

To make sure you are in compliance, review job descriptions of company positions and make sure they are accurate. Make a job analysis of each position and list of tasks necessary to perform the job. Next, answer the following questions about each task: What is the task performed? How often is it performed? How is it performed? What methods, techniques, or tools are used? How much time does it take? Does it consistently take this much time? How do you measure whether the task was accomplished or not? What happens if the task is done wrong? What aptitudes (potential to learn and accomplish a skill) are necessary? How much physical exertion (lifting, standing, sitting, etc.) is needed?

Once you answer these questions about the position, determine the bottom-line qualifications that would be needed to perform the essential functions of the job. Then determine the qualifications which would be nice to have, but which are not strictly necessary for success.

In an interview the only questions to ask are those that deal with the essential functions of the job. Do not ask about the person's disability unless the disability might affect their ability to perform an essential function. Permissible questions are: "This job requires that you be able to lift 50-pound boxes. Can you do that?" "An important part of this job is word processing. We use WordPerfect; do you know WordPerfect?" "The job requires all employees to be at work at 8 a.m. Is there any reason that you would be unable to do this?"

If the applicant is unable to perform an essential function of the job, ask whether there are any reasonable accommodations, such as special equipment, that would enable him or her to do the job more effectively. Do not raise the question of accommodation unless the individual is determined to be qualified as a potential candidate. If the person is not qualified, you should state why, and make it clear that the reason for rejection is due to lack of qualifications and not due to a disability. Finally, keep a record of the interviews.

The ADA law gives only vague guidelines on the type of "reasonable accommodations" you must make for disabled employees. Accommodations that would impose an "undue hardship" on the employer are not considered "reasonable" and thus are not required. Factors that the Equal Employment Opportunity Commission may consider as evidence of undue hardship are the net cost of making the accommodation (taking into account government assistance and insurance coverage), the disruption to business operations that would be caused, safety hazards that could be caused by making the accommodation, and generally any proof that the proposed accommodation would not accomplish the goal of enabling the individual to perform the job adequately.

Maintaining Good Relations with Your Employees

Communication with employees on company policies should be prompt and thorough. If you do not keep your workers posted on new developments, they will get their facts through other means, often garbled by rumors and misinformation.

Informal chats with employees help create a friendly atmosphere and give you a chance to uncover dissatisfactions. Even small companies need the regularity and definiteness of formal communications. Meet with your entire staff at regular intervals to impart general information and answer questions. Be sure that notices of holidays, schedule changes, and training and other educational opportunities are posted on bulletin boards. An in-house newspaper or magazine can serve to tell employees what is currently happening to their fellow workers and to the company. You might mail an annual letter to each employee, giving information about the company's status and expressing appreciation for past efforts. Some companies send greeting cards to employees on birthdays, their anniversaries with the company, and at Christmas time.

Encourage your workers to come forward with their complaints. They should feel assured that stating their grievances will not prejudice their positions with their immediate supervisors. You might have an employees' suggestion box. Choose an administrator to gather suggestions, and let the employees select a committee to consider new ideas and possibly make awards for ones that are adopted.

Discharging Employees

Sometimes a reduction in business or an employee's total unsuitability for the job makes it necessary to terminate the person's employment.

This creates an unpleasant task for both of you. Try to schedule your talk for the end of the day when you can be free from interruptions. Give the employee your exact reasons for termination, mentioning the benefits available in both severance pay and unemployment compensation. Help the employee find a new job if he or she has some skills which you can honestly recommend. Do not forget that any lack of tact or feeling you might show when discharging an employee will cause resentment among other employees whom you need to retain. You must be very careful when discharging an employee to avoid the discriminatory aspects—focusing on people over the age of 40, terminating blacks in a higher proportion than whites, or more women than men.

Using a Temporary Employment Agency

If your need for office help is usually light or only periodically heavy, you may be able to use a temporary employment agency, as do 80 percent of American companies at one time or another. Although the rate you pay the agency that provides the temporaries may seem high, you are probably saving money because the agency takes care of the workers' insurance, pension plans, and other fringe benefits and bookkeeping, payroll, and tax deductions, which can add an additional 40 percent in extra employee costs on top of wages.

Proper use of temporaries can keep an employer's unemployment tax from rising. The rate of unemployment tax you pay to the state and federal governments depends upon how often you hire and fire your employees. Because temporaries are the employees of the agency from which you hired them, moving them in and out of your work force will have no adverse effect on your unemployment tax rate. Moreover, temporaries may be well-suited for certain types of jobs that do not require the background of your regular work force.

However, if the position requires extensive training and you cannot keep the same temporary for a sufficient time, your work output suffers. Many established firms prefer to hire a full-time "floater" who goes from one temporary assignment to another as workloads develop within the office. Temporary help can also be used on a trial basis, to determine if an individual will work out in the organization before making any long-term permanent commitments. This arrangement should be negotiated with the agency before the temporary starts work.

16

Dealing with Fraud, Theft, and Robbery

The profits of small business are substantially cut each year by internal theft. Forgeries, embezzlements, and manipulations of trusted employees siphon off sums sometimes substantial enough to drive even long-established firms into bankruptcy. Theft by their own employees accounts for 30 percent of the losses suffered by small businesses. In the plant, workers express dissatisfaction with their jobs by making off with tools, parts, or finished products.

In addition to the take of internal thieves, small businesses must deal with the threats from burglary, robbery, and swindle. Retailers must also deal with the hazard of shoplifting. Although some loss by theft is inevitable, the individual business owner must manage the loss if the profitability of the firm is to survive. The loss from theft swells in proportion to the opportunity to steal.

This chapter is on how small business owners can *manage* losses from theft and pilferage.

Curtailing Employee Theft and Pilferage

The first step in preventing inside theft is to do a good job of screening job applicants. Small firms should emulate the practice of large organizations by providing a form for job applicants to complete which facilitates holding meaningful job interviews and checking references. All previous employment should be listed so that dates can be validated and lapses between jobs accounted for.

The prospective employer should insist on obtaining relevant personal and business references and follow up on them with telephone calls and searching questions. Because of the fear of lawsuits alleging damage to an individual's employability, previous employers and personnel managers are more open and objective on the phone than in letters. To offset the tendency of previous employers to give innocuous assessments of the performance of former employees, when calling, clearly state your purpose, the importance to the firm and the job applicant of avoiding a mismatch in hiring him or her, and the fact that the interview will not in any way be recorded.

Lie detectors are used by some firms to test the trustworthiness of employees. However, the tests are expensive and of questionable validity. Moreover, it is generally illegal not to hire someone solely because they refuse to take a polygraph test. Handwriting analysis does not fare any better than, if as well as, polygraph tests.

In the effort to keep losses from theft and pilferage within bounds, keep in mind the fact that there are few pathological or professional thieves among employees. Employees steal mainly to punish the employer for real or imagined grievances. Theft is usually a function of feelings of boredom, of being underpaid, underrespected, or underutilized, and these feelings can lead to major theft (how else can the employer be punished?). In addition, low employee morale may also lead to pilferage of items such as desk paraphernalia (pencils, pens, staples, tape), odds and ends (self-adhering computer labels, stamps), and plant supplies (rope, packing, lubricants).

Preventing major thefts is a matter of establishing effective procedures for preventing them and, much more importantly (because even the best of procedures cannot protect completely), removing the main causes for bad feelings toward the firm. Consider job enrichment, respect for all forms of work performed, concerns of management as essential to productivity as plant layout, salary administration, and cost control. Act on those considerations, and you will have happier employees who are less likely to steal.

As to what is lightly called (and usually ignored) pilferage, the taking of low-cost items is not viewed as theft by most takers, not usually even by management, but purloins which, being so small, are not worthy of notice. However, the pilferage, ungoverned, can exceed the cost of grand theft to the company.

In closing the subject of why employees steal, look at your own standards of behavior. If you purchase through the firm items for personal use, take home materials out of stock without paying for them, or put your son's or daughter's car used at college on the books as a company vehicle, don't blame employees for emulating that behavior as much as they can.

How Employees Steal

The following are the most common forms of employee theft over which employers should establish control:

- Stealing petty cash and covering theft by false vouchers.
- Stealing cash payments received by mail.
- Stealing cash payments by customers for sales in store, or on the road.
- "Lapping" cash by using today's receipts to cover yesterday's embezzlements.
- Purloining stamps, large quantities of which can be sold on the black market.
- Manipulating payroll, including salaries for fictional, discharged, or deceased employees.
- Forging a company check to one's own order and destroying the check on return by bank.
- Cashing company checks made out for fictitious bills from nonexistent vendors.
- Altering legitimate bills to get an additional payment that is cashed by the thief.
- Lowering amount of customer's bill in book entry and keeping the difference when customer pays full amount.
- Adjusting or writing off customers' accounts, sometimes in collusion with customers.
- Sending goods to nonexistent customers that are then sold for personal profit.
- Directly stealing company supplies or stock.
- Selling company property (by-products, fixtures, machinery, automobiles, investments) and withholding proceeds.
- Taking kickbacks, splitting commissions, or making other deals with suppliers or customers.
- Using correctable typewriters to change the figures on checks.

Total protection against the ingenuity of the determined internal thief is beyond reach. You can, however, make theft hazardous and limit your losses by appropriate procedures controlling the handling of cash, checks, or other instruments and curtailing opportunities for impulse thievery.

Safeguards in Office Procedures

In general, the possibility of fraud in the office can be cut by instituting methods such as the following:

- Have one employee record a sale, but another charge the customer's account.
- Have one employee receive the collection, but another record the credit to the customer.
- Have one employee handle cash, but another keep the cash-ledger account.
- Have one employee accept an order, but another issue the goods.
- Have one employee approve invoices for payment, but another issue the checks.
- Have one employee make up the payroll, but another issue the paychecks and take receipts.
- Have all extensions and additions on purchase orders and invoices checked manually or by computer.
- Institute a procedure to see that invoices are paid only once.

Of course, two or more employees acting in concert can circumvent safeguards. Good friends or relatives can be tempted to act together to steal if their jobs combine to give them the opportunity, for example, if one employee is the bookkeeper and his or her spouse works in shipping and receiving.

Business owners with few employees should themselves supervise their employees as much as possible and spring spot checks so that the employees are aware of the owner's watchfulness. However, one should avoid making such supervision appear to be anything but a businesslike caring for fulfillment of procedures. Obvious suspicion will only stir up the antagonism of honest employees and turn the minds of the dishonest to devising new ways to steal.

Theft of petty cash is the most common form of employee larceny, made easy by some employers who allow vouchers to be made out in pencil, so that the amount can be altered. Unmarked vouchers can be reused by the petty-cash manipulator. Take these four simple precautionary steps, which auditors consider essential:

1. Requests for payment from petty cash must be made out in ink to prevent forgery. As a further precaution, all slips over $5 must have the amount written in both longhand and figures.

2. In every possible case, the request should be supported by invoices or receipts and approved by a designated official.

3. After each petty-cash voucher has been paid and date of payment entered, it must be stamped or punched to prevent reuse.

4. The vouchers must not remain under the control of the cashier.

Safeguarding Mail Receipts

If your mail customarily contains checks, cash, or stamps, you need a strong protective system. Find out whether a registering machine, which creates a cash record and registers the customer's remittance documents, would be an economic safeguard in your business. Install these office routines:

- Mail is opened under competent supervision away from other staff.

- Mail openers sort orders or payments immediately. All papers and mailing documents are fastened together with cash or check.

- Coins or stamps are put into envelopes for attachment to other papers.

- Amount of money received is marked on the papers.

- Checks and money orders are endorsed "for deposit only." Company endorsement stamp is used.

- Other employees take over. Paid orders are channeled one way; payments another. A clerk who opens mail should not be the person making book entries of the receipts.

- Staff is rotated so that no one person can easily set up a system of pilferage or book falsification.

- Customer complaints of unfilled orders or bills rendered again after payment should be investigated immediately. Have such complaints directed away from mail openers or bookkeepers who might have reason to suppress them. If complaints make you suspect mail pilferage, you might want to plant a couple of pieces of mail containing cash in the incoming mail.

- Tighten security and let employees know you are watchful.

Cash-Handling Protection

Take the strongest measures possible to safeguard cash:

- Bond all cash-handling employees from cashier to outside sales-people.
- Install a modern cash register. Use of a till or cash box invites larceny.
- Demand a regular check of petty-cash funds.
- See that the cashier does not make disbursements from receipts; an imprest fund is usually more advisable.
- Make sure that the cashiers are required to give a full receipt for all funds taken in.
- Educate the payer of funds to get a receipt for proper credit of payment.
- See that the cashier registers funds immediately upon receipt.
- If the registry is by a duplicate receipt, number it serially so as to control it fully.
- Make certain that lapping, the holding back of funds despite entry in the receipt records, is not possible.
- Compare your receipts with budgets, standards, and ratios in daily or periodical reports. Investigate all unusual divergences from forecasts or normal trends.
- Make certain that it is impossible for cash to be taken by a clerk not reporting sales.
- Be sure that unauthorized or improper allowances cannot be entered.
- Make certain that it is not possible for cashbooks to be juggled or forced, particularly in the discount columns.
- Be certain that it is not possible for a charge to be made to an expense account to cover stolen cash.
- Have independent office personnel or accountants balance the cashier's funds and salespeople's registers.
- See that the person receiving money on charge accounts does not have access to the ledgers.
- Segregate the person handling cash and cash operations from the rest of the office.
- Provide an adequate safe room; make certain that the safes are modern, burglarproof, and fireproof; permit only authorized persons to know the combinations; and change the combinations periodically.

- Make use of the protection given by mechanical equipment—cash registers, analysis machines, autographic registers, check registers, automatic cashiers, paying machines, and change-making machines.
- Avoid any "payouts" from receipts which should be deposited in the bank intact.
- Avoid cash collections by outside salespeople if you can. Bond any collecting salesperson. Have sales force's receipt books serially controlled in duplicate. Have orders and cash balanced by someone outside the sales department. Investigate quickly if customers complain that cash payments were not credited to their accounts or if they fail to pay for a salesperson's order. If salespersons must use customer cash payments for their expenses, ironclad control and recording are needed. Spot-check from time to time to prevent salespersons from overcharging customers and pocketing the difference.
- Banking should be done by a bonded person other than the cashier. Have that person accompanied to the bank, and make sure the money is carried unobtrusively. Bank nearby and insure against crime loss.
- Make deposit slips in duplicate to receive bank proof and prevent forgery.
- Check daily deposits through bank records. If possible, have this done by someone other than the person receiving the cash.
- Reconcile all bank statements regularly. If possible, have the reconciliation made by a person other than the cashier.
- Reconcile the bank balances occasionally at periods other than the close of the month.
- Review all bank accounts yourself or have an accountant do so to guard against borrowing from one account to cover a shortage in another. Question all transfers between banks, particularly those at the end of the month.

Safeguarding the Use of Checks

Permissive use of checks leaves the door wide open to the forger. Install positive routines and a sound verification system in the writing of checks. Remember that in too many cases the trusted, long-time employee has proved to be an embezzler. These protective measures guard management from loss and the employee from unjustified suspicion:

- Require more than one signature on a check. Have at least one of the authorized signers thoroughly audit the vouchers. This prevents the use of false, previously paid, or raised invoices. The latter are sometimes rendered by vendors who conspire with employees to defraud a company.

- Have checks numbered serially and prepared with a checkwriter; retain all voided checks; and route checks returned by the bank to a person other than the issuing employee. Have the bank reconciliation made by a disinterested person.

- Permit no checks to be made out to "cash" or "bearer," no presigning of blank checks, and no signing of checks without seeing the bills to which they correspond.

- Blank checks must be locked up safely.

Supervising Your Accounts

Constant supervision of your accounting system is necessary. The new business owner needs a qualified accountant for guidance in setting up a system; the established company needs the auditor's eye. Sloppy bookkeeping and indifferent checking up enable the embezzler to cover tracks for years. Note these pointers:

- Review all reductions of accounts carefully. Bad debts, allowances, discounts, and all kinds of write-offs should be properly authorized and subsequently audited.

- Make sure that reductions can be charged nowhere but to the account provided.

- Check all deductions from remittances, such as cash discounts and commissions. Make certain that a cashier or salesperson cannot misappropriate any payments received on accounts that have been charged off.

- Be sure that items cannot be lost. Points to watch include goods sold without an entry in your books; interest received from customers on their notes and accounts and not entered; proceeds from sales of by-products, waste, etc., that have not been properly protected; and interest or dividends due on investments that have not been received.

The computer has opened up new areas in employee fraud. Computerized embezzling is more difficult to detect than earlier varieties of embezzlement, particularly because some auditors are not fully attuned to unraveling that type of fraud. Control and audit techniques have to be built into the system from the start. When one person or one group follows a transaction from beginning to end, the possibility of manipulation exists.

Computer manufacturers are at work to incorporate security checks into their systems. In the meantime, experts have some advice for business owners who use computers:

- The programmer and the operator of the computer should not be the same person. Both should be carefully screened when first employed, the programmer in particular.

- The officers who authorize checks should be in a department apart from computerized check-writing operations so that a dishonest company officer cannot easily convert falsified data into checks.

- Change job responsibility frequently. When programmers and operators do not work on the same job for long, they have less opportunity to set up a system of fraud.

- Require that programmers and operators take their annual vacation at different times; most computer theft schemes fall apart without constant monitoring.

If computers are used in your accounting system, you need auditors who have been trained as programmers and are experts in checking through all phases of a computerized operation to detect fraud.

Workers, not inherently dishonest, may be tempted to steal if your methods of loss prevention are slack. People who begin by taking a few nails for a job at home may eventually cost you thousands of dollars in inventory or equipment.

Let your employees see that you mean business regarding security, whether that means a ban on lunch boxes at the job area or sophisticated methods of inventory control. *See that rules apply to all.* If the system requires that everyone sign for stockroom items, then you, and members of your family also in the business, should comply too. Here is a checklist of essential security measures:

- Control keys effectively; install time locks and alarms. Use locks that need a key on both sides if permitted by local regulations. Employ a central-station alarm system, motion detector, or electric eye. You need every protection against the employee-thief who hides until the plant is closed and then leaves freely without evidence of forced entry.

- Guard against collusion between employees and outsiders. Rotation of security guards should be established. Make spot checks of truck loading to see that no stolen goods are on the truck. Consider closed-circuit television to guard the loading area. Supervisors should have a clear view of operations from their desks.

- Employees must not park cars in the receiving area.

- Trash cartons should be flattened; trash bins should be checked at unexpected times. Have trash collections supervised in case employees and collectors have a theft deal going.

- Make sure the receiving door is shut and locked when not in use. An alarm should ring when it is opened, and only managerial employees should have a key to turn the alarm off.

Top security areas should be guarded by a card entry system to prevent access by other than needed personnel. The latest entry systems employ fingerprint scanners and even voice-activated controls. Card systems, run in conjunction with a computer system, are cheaper and usually sufficient for most security needs.

Prosecution of employee-thieves is advised; to settle for less would encourage others to steal. Many companies now sue the thieves to recover what monies they can. Formerly, companies would hesitate to press for recovery; some even dropped criminal charges because of the fear of adverse publicity. However, because insurance companies rarely pay the full amount of the loss, more companies now try to recover for the theft by any means possible.

Protecting against Theft in the Plant

While plant theft is seldom as startling and as major as a suddenly discovered defalcation by a bookkeeper or accountant, it can, over time, reach similar proportions. And, wherever the items made, passing through, or used in the plant are commonly usable, such as hardware and auto parts, theft *always* occurs, usually in direct proportion to the lack of care taken to prevent it.

In a manufacturing plant, small tools, incoming materials, and finished goods are the common objects of theft. Inventory and returned items are usually the booty from warehouses.

Theft of incoming materials is easily controlled procedurally, although few small companies take the trouble to install them. A sample of the kinds of procedures needed follow:

- Are invoices and pick-tickets prenumbered and accounted for?

- Is incoming freight checked against purchase orders?
- Are claims made immediately for shortages?
- Are returns credited immediately?

Shrinkage is the most commonly used measure of theft of stock items. But to benefit from the measure it has to be timely and accurate. Estimating shrinkage once a year after the taking of the annual inventory is useful only for accounting purposes, not for the detection and prevention of theft. Few small businesses measure shrinkage often enough to have a preventative impact on stealing.

An important aspect of inventory control is detecting theft. Wholesale theft can put a company handling large numbers of items at slender margins—such as an auto parts distributor—out of business. The computer can help. It can make light work of taking physical counts of appropriate sample strength and reconciling them to the inventory record on a timely basis. That is much more difficult to do manually on a timely basis. Taking inventory on a rolling basis by hand often gets interrupted when business activities intensify, thus defeating the purpose of taking inventory on that basis.

Theft of hand tools is especially hard to control since they are indispensable to doing the work, hard to hold individuals responsible for, and costly to control from a tool crib. The best means of control is probably through the budgeting process tied in with some form of incentive for keeping tool costs within the budget.

Guarding against Burglary and Robbery

Crime prevention begins with elementary measures that are too often overlooked. Business premises should be thoroughly inspected when acquired for ease of access to thieves. Locks may easily be picked, doors pried from hinges, and windows and skylights broken. If you do not know who might now hold the keys to your premises, you should have the locks changed. Changing the locks from time to time is one method of preventing use of old keys by former employees or other persons.

Sheer carelessness can invite burglary. Doors, windows, and even safes are sometimes left open after closing hours. A regular routine of double-checking the premises should be established. When the owner or supervisor will be absent, other responsible persons should be designated for this duty.

Be sure that no unauthorized person is concealed on the premises at closing time; that certain lights inside and outside are left on, particularly those illuminating the safe, which should be visible to a patrolling security guard or police officer from outside; and that any adjacent alleys are also adequately lighted.

In high-crime areas, retail storefronts are now protected by various types of folding metal gates. Similar gates can be installed at particularly vulnerable windows of offices and plants. Where the glass of doors or windows can easily be broken and access gained to a lock, such protective measures should be taken.

Check with your police department as to whether it links up with alarm systems of local businesses. In your area there may be a commercial center which provides response to alarms. For both police and commercial alarm centers, false signals provide a real problem. If you have an alarm system installed at your business premises, make thorough arrangements for its use. Designate who will activate the system and turn it off; cover absence of the responsible person; and guard against accidental triggering of the alarm. Sometimes nothing more than the wind rattling poorly fitting doors and windows activates the alarm. Tests at set intervals will be necessary to check on a system and on its power sources.

Maintenance of an alarm system may seem costly, but it can reduce your insurance premiums. The more you do to stop crime, the less risk the insurance company will be taking, and they may be able to reflect this in your rates. An alarm system is a kind of insurance, one that may save you grief and money in the long run. In areas where crime insurance is unavailable, the preventive measures you take yourself are your only protection. These may include dogs, alarms, and private security guards.

Among your antiburglary measures, list these precautions: Leave cash registers empty and open so they are not damaged by hopeful thieves. Bank frequently so that little cash remains in a safe overnight. Keep the safe combination out of unauthorized hands, and change that combination when employees who know it are shifted or leave.

Armed robbery is an ever-present danger at many retail stores and at other places of business where cash or high-price merchandise is available. Large cash payrolls have proved to be a temptation to armed bandits; when possible, payment by check is preferable.

Prevention of a holdup may not be possible, but you can take reasonable precautions and instruct your staff on their conduct in the face of robbery. In general, individuals should not resist or do anything that would provoke a robber's use of arms. But if possible, a silent alarm should be triggered or, through prearranged signals, other employees alerted to the situation. Whatever happens, observation of the robber's appearance and methods of robbery and getaway can provide police with necessary clues.

Hazards of Cashing Checks

If you intend to accept checks in your business, you should establish a specific procedure that will help to weed out fraud:

- *Know your state law.* Be especially knowledgeable regarding fraudulent checks.

- *Decide if checks made out for more than the cost of goods or service will be accepted.* Establish the limit.

- *Examine all checks carefully.* Refuse those which show signs of alteration or an illegible name, have more than one endorsement, differ in figure and written amount, are stamped or typed with a company name, are not properly imprinted with the bank name and location, are not dated or are postdated, or are more than 30 days old.

- *Require identification from the check passer.* Preferably require a driver's license or government or military identification. Compare the signature on the identification with that on the check; record the identification number on the check. The person passing the check should record his or her address and telephone number on the back.

- *Know the check passer.* Refusing to cash a stranger's check may lose some business, but the loss on a bad check may be greater. Government checks are sometimes stolen, so use particular care before cashing them. Even certified checks have been altered by forgery. Check with the issuer when in doubt.

- *Verify credit cards.* Acceptance of invalid credit cards can also result in losses. The issuing company should provide a phone verification service so you can quickly find out the maximum that can be charged on that card, or whether the card has been stolen.

Protection through Insurance

It is preferable to have all employees, not only those directly involved with financial transactions, covered by fidelity bond. There are many ways in which a dishonest employee can operate, quite apart from "dipping fingers in the till." Nor should long-time, trusted employees be excluded from coverage. Change of circumstance and unusual pressures have driven many a formerly honest person to crime.

Loss through forgery may be covered in separate categories. You may protect your checks, bank drafts, etc., and forget that you have other negotiable instruments, such as bills of lading and warehouse receipts, that are also vulnerable. Where a hazard exists, you may decide to expand your coverage.

Know the terms of your insurance. You may think you have the situation covered, but after your employees are held up on the way to the bank, you may discover that all the conditions laid down by the insurers have not been fulfilled. See that your employees know special precautions demanded of them and that they do not become slack in carrying out their assignments.

Stopping Over-the-Counter Sales Thefts

The owner of the retail store must protect over-the-counter sales from the light-fingered salesclerk as well as from customer theft.

Employee theft at the retail level may take the form of ringing up items for friends and relatives at less than the ticketed price. The salesclerk who is too popular with customers or who has many friends visit the store may be doing favors that are costly to the store owner.

If clerks are permitted to buy store-damaged or returned items at a discount, see that they do not go home with substituted first-class merchandise. At no time should a clerk be allowed to ring up his or her own purchases on the cash register. These steps may also help reduce employee theft:

- Use modern equipment for counter sales, particularly cash registers, autographic registers, and charge registers. Balance the sales that are registered against cashier's funds daily. Such balancing should preferably be done by persons not in the sales or cashier's group.

- Do not permit counter salespeople to disburse any funds received.

- See that customers know they are entitled to a receipt. Advise them that subsequent adjustment depends on showing their receipts.

- Salespeople taking cash should give a receipt that is serially controlled in duplicate.

- Maintain a perpetual inventory of stock in stores where counter sales are made.

The Menace of Shoplifting

Shoplifting costs retail merchants some $8 billion annually. Merchants can expect losses to run between 2 and 15 percent. Some security people claim that one out of every three small business bankruptcies can be attributed to shoplifting losses. Some city jewelry firms now only let one customer at a time into the store. Other firms are trying to derive more of their income from mail orders.

The shoplifter is 20 percent more likely to be female than male. One survey of teenagers revealed that 70 percent had some shoplifting experience. As many as one customer in every ten may be leaving your store with merchandise for which he or she has not paid. While professional shoplifters can clear whole racks at a time, amateurs, by their sheer numbers, will account for most of your losses.

The small retailer is more vulnerable than the large corporation. The merchant may be unable to afford the more sophisticated protection devices. Moreover, a local merchant who catches a member of the community shoplifting, or possibly the son or daughter of an important customer, will think twice about a theft charge. Large department stores have become less hesitant, believing that a reputation for prosecution lowers shoplifting losses. Even though convictions occur at about a 95 percent rate, time-consuming court proceedings may represent a financial loss to the small merchant. If you are actively going to combat, arrest, and prosecute shoplifters (as opposed to figuring your losses into the cost of doing business), make sure your confrontations take place according to local law. Also, have your business insurance cover you for damages relating to suits for false arrest. Settlements of several hundred thousand dollars have been won by people falsely arrested.

Alerting Employees to Shoplifting Techniques

All salespeople and cashiers should be aware of typical shoplifting methods. Let them know that the failure to report acquaintances who steal will result in the loss of their own jobs. Your employees may know which of their friends shoplift and give them the message.

The most common shoplifting method is to conceal the merchandise in an innocent-appearing object, such as a handbag, shopping bag, box, briefcase, or closed umbrella. Ambitious shoplifters sometimes prepare boxes with ingenious fake tops or bottoms. They slip stolen items into the boxes by raising the false tops or bottoms which are pulled back into place by strong rubber bands attached to the inside of the package.

The second most common method is to conceal the merchandise in clothing. A raincoat over one arm is a useful screen. Pockets are, of course, invaluable to the youngster stealing at the local variety store and to the professional, who may wear specially prepared clothing with concealed pockets. A slit in one pocket of a coat may enable the shoplifter to transfer merchandise to a larger one inside.

Another technique is the switching of price tags. This can be foiled by the merchant who is also the cashier and remembers the price of each item in the store, which is only possible if the price is not changed frequently. Computerized price markings used by supermarkets and other retailers help to combat this ploy. The optical scanner used by the computer-assisted checkout system verifies the proper price for the item.

Baby carriages or strollers are often banned in stores, not only because they block the aisles, but also because they are used as a cache by the shoplifter. Collapsible shopping carts are also sometimes used for store theft.

Stout thieves need no special equipment. Their clothing often contains sufficient space to hold merchandise they intend to remove from the store. The change in their gait is hard to discern, though short steps may be a clue.

In apparel stores, fitting rooms are, of course, invaluable to the clothing thief who walks out wearing more clothes than on entering the fitting room.

Jewelry shoplifting has some specialized techniques. One involves the accomplice who distracts the salesperson while the theft is made by sleight-of-hand substitution of a cheap but accurate imitation of a valuable piece. In another method, a shoplifter conceals in one hand a clamp attached to strong rubber bands which run up the sleeve and are fastened securely. While examining a ring or some other piece of jewelry, the thief fastens the clamp to it and so whisks the prize up his or her sleeve.

Pairs and groups of shoplifters will often work together to divert attention. Young people particularly, not necessarily professional shoplifters, may enter a store en masse. A disturbance is a favorite cover for theft.

Devices other than "lifting" an article may be employed by the store thief. Returning an item for refund that was in fact taken from the shelves is one method. The clerk accepting the returned merchandise should see that it comes in a bag and has the sales check with it and that the customer has not been roving the store before coming to the checkout counter. Insistence on the return of sales checks helps retailers to protect themselves from giving refunds on merchandise stolen from other stores, as well as from their own.

Retailers need the cooperation of employees in antishoplifting tactics. Employees should be trained to recognize likely theft devices and to be alert for new ploys. Watchful employees patrolling the aisles, particularly when the store is busy, can help to safeguard stock against the amateur or impulse shoplifter. The determined thief is full of tricks. Salesclerks should try to keep the customer in view when filling a request and reckon with the fact that people who appear to be strangers to one another may in fact be accomplices.

Antishoplifting Devices and Methods

The interior arrangement of the retail store should provide maximum visibility. Racks, counters, and tables should be as low as possible and not offer cover to the shoplifter. Convex wall mirrors that enable store personnel to watch the aisles are necessary in many types of businesses.

Locked display cabinets should be used for expensive merchandise. The checkout counter where cashiers are in attendance is frequently used for the display of items that are easily stolen.

Signs warning against shoplifting may usefully be posted in some types of business. Letting the potential thief know you are alert and employing protective devices may serve as a deterrent.

A customer going to a fitting room should be handed a tag corresponding in number to the number of garments taken in. When the customer leaves the fitting room, a clerk checks that the number on the tag and the number of garments are the same. Shoplifters may try to take more garments than are permitted into the fitting room. Salesclerks should be alert to this possibility.

Doors not in regular use should be locked unless such locking would violate fire ordinances. Check with your local authorities.

Fast service is recommended as a deterrent to shoplifting. Sales checks should be given to the customer to confirm payment and should not be discarded by the cashier. Shoplifters watch for sales checks scattered around. They use them to protect themselves or to return a stolen item for "refund."

When shoplifters are suspected in a store, the staff should be able to alert one another by the use of a prearranged signal or code.

The arrangement of merchandise and its tidiness are important. Do not stack goods so that they obscure the view or make it easy for a thief to sweep items into a bag or pocket.

Lifting from the cash register, a type of theft known as "till tapping," can be discouraged by placing registers away from customer access and keeping the amount of cash at a low level. Drill employees in a register routine which calls for closing the drawer immediately after giving change. Employees should avoid being distracted by a customer while the drawer is open, thus making it easy for an accomplice to rifle the till. A register not in use must be locked.

The marking of merchandise with sensitized tags has proved to be a useful deterrent to retail-store theft. The tags cannot be removed by a would-be shoplifter without damage to the merchandise. The thief trying to sneak out of the door with stolen items that are still tagged would set off an alarm system.

At larger stores, many devices and systems are being used in the antishoplifting war, many of which are beyond the means of small firms. But closed-circuit television is not beyond the range of business owners' pocketbooks. The use of television to keep its ever-present eye on cashiers, clerks, and customers alike is increasing. The cost of TV surveillance systems has plummeted in recent years, making them worthwhile in operations where losses can be extensive, as on shipping docks and out-of-sight aisles in warehouses and retail stores.

Apprehending Shoplifters

Many retailers shrink from confronting shoplifters, but that is a mistake that only encourages more shoplifting. Consult with the police to determine what local law permits in such confrontations. Less than half the states have criminal legislation specifically covering shoplifting. You may have to make a citizen's arrest, or you may be able simply to detain the suspect until the police arrive. Find out for sure before you open your doors. A storekeeper should fear accusations of false arrest or defamation of character.

In some cases in which the store owner is certain of the theft, he or she or a representative may follow the shoplifter outside and say, "I believe you forgot to pay for something." To wait until the thief leaves the store makes sure there is no intention to pay and no opportunity to get rid of stolen goods. Many states allow arrests inside the store if the retailer can prove intent. Intent may be shown if the customer has taken the item past the cash register for that department or has secreted the item inside his or her clothing. Check with authorities to see how local law views arrests when the customer has merely put an item in his or her pocket. After all, the customer may be legitimately absentminded.

Some shoplifting laws allow retailers to detain someone for a reasonable time in a reasonable manner. Some laws allow a retailer to deny a suspect telephone calls.

17

Office Management and Efficiency

The office is the nerve center of most businesses. From it the activities of the typical business are coordinated: Orders are received and entered, purchases are made to fill the orders, records are maintained and stored. The office is where management decisions are planned and executed, and where the activities of the enterprise are coordinated.

Physically the office may be one room, a suite of rooms, or extend over several floors (an arrangement to be avoided, if possible). The size and physical layout of the office varies with the nature, size, and maturity of the firm, but the basic furniture and equipment—desks, telephones, fax machines, typewriters, calculators, computers, and filing cabinets—do not. They are common to all offices and are significant considerations in meeting the need for efficiency in coping with the communications deluge—the high volumes of paperwork, telephone messages, and mail inherent in being in business.

Offices very much reflect the management styles of the people that run the companies. Some are attractive, some are messes, others are somewhere in between. As there are people who consciously dress to impress, there are also offices which are laid out and designed to impress.

Which is the more efficient cannot be settled by appearances alone. The facts are that attractiveness and neatness do not of themselves make an office efficient. But this much can be concluded: The office is the place where many people have their first contacts with a business, and initial impressions hold importance for a company. So, moderate attention to detail can make a positive public image. Orderliness is also a prime factor in the creation of efficiency.

Designing the Office Space

Whatever your aesthetic or management style choices are, the layout of your office should be designed to be efficient. Layout is a good place to start. Also, consider which tasks can be performed better if personnel performing related duties were located next to each other or next to a frequently utilized machine. When you employ a large office staff, you generally have to decide between having (1) separate rooms for each worker or group of workers or (2) an open office space in which the staff works, and which may be divided by partitions to separate space according to an overall organizational plan. Many manufacturers offer freestanding screens and panels, modular and L-shaped work units, and furniture with built-in shelving and filing space, all of which can be easily combined into any pattern the business finds convenient. The open office is popular because it permits less-expensive changes and because the partitions can be easily shifted. Only one temperature control system is needed for the comfort of many workers. Wiring for electric power, computers, and telephone equipment is less costly to pull up and rearrange.

However, some workers require a separate office, especially those who are often on the telephone as part of their job and who may disturb other workers unless situated in separate quarters. Individual offices also help insulate those who need a quiet atmosphere to concentrate or need privacy because of the nature of their work. The addition of sound-and-noise reduction materials may be a good investment to increase productivity. Managers and executives also prefer separate office space, if only to reinforce their image and status.

When planning your firm's office space, make adequate provision for reception room, conference room, storage, and vaults. The reception room should have 10 square feet per person for the maximum number of people who may come at one time and a minimum size of 50 square feet.

Your office should contain adequate personal comfort facilities: restrooms, coatrooms, locker space, drinking fountains, and coffee machines. The average office needs at least one toilet and one sink for every 15 persons; more sinks may be necessary depending upon the type of work being done. Local regulations may require two toilet facilities: one for males and one for females. Under the new Americans with Disabilities Act, additional facilities may be required for the handicapped. Offices sometimes provide shower facilities as a consideration and encouragement for employees who jog or bicycle to work.

Filling Lighting Requirements

Be sure you have adequate lighting in the office. Poor lighting means eyestrain and tired and grumbling employees. Fatigue can be reduced by better lighting. Compare your existing light with accepted standards by use of a light meter. The electric company in your vicinity will aid you willingly in your study. In looking ahead and planning for the future, you may want to consider installing lighting fixtures that conserve energy. Generally, commercial and industrial customers who receive subsidies from public utilities for installing energy-saving lighting equipment are taxed on the value of the subsidy received. However, starting in 1995, under the Energy Policy Act, 40 percent of any subsidy received from a public utility may be excluded from income. The exclusion is increased to 50 percent in 1996 and to 65 percent in all future years.

Fine, detailed work requires more light. For instance, drafting workers need 6 times as much light as mail room workers. Artificial lighting should be of good quality to avoid glare and shadows and to increase efficiency of workers. Fluorescent lighting is available and closely approximates natural light; it is commonly marketed for indoor garden use, but also serves well as office lighting.

Study equipment to obtain fixtures that will properly direct the light. Glass-top or highly polished desks cause glare. Avoid too great a contrast of light in different parts of the same room. Consider use of indirect lighting and translucent bowls or fluorescent lighting to increase diffusion of light.

Efficiency of lighting may depend largely on getting maximum reflection from ceiling and walls. Flat white is the most satisfactory color for the ceiling, but flat white paint on the walls reflects up to 90 percent of the light, causing glare. Buff, light blue, or green will reflect about 60 percent of the light, creating a more restful condition for the eyes. Much work has been done by psychologists on the impact of colors in the workplace. Investigate the best choices for you.

Equipping the Office

To determine standards for buying office equipment, ask yourself the following questions: Does the item speed up office work by making records easier to find, fill out, or understand? Does it promote greater accuracy or provide greater protection in the handling of cash, securities, mail, and other office valuables?

If you are considering equipment which will change routine operations, first seek an office demonstration of the equipment, especially with the employees who will use it. Listen to their comments; do not buy equipment which they will not feel comfortable with and which they may resist using, unless you believe they will accommodate themselves to the equipment in a short time.

Before buying new office machinery, find out if there is used equipment available that will meet your needs at less cost. There are dealers who specialize in renting or selling used equipment, in addition to the nationwide brokers who handle used office machinery. Less expensive still are sources of used machinery available from bankruptcy auctions and General Service Administration (GSA) auctions of used government equipment. Here, however, the machinery comes "as is," so that repair costs may cancel out your savings.

In acquiring office equipment, do not buy equipment that does not use the same standard supplies as other equipment in the office. Do not buy equipment for which use, though advantageous, is confined to short periods. Machinery is often acquired in the mistaken hope that it can be used more extensively.

The desks and chairs of your office workers, secretaries, typists, and clerks should conform to certain standards of comfort to eliminate backache and general fatigue. Desks should be about 29 inches high—a natural working height, should have adequate drawer space and compartments, racks for cards, stationery, and accessories, letter and filing trays, and partitions for particular jobs to be done.

To facilitate asset control make a card for each piece of equipment, recording the manufacturer, serial number, model, cost, date of purchase, type of work performed, location, etc. Keep a record also of maintenance costs, perhaps on the reverse side of the equipment card, showing the dates of repairs. Such records can be conveniently maintained with a simple computer database system.

If you enter into a maintenance contract with the manufacturer who made your equipment, see that repair people come regularly to clean and oil machines and that they respond to emergency calls as well.

Maintenance can drain finances. If repair of a purchased machine is running more than 15 percent of its cost, consider replacing it.

The rental of office equipment may save costs. Some machines are, in fact, usually rented rather than sold to small businesses, for example, photocopying machines. Check into rentals for your office needs before committing yourself to a purchase.

Computers and Automation

No discussion of office management would be complete without recognizing automation and computerization. Technological breakthroughs have expanded common office equipment (i.e., typewriters, copying machines, calculators, etc.) capabilities to the point where serious management consideration should be given to upgrading the routine office tasks.

Without question, the introduction of computers in smaller, more powerful, and economically usable forms has created what may be considered to be a most powerful tool for small, as well as larger, businesses. For this reason, we have devoted the next chapter of this book to selecting and using computers.

Efficient Work Habits

Although the capital investment for office equipment and overhead can be sizable, the cost of labor contributes the largest part of the expense of running an office. Work efficiency can lower costs.

Check for wasted motions and duplicated efforts:

- Is there a specific and understood purpose for each office operation?

- Does work move directly from one person to another without unnecessary repetition, duplication, or delays?

- Do certain details or records require more time than the results are worth?

- Are personnel supplied with the necessary materials to perform the step or operation without unnecessary delays to get material?

- How does your staff work? Can you eliminate unnecessary interruptions, arguments and gossiping, absences from desks, delays in answering questions, procrastination, or unnecessary questions?

If your salespeople or executives dictate their letters, instruct them to organize their thoughts and make meaningful notes before dictating. They should try to adhere to a definite dictating schedule, preferably at the same time each day. They should make a practice of spelling out all technical terms and proper names. An office dictionary is a necessity, as well as a spelling checker with your word processing program.

Sometimes time may be wasted in preparing individualized business letters when phone calls may be quicker and cheaper. But if you want your instructions or discussion on record, written correspondence is most effective.

When possible, standard form letters and paragraphs should be used. Keep these on file. Specialized word processor equipment with suitable software programs provide storage and easy access to standard form responses.

A style manual will help your stenographers to prepare neat, well-organized letters. The stenographic station should also contain a file of names, addresses, and telephone numbers of all clients and suppliers and a list of difficult spellings and terms that commonly appear in your business correspondence.

Insist on written messages; concise interoffice memos save time, minimize misunderstandings, and serve as reminders. A three-tiered basket on each desk can receive all incoming, outgoing, and file papers.

Be sure your senior office personnel impart to their juniors the tricks of the trade, and that the tools of the trade are properly and fully used. For example, experienced clerks who send mail to the same branch offices every day know to address a supply of envelopes to the branch offices in their slack time. Rubber stamps are also available for commonly used addresses. However, be on the alert for employees who withhold information from others for job protection or other reasons. This can cripple an operation.

Economical Habits

Teach your staff to use office supplies as sparingly as if they were personally paying for them. Recognize that waste in supplies can be due to mere lack of control. Avoid serious waste in deterioration or obsolescence of supplies, and issue supplies in limited quantities to each desk to reduce spoilage and waste. With sufficient tact, you can discourage wasteful habits on the part of your staff. Of course, you do not want your company to become known for a petty attitude over minor concerns. A contented staff will be willing to observe little economies out of habit. Encourage your workers to turn off lights and electrically driven machines when leaving their desks, at noon, at rest periods, and at closing time. Nothing that can be reused for another purpose should be thrown away. Discarded photocopies and obsolete forms can be used for scratch paper.

Select the most economical grade and size of paper for each purpose except in situations in which quality paper is necessary to create an impression.

Copy machines may be used to reduce costs. Copy machines can be used to produce form letters, business forms, or even artwork. Many copy machines today do not require special paper, which thus reduces costs.

Review Office Expenses

Periodically review office expenses by examining payroll records, purchase records, and service-charge records to determine payments for office rental, light and heat, machines, supplies, postage, clerical help, and telephone use. Translate each expense into a percentage of the total.

The use of outside services for particular jobs such as addressing and mailing may be more economical than using skilled employees. Some savings may be made by using part-time help, such as students working after school, who can be paid the minimum wage for unskilled work and short-term routine jobs.

The Office Manager

The larger your office, the more you need someone to serve as an office manager. There should be someone to help facilitate office procedures by assigning and overseeing the work, to see that supplies are distributed and accounted for, to make sure that all relevant memos are circulated, to make sure that the proper reference publications are subscribed to, and to act as a troubleshooter in making temporary adjustments to office equipment. In many small offices, these matters are too trivial for the chief executive's attention, so the responsibility of maintaining office functions should be delegated to the head clerk or secretary.

Filing Procedures

- Devise an overall filing plan and adhere to it. Train your personnel to sort papers before filing, through the use of sorter trays, etc.

- File promptly, preferably daily, so that work does not pile up. When folders are full, use expansion folders or divide folders; this will conserve supplies.

- Insist that folders taken from the files be returned as soon as possible. If you have difficulty with this, consider making a rule that all outstanding records be returned to the files at the close of each working day.

- Keep track of records through the use of a tickler system, so that you will know when records are outstanding for more than the usual length of time.

- Examine the contents of file drawers occasionally to see if all papers are worth saving. Material with a limited usefulness should be purged periodically.

- Do not fill drawers so full that papers cannot be removed easily or without pulling out unwanted material.

Establish and adhere to a time schedule for the retention of records in the files. Clean out the files regularly. Organize the transfer system carefully. Appoint someone to work out the procedures and be responsible for the follow-up. Work this way:

- Classify what is to be destroyed and what is to be transferred. Decide how long various types of papers and records are to be kept. Observe financial and legal guidelines.

- Mark on the copy, at the time written, the date for its disposal. Have the filing department remove outdated material from the files as they file new material.

- Recognize that filing affects a good many departments and people with differing views and requirements.

- Survey what is being filed. Eliminate from permanent files unnecessary duplicates that may come back to the filing department from several departments. Decide which copy to keep—preferably one of distinctive color.

- Set up a routine for automatically disposing of unneeded carbons or photocopies after some established interval has passed.

Consider these three methods of sorting outdated material for the needs of your business and choose the most economical one:

- Regularly switch the entire contents from current files to transfer boxes.

- Regularly transfer out of current files only the material over a given age (say 1 year old) to transfer boxes.

- Maintain two sets of filing cabinets; use the upper row of drawers for current files and the lower for transferred documents. This expedites reference to recent files and material not recently transferred. At fixed periods transfer the old files to storage. Always maintain a cross index of materials in transfer files and their storage location.

Consider the use of microfilm. Many firms save on storage costs by having their records microfilmed. A roomful of records can be condensed to small rolls of film occupying a mere cabinet of space. These rolls can also be safely stored in bank vaults. Film has the advantage of binding records in a definite, unchangeable order, making loss of one record in a group impossible. Fraudulent alteration of records becomes impossible, and the transportation and transfer of records are accomplished more economically.

Microfilming can be handled by outside services, but if use justifies the cost, obtain a microfilmer for your offices through lease or purchase.

Designing Forms for Your Business

The stationery, documents, and other forms you choose for your business should simplify your company's activities. Clarity is an objective of good form design. The instructions, printed across the top, should leave no question as to procedure and purpose. Columns should be aligned under their proper titles, with an occasional horizontal line to break up the page and keep the divisions separated.

Assorted forms, labels, folders, letters, and memos are sold in stationery supply stores or are available more cheaply from mail-order firms. Businesses can choose unadorned letterheads or designer forms. Carbon duplicates offer a savings over the more popular, less messy, carbonless paper products. Money can be saved by ordering the correct size paper products to suit your business. For example, an invoice may have 8 lines or 20. If your typical customer purchases only one or two items, the smaller pads offer a savings. Consider the average size of your memos for the most efficient memo pads. The same forethought can save you money when ordering stationery, folders, ledgers, etc. No forms should be ordered without consulting the workers who do your paperwork every day. They are in the best position to know your needs and requirements.

Inexpensive computer programs are available that permit you to easily prepare your own forms, tailored to your own needs. The forms are filled out right on the computer screen, allowing a record of the form and a printed copy to be prepared at the same time. An inventory of preprinted forms is not needed, and the required forms can be modified at any time.

Review your paper requirements periodically. Some forms and documents may no longer be essential and can be eliminated or adapted to other paper documents. Self-copying documents may become unnecessary as photocopying or multiple-entry bookkeeping practices become routine. Also, rubberstamping certain information may be cheaper than printing certain special, seldom-used letterheads. Paperwork is the biggest problem for many entrepreneurs. The forms you must file for others are troublesome enough. Do not create more of your own paperwork than is really necessary.

Duplicating and Printing Services

Your needs for duplicated or printed material may be small. A laser printer or photocopying machine is sufficient for many offices; others with greater needs find it cheaper to install more complex equipment, even to set up a small offset print shop or phototypesetter on their premises. You should consider leasing rather than purchasing certain types of equipment, especially if your needs arise only at particular times of the year.

Outside services are available for all types of copying and duplicating, as well as printing. Check the yellow pages of your telephone directory under letter shop services, copying and duplicating services, duplicating machines and supplies, photocopying, data processing services, and typesetting (which includes computerized typesetting). Request brochures, and watch for new developments which take place constantly in the equipment and services offered in this area.

Every year improved technology expands the capabilities of electronic paper copiers. Each year new purchasers looking for a copier to suit their needs generally find more choices and better bargains. Machines can copy on both sides of the page, change the size of the material being copied, copy materials of many different sizes, and make color copies and transparencies. Copiers can also sort and collate the documents being reproduced. Also available are all-in-one devices that operate as a computer printer, fax machine, and copier.

In determining the cost of a copier, do not overlook the cost of processing a copy. The paper, electricity, and developing chemicals may run anywhere from 1 to 10 cents a page. The more copies you make, the better it is for you to purchase a machine with a low cost per copy. A business making infrequent copies might get a copier with a high cost per copy but a low initial purchase price, making the overall copier costs inexpensive. A copier can cost anywhere from $400 to $10,000, so an infrequent user may indeed find savings in an inexpensive machine with higher operating costs.

Dealing with Your Printer

Your printing needs will be best served if you can locate a printer who can fill all your requirements quickly and to your specifications.

Invite bids from printers who are properly equipped to do your type of work. Ordinarily they will be able to turn out the work at the best price. When seeking estimates, give complete specifications. Get bids from at least two sources. If one bid is unreasonably higher than the other, you can assume that the printer does not have the necessary equipment to do your work economically. Among reputable printing establishments, higher costs do not necessarily indicate better quality.

Consult with your printer before planning a job in detail. You can get valuable tips on effective type size, paper, folding, and mailing. Weigh the advantages against the cost whenever you consider the use of extra color, tricky layouts, oversized pages, or excessive corrections.

To control your composition costs, make sure all the printed or typed copy you submit is clean. If you use a computer to input your copy, you may be able to save money by submitting a disk to the printer. Edit all copy carefully. Corrections after your information has been typeset may be expensive. It does not pay to send copy to the printer long in advance of publication. Changes may occur which make it necessary to alter the material; and these changes can be very costly.

Be aware that an unspoken custom in the printing trade permits the printer up to a 10 percent deviation from the number of copies ordered by the customer. On small orders, a 10 percent deviation is common; on large orders, it is usually smaller. For example, it is not uncommon for an order of 3000 pamphlets to produce as few as 2700 or as many as 3300 copies. You are charged for the actual number of copies produced. Take such possible deviations into account when planning your orders.

Do not overlook your computer system. It may have a printer whose print quality is adequate for your printing needs and have a program allowing for attractive, customized formats. Thus time and money can be saved, in addition to having greater control over the job—particularly for last-minute changes.

Reducing Mailing Costs

Watch these details to cut your mailing costs:

- If you want an envelope to hold no more than 1 ounce, you need not necessarily confine the contents to one sheet. With some lightweight paper, especially useful for airmail, nine sheets weigh only $\frac{1}{2}$ ounce.

- Large first-class envelopes should be clearly marked or stamped "first class"; otherwise, they may be mistaken for slower mail and delayed in transit.

- In place of stamped, self-addressed envelopes for reply, business-reply cards and envelopes permit you to pay only on those actually returned.

- Demurrage charges on c.o.d. mail can be avoided by using address labels recommended by the U.S. Postal Service, giving specific instructions if undelivered.

- Check with the post office for the least expensive mailing arrangements when mailing books or catalogs. Here are some examples: Send books and tapes at book or fourth-class rates; if your airmail packages weigh less than 4 pounds, you can save by using small packet rates. Also use, when possible, a priority envelope. For a modest charge, you can put in as much weight as the envelope will hold. Priority mail is generally delivered in 2 days.

- Your covering invoice, if it applies strictly to the package contents, can be enclosed in the package. That saves postage and the time of preparation that would be required if the invoice were mailed first class later.

- Special delivery should not be confused with special handling: Special handling gets extra speed in handling only to the post office in the addressed area; special-delivery mail is also speeded to the addressee's post office, but it is delivered directly to that address by other than the usual letter carrier. Check what actually happens with special-delivery mail to the areas that you service. In some areas, special delivery means later delivery. You and your mail contacts may find time and money saved by using regular mail delivery instead of special delivery.

Investigate mechanical aids that might save money and time in handling, such as hand stamp affixers, envelope openers, sorting racks and tables to facilitate sorting and dispatching mail to various departments, folding and inserting machines, addressing machines, postage scales, parcel post machines, scaling machines, combined sealing and stamping machines, metering permit machines, nonmetering permit machines, and tying and bundling machines.

Remember that your computer can also serve as an addressing machine. Most word processing programs have a mail-merge feature that individually addresses and alters text for form letters. These programs also can prepare mailing labels, sorted by zip code so that you can save money by presorting bulk mailings.

Avoid the use of clips or other weighty material in your mail. Charge postage to the department sending out the mail. If you request periodic reports on the postage ordered, your department heads will be more careful about usage. Finally, investigate the services of private carriers. For certain deliveries, you may find that they offer faster and more economical service than regular mail, with greater reliability and better insurance on the delivery.

Telephone and Electronic Communications

The range of telephone service and equipment is constantly changing, and as in the case of computers, the wide choice of equipment may be initially bewildering until you become generally familiar with what is available and determine what might meet your needs.

Even before you invest in equipment, you must deal with your local telephone company, which will provide the link from your business to the outside. Inquire about the fees charged and the various types of services provided by the company. You cannot avoid the cost of the initial hookup, but before placing your order, determine the number of lines that you will need. If you are first starting out, one line may be sufficient. The cost of installation will not cover additional outlets on your premises. The number of outlets will depend on the necessary locations of use. You may have the telephone company install them, but before you do get an estimate of their charges. If the installation charges will be high, you may save by installing the outlets yourself. Local electronic stores offer a wide selection of hookup devices and outlets.

If you install several telephone lines, it is advisable to list only one number in the yellow pages; this frees the remaining lines for placing calls.

You must also decide on long distance service. Rates and services are competitive. Special offers can save you substantial money. Call each company offering long distance service for rates and plans.

Telephone devices have developed far beyond the traditional handset. There are portable phones, answering machines, and fax machines. Efficient, inexpensive fax machines are widely available and should be considered for the instant sending and receiving of business correspondence. If your volume of fax use is low, the fax machine can be hooked into your regular telephone line. Most fax machines allow for both telephone and fax use, and sometimes an electronic splitter may be used to distinguish between fax and telephone calls on a single line. However, if volume is frequent during the work day, use a separate line and number for the fax. If you are planning to invest in a copier and computer printer, consider a machine that incorporates the three functions of computer printer, copier, and fax. If such a unit is possible given your needs, you may save both money and space.

Telephone systems are costly to maintain, and it is important to review all monthly bills. Such a review will uncover any telephone company errors, which can then be corrected. It may also reveal employee abuse of the system for personal calls. Inexpensive devices can be added to a business telephone system that will restrict outgoing calls to certain exchanges or area codes.

18

Computers in Small Business

Computers now dominate our personal and business life. If you are already familiar with computers, you do not have to be convinced of their incredible versatility and utility. If you are not, you are failing to take advantage of a device that can serve you in every phase of your business. You can make up for your inexperience by taking courses available in your community or you can with a modest investment—often under $1000—buy a personal computer package with "user-friendly" software that is especially designed for beginners to operate powerful applications. In the light of the current state of computer art, ignorance is no excuse for not taking advantage of the latest computer technology.

Type of System

There are two levels of computer use: (1) general utility and (2) intensive business application.

General Utility

You can invest in a moderately priced personal computer which you can use to do all of your business correspondence, such as letter and memos; keep an accurate and running list of customers and clients; maintain and print mailing addresses; and even run an inexpensive and efficient accounting system. Mastering a personal computer is simply a matter of practice—a valuable learning experience that is within the reach of everyone. Such experience will teach you at first hand the capacity and shortcomings of computers and programs and help you to develop a sophisticated system when your business requires such a system.

Almost daily, advertisements feature personal computer systems which can be bought not only in specialized computer stores but also in general department stores. This wide availability gives you the opportunity to review the latest models and become acquainted with features and prices. The market tends to offer computers in price ranges set according to features such as speed, memory, and monitor quality. All currently available personal computers are fast and come with substantial memory capacity. However, the development of software designed for vast amounts of data and screen representation has required the development of fast machines with enormous memory capacity. You may have no need for such capacity, especially in the beginning. If you think you may later need such capacity, try to invest in equipment that will allow for later expansion.

Review a system not only for its speed and memory but also for the number of ports, which allow for connection of printers, a mouse, and other devices. A modem, an electronic device that allows the transmission of data over telephone lines, is a must for outside communication. Buying a computer with an internal modem will save you the cost of installing one. Check the quality of the monitor. Select one that reproduces a clearly defined screen. Do not skimp here, because eyestrain may interfere with your operation of the computer. Make sure that the system comes with at least a 1-year warranty that provides for local service. Equally important is the support service offered by the computer and the software manufacturer. Can you use a free "800" telephone number to get answers to your questions? Some companies skimp, and will answer only at *your* expense. As for software programs, almost all personal computer systems now offered for sale come packaged with basic and useful software. As for price, a system offered by a major computer company may cost slightly more than lowered-price units of a "clone" producer. However, the quality and support service of a major producer may be worth the extra cost.

Finally, as a beginner, do not be discouraged by the surface complexity of computer systems and the jargon you will encounter. Make it a habit to read magazines, such as *PC Magazine* or *Byte,* for product reviews or computer equipment and software. Not all devices are equally efficient, although to the beginner they may all look alike. Intensively advertised new software may have bugs; look for reviews, which will warn you of any specific problems a software package may have. Keeping current will also have a positive consequence by alerting you to new products that can improve your business efficiency.

Intensive Business Applications

Depending upon the capacity of the system and the needs of management, a business can use a computer for a great range of functions, including counting yesterday's cash intake; routine and specialized accounting; inventory control and purchasing; analysis; filing of statistics, documents, and correspondence; electronic mailing; coordinating and implementing schedules and calendars; calculating or modeling; and linking offices.

Unless extreme care is taken in computerizing your business functions, the increased capabilities of computers and their decreasing hardware costs may accelerate the generation of useless data. Your installation need not experience such shortcomings if you recognize and seek to implement the following principles. The installation that cuts paper proliferation has this configuration:

- It is tailored to the current and forecasted needs of the firm.
- It has software which exceeds the demand on it.
- It has hardware with excess capacity.
- It has clear documentation.
- It has users who understand what it can do.
- It is responsive to users' requirements.
- It is well controlled (that is, run on schedule and protected against intrusion upon its time and application).

The steps in selecting a computer system are the following:

1. Determine the types and schedules of reports that will be *required* to run the business.
2. Define the reports that can be accessed by computer.
3. Employ the services of a system professional, perhaps from your accounting firm, to review and confirm your individual business's requirements and assist in selecting software and hardware.
4. Prepare system flowcharts depicting the sources, movement, and application of data.
5. Review the commercially available software packages which will produce the reports. Determine which packages may best suit your projected requirements.

6. Select the computer hardware that can utilize the software. Determine which equipment offers the best price performance and can still provide for future growth or expansion. Expansion may not be as simple as just adding another computer because the software for one computer may not be compatible with a different computer type.

Judging Future Needs

Before you select a computer system, you must understand how you plan to use it, looking from the present into the future. Will your business be the same in 3 years? If not, how will it change or expand? In the broadest terms, what informational needs do you have now and what needs will you have in 3 years? Computerizing your manual systems will require all the information now in manually created files to be put into a computer-readable language. This requires someone to "keystroke" all the data. In many installations this will have to be done several times because inadequate planning and thought have gone into analyzing what the business is doing today and what it will be doing in 3 years. Careful thought and homework at the outset will save future problems.

When you started your business, you probably prepared a business plan. Now you must develop a computer plan. In the language of information managers, this is called a system study. As the owner of a small business, you may elect to develop your system requirements entirely by yourself. But that is a mistake. Have the people whose activities produce information and those who need to be informed about the activities describe the activities performed, what they need to know about them, and suggest how a computer can assist them as well. On the other hand, don't risk losing control over the design. Although you want as many inputs as possible, make certain that only you or your designated specialist selects and sequences the output of the system.

At this point, it is essential to organize the data and information requests using a schematic diagram that identifies the departmental functions and the movement of information amongst these entities. This schematic is called a *flowchart* because it pictorially shows the transfer or "flow" of data created by business transactions and the recording and reporting requirements of the respective organizational units.

Accuracy and efficiency of data and generated information are dramatically enhanced when data can be entered only once into your system and automatically carried throughout all the necessary related subfunctions. This is called *integration,* and its significance is apparent when selecting the computer hardware and software required to service management's needs.

Figure 18.1 reflects the flow of information between functional modules in a fully integrated system: Completing a chart like this for your organization will help you understand your information requirements. It will show how the functions interrelate and assist in determining a

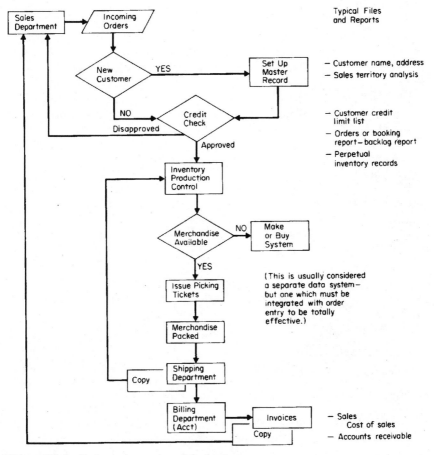

Figure 18-1. Order-entry system flowchart.

logical sequence and priority for automating them. From the "wish list" feedback described above, you can define the actual report formats to satisfy the demands of your management personnel and those of governmental or financial institutions.

Figure 18.1 is a simplified pictorial representation of one particular system—order entry. Each major system should be described in as much detail as possible.

Figure 18.2, using an alternative method of flowcharting, depicts each class of transactions in their relationships of one department to another. The specific files and reports must each be described in sufficient detail to ensure that the software system ultimately selected will fulfill the total needs of each group.

The flowchart is intended to show the types of transactions occurring in each organizational unit, how and at what point the system should be informed about the transactions, the use the system will make of the input, and the output the system will provide. It is vital that each organizational unit understand its own information needs and the dependence other departments have on that information.

It is necessary to organize the various divisions into recognized subsystems. For example:

General ledger accounting

Payroll

Inventory control

Order entry

Production scheduling

Bills of material

Purchasing (including make-or-buy evaluations)

Accounts receivable

Accounts payable

Cost accounting

Sales forecasting and analyses

Financial planning and budgeting

Give priority to implementing systems with given significant economic payback in terms of greater operating efficiencies, better and faster management information, and the development and maintenance of more accurate records.

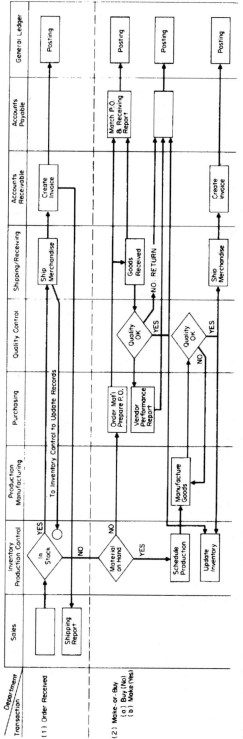

Figure 18-2. Transaction flowchart diagram. (In the illustration for item 1, order received, we have omitted the initiation of a customer master file and the credit-checking procedure. If you select this diagramming approach, you would, of course, show the data flow relationships among several departments for various report requirements.)

Software Selection

Once you have completed the initial systems plan and established priorities, you can turn your attention to software selection. While it may seem backward to investigate software before selecting hardware, keep in mind that the computer you buy must be suited to the program that can do your work. Finding the right hardware is the easiest part of finding the right computer for the job. Software and hardware are not entirely sequential tasks. Consideration of the hardware (computer type and model) should always be kept near the surface of the software selection process.

There are thousands of software packages available to today's computer user. It is worthwhile to take the time to find the ones most suited to your needs. Why reinvent the wheel? In today's computer environment, it is usually not necessary to have someone create software just for your business. Well-documented programs are available for purchase (or rent) for almost every kind of business.

Preprogrammed packages are almost always more reliable than do-it-yourself system analysis and programming. An off-the-shelf package can be seen in operation at another noncompeting firm in your industry. In-house created programs are usually developed by programmers whose experience is limited to the needs at hand, who have little exposure to the mistakes other programmers working to develop similar software have made, and whose general programming backgrounds are limited. The programs they produce are seldom documented properly and require frequent revisions or patching to make them operational. Purchased software packages have more substantial guarantees to work, and usually do.

Some software packages may offer certain flexible options that may prove valuable for your needs. Steer clear of modifying packaged software systems because you may lose the capability of automatic program updating (from the suppliers) and the facility to change to other larger or more powerful equipment in the future.

Where to Find the Software

Ask the help of your computer vendor, visit computer stores, go to the library, get some personal computer magazines, ask your accountant, contact computer consultants, and most important of all, speak to users in your industry. Whatever you do, be certain your system has the capacity and flexibility to do much more than you need today.

Carefully evaluate or have the documentation for both the hardware and the software evaluated before you commit yourself to a purchase.

One need not be a computer scientist to comprehend it. The documentation helps you and your employees learn to use the hardware and software and serves as reference material in the future. If any offered material is not understandable to you, continue to look for products that are understandable.

Selecting the Computer

What will it cost you to learn how to use the system? For comparative purposes, figure the cost of the time you must spend operating the computer. Measure that against the cost of doing the same tasks your regular way. You may well find that programs written for a particular routine, say accounts receivable, are more work than they are worth.

Some computer experts recommend buying machines that have been proven in service (but this means these units may be outmoded sooner). Be certain to contact other users, whose names can be obtained from the prospective equipment suppliers. Seek out users whose business is the same or similar to yours and discuss their favorable and unfavorable experiences with the hardware and the software. This should help you in your selection process.

Try to establish how many user terminals, known as CRTs (cathode ray tubes), and printers you will require in your system to achieve your data processing objectives. Make certain that the hardware you select can accommodate the total number of devices that you specify and perhaps provide the capacity to add additional units in the future as your system needs grow and expand.

Select the printer, or combination of printers, that will exceed your long-range requirements for print quality and speed. Look for speed, print quality, price, and noise level. The laser printer is the printer of choice, replacing the "daisy-wheel" and dot-matrix printers for letters, memos, and routine office communication. The speed and versatility of a laser printer make it an overwhelming favorite. As previously discussed, you may want to purchase a unit that will combine the functions of high-speed laser printing with fax-machine capabilities.

Computer Maintenance

Two types of maintenance contracts are available once the warranty period expires: on site and carry in.

On site means that you can call a service person whenever you have a problem or want the equipment cleaned. It is expensive. It may cost one-fourth to one-half the original cost of your hardware per year. Depending on available personnel, service may range from excellent to poor. *Carry in* prepaid maintenance, where you bring the equipment to the service company, is far cheaper and quite popular. But as prices on personal computers continue to go down, people are increasingly opting to pay for maintenance as things break.

In many stores where computers are sold, their personnel may not be fully trained in the operations and maintenance of the units. In addition, their service departments give first priority to their prepaid customers. As a result, you may have to pay a premium to have their service person look at your machine. One thing is probable: Your computer will break down when you need it the most. Therefore, address the maintenance problem before you buy the equipment.

Installation and Training

Each system should be run in parallel with the manual systems for at least 2 months until the computer system seems to work without a hitch. During this period, users are taught how to read and understand the manual, how to use the equipment, and how to get out of trouble should a problem arise during operations.

Data can be lost through electric surges, mechanical failure, dust, static electricity, and heat. Surge protectors, antistatic mats, and, sometimes, air conditioning will reduce failure. Therefore, users must be trained to create a backup on disk or tape so that it will not take more than 8 working hours to recreate lost data.

It is best to have an uninterruptible power supply for your computer. If a power failure should cause the computer to shut down, data vital to your business may be destroyed. Be aware that computer data is stored on magnetic media, either disk or tape, and that the magnetic fields on such media are subject to weakening, thus resulting in loss of data. Therefore, data should be refreshed, or backed up, by recopying on a regular basis, usually daily. For safety's sake, a duplicate set of data and programs should be stored in a vault or fireproof file.

Security

After the system is installed and running, it is important to police the uses to which the computer is put. Many additional demands on the system will be created. Some demands will be for the good of the business, but others will be self-serving, useless, and expensive. All requests for special reports, additional programs, or special-purpose systems must be reviewed and approved by the manager or owner of the business based on economic justification.

The worst computer stories concern security breaches. Unscrupulous computer programmers have stolen money by setting up dummy pay-rolls and bogus disbursements, or have stolen company secrets stored on computer tapes. Since most computer crimes go undetected (although discrepancies should be obvious in a small company), the nationwide scope of these abuses is much larger than actually reported. The business person should check noncomputerized records often against the computer figures, both to stop theft and to spot errors. The misplaced decimal point is a common mistake between the computer, programmers, and transcribers.

Communicating through Your Computer

A modem installed in your computer links you to data and services beyond the confines of your own establishment. A modem is an electronic device installed in your computer that allows it access to a telephone line for the transmission and receiving of data.

Through a modem, you can always be in contact with your business while on the road, provided you also have a computer, such as a laptop or a palm-size computer. A palm-size computer that can fit in a jacket pocket can duplicate the programs of your office computer and also be used to write letters or memos that can be transmitted to your office.

If you have several business locations, modems can link the computers of each place and give you the advantage of quick communication within your own company.

Finally, a computer and modem allow you to subscribe to and take advantage of a wide array of data banks providing research materials, stock market quotes and reports, news services, travel information, and other data that may be of use in your business.

19
Selling the Product

In less-developed areas one can still see simple and straightforward methods of selling. Marketing problems are quite simple. A seller sits by a road and sets up his or her wares: baskets, weaving, or produce. The few products are clearly displayed to the potential buyer. On the spot, the seller can tout the wares, set and alter prices, complete transactions, and, after the day, count the profit or loss.

The modern world, with its multiplicity of products, markets, methods of distribution, and legal restrictions, is much more complicated. To profitably sell your merchandise you must determine your market, which may be in one, dozens, or thousands of locations. It may be segmented by personal or family income or even have ethnic ties; bring the product to the attention of potential buyers; and transport the product. You must master the sophistications of pricing for profit, offer profit-supporting discounts and credit, stave off competition, tailor your products and services to customer needs, satisfy the requirements of numerous and complex laws, and be prepared to change your methods as needed. Doing this and all that goes with it successfully makes selling a consummate art!

Setting Sales Objectives

If you are new in business, you should have a business plan. If you have been in business for more than a year, then you should also have developed a budget. To have an effective business plan you must either forecast or determine the profitability of what you plan to sell or have sold. If you are selling more than one item, then you need to know what it will cost to sell each item, the profitability of each, which will be sold locally and which nationally (or, possibly, internationally), and which need to be revitalized or replaced by new items.

Some of these items may have been tested locally or in a small number of stores throughout the country and are now ready for a national rollout. Or you may just be on the threshold with your first new product. In any case, you should set firm sales objectives which spell out what you are planning to sell, when, how, and at what price(s). The plan should result in a spread sheet which lists, by months, how you plan to spend sales dollars. This gives you the ability, as time progresses, to compare actual amounts spent against budgeted amounts. You can analyze the variances and make judgments on your sales costs in various areas. Let your accountant help you set up the best format for you.

But what is it that you need to be aware of when you consider introducing a new product? Let's follow this product from beginning to end.

Developing a Corporate Image

Today, selling is more than pushing products. It also often involves brand recognition, company reputation, and ethics. You will do well to consider what people may want to know about your company and your product. Try to be as specific as possible. Buyers seldom research what they buy, and you cannot be everything to everyone. Decide whether you want to be seen as a producer of high-priced, premium quality goods or services, or a producer of products everyone can afford.

Once you have given your business a specific image, everything you do must stay within character. The logo, package, merchandise, price, customer, advertising, mode of sales, letterhead, your vehicles, and the way you and your people dress must all come from the same mold. Give considerable thought to defining and holding to the image, since a change will confuse customers and might destroy their loyalty.

Developing and Keeping a Customer

No matter what you sell, remember the p's and q's of selling: *Plan* every sales call. Be *personal, pleasant, persistent, persuasive,* and *patient.*

Be *persevering* and *perspicacious*. *Perform* and deliver the best *quality* affordable. Live up to your *promises*. You and everyone in your company must be *proud* of your *product* and *never quit* trying to improve it.

Marketing a New Product

Before introducing a new product, you should answer the following questions:

1. What consumers will use the product? What are their ages, locations, and occupations? How many are likely to ignore the product because it is too expensive or not expensive enough for them? What makes your product unique? How many similar items are already being sold? Remember, customers often resist changes in their buying patterns, and frequently they will be satisfied with a product which doesn't have all your improvements simply because they are familiar with it.

2. Can your product compete favorably with similar products already on the market with regard to quality, style, and service? Will its price compare favorably with those of existing products of its kind? Are other manufacturers likely to enter the field with products similar to yours or which serve the same purposes? What is the present consumption of items of this type? Is consumption likely to expand in the next 2, 5, or 10 years? How often will customers buy it; is it durable or does it need frequent replacement? At what season does it reach peak sales?

3. Through what channels are customers accustomed to buying products of this kind? You will want to discover the basis on which your competitors distribute their products to retailers. You might choose to sell through established wholesalers, through exclusive distributors, or through your own sales force. Some manufacturers use a combination of these.

Effective Packaging

Packaging should supply adequate protection against rough handling in transit and delivery to users. It should be able to withstand climate and temperature changes, provide interior reinforcement and cushioning, and be of minimum weight for proper protection.

Your package should allow you the greatest possible shipping economy. Occasional breakage and replacement may be more economical than penalizing every shipment by the cost and weight of damage-proof containers. Your shipping department should observe standard practices which eliminate extravagant use of crates, nails, padding, wrappings, tape, etc. If your container can be used by the purchaser for display or some other purpose, be sure to explain this in prominent lettering on the exterior of the package.

When designing for retail display, make sure the package will be acceptable to the stores and will be distinct and visible on shelves and counters and in windows. It should "look its price"—that is, give the impression of being worth what is asked for it. If it contains one of a line of similar items, it should probably bear a "family resemblance" to the packages of the other items. If the appearance of the contents is a sales asset, consider transparent wrappings, a box with a clear plastic window, or a bulk display of packages with one sample exposed to view. Make sure that the labeling on your package is informative as well as distinctive and that it includes all the information required by law. Experimentation may show you whether you might enlarge your sales market with cartons of a different size or containing a different quantity.

Generally speaking, your packaging costs should be modest in comparison with the ultimate prices of what you are selling. For example, cosmetic producers often spend nearly as much on the packaging of their products as on the products themselves. If you package for ultimate retail purchase, try to keep the tone consistent with the style of the merchandise. Some commodities, such as jams, are effectively merchandised in the wooden crates in which they are shipped.

Setting a Price

The price you establish for a new product may be the pivot on which the success of your marketing efforts will turn. Prices must be in line with perceptions of the quality, style, and service you provide and of those of competitors.

If the product cannot be differentiated from that of competitors, price may be the only variable available to you. Accordingly, you may find it necessary to set up a schedule of discounts and allowances to wholesalers, retailers, and others as an inducement for them to carry your line.

Do not set your prices simply on the basis of competitors' prices. Your pricing policies should embrace everything that goes into the establishment of a true price. In addition to your product cost, include such items as credit and collection costs, delivery costs (if there are any), consignment and returned goods costs, the costs of order cancellations, and credit for damaged or unsatisfactory goods.

Legal Advice

Legal counsel can be of help to you in establishing marketing plans and policies. It can examine your product, labeling, and advertising, as well as your sales agreements and price policies, to see what in the product can be patented, what on the package can be trademarked, and whether or not you have abided by regulations set up by the Food and Drug Administration for industries engaged in interstate commerce. It can identify any statutes in your area governing the use of premiums and contests to promote your merchandise. State laws vary widely in their restrictions on advertising and display material on alcoholic beverages and various other products. In many states, particular items, such as drugs, may be sold only in specified types of retail outlets. A substantial number of cities throughout the country have adopted ordinances circumscribing the activities of house-to-house canvassers, and many require a license for such activities. In other states, restrictive laws have been passed which tend to cut down or eliminate sales of out-of-state products competing with dominant local industries.

Health laws, building codes, and sanitary codes are in operation in most, if not all, cities. In many instances, these laws prohibit the use of certain types of products in the construction of homes, offices, and factories.

Avoiding Sales Terms That Discriminate

The law forbids price discrimination that injures competition. Special sales terms that amount to price reductions, or price increases, should be quoted to all purchasers on an equitable and consistent basis. Special terms may be granted in good faith where necessary to meet competition, but shaded prices or discounts should normally be applied uniformly to all competing customers who purchase the same product in the same period of time.

Rebates in a Market Decline

The law permits a seller to give a buyer a guarantee against a price decline. However, the seller must give the same terms to all customers who place orders on a single date and have rebates computed as of a single future date. Any shift in the initial date, or the rebate date, justifies a change in terms—provided changes in the seller's cost or in future market conditions have occurred.

Future Delivery Contracts

A price quoted for future delivery need not be the same as a price quoted for immediate delivery. This is so because the law does not prevent changes in price based on changes in market conditions. The seller may, for example, take an order from a customer for delivery 1 or 2 months ahead, at either more or less than the price prevailing on the day when the order is placed. On the other hand, if the seller quotes different prices to different purchasers who place orders for the same amount of the same product for delivery on the same advance date, the seller runs the risk of violating the law.

Options for Future Purchases

A seller may give a buyer an option to purchase a given amount of an item at any time up to a given future date at the price prevailing on an earlier date. It is true, in this case, that a buyer who does not have such an option may be paying a different price when purchasing on the same date as the buyer who has the option. This fact will, however, not result in violation of the law if all buyers have had the same rights and opportunities to enter into a like option.

Special Discounts for Large Orders

Quantity discounts are legal if they do not restrain competition or if they are based on specific cost, market, or competitive considerations. They are permissible when a seller's costs actually vary with order size. However, difficulties may be encountered if a seller's discounts for large orders have no reasonable relationship to discounts on smaller orders.

Credit terms and special delivery services must also be extended to all customers without discrimination.

Market Test

Introducing a new product is risky and costly. To reduce the amount of loss that might follow a failure, manufacturers test their products and the methods used to sell them.

In the broadest sense, there are two ways to test consumer reaction: focus groups and market surveys. Focus group tests are done in conference rooms which have hidden microphones, TV cameras, and two-way mirrors. Using accepted sampling techniques based on specific criteria, members are found in shopping centers. They are paid a small stipend. These people do not actually purchase the product but can provide feedback to the manufacturer in a confidential environment. Market surveys cannot be conducted in private and court the danger that your competitors will be tipped off. The competitor can audit one of your test areas and, if they are impressed, enter the market at the same time you do. That will deprive you of the benefit of being first and getting the largest share of the market. Surveys are considered more reliable since buyers actually purchase the items before being interviewed.

By testing in several cities, manufacturers can note the possibly differing results of advertising slogans, techniques, and packaging. They can also test the consumer's reaction to different colors and smells, unit assembling, and prices. Advertising can be tested with focus groups. You might try different combinations of light, average, and heavy advertising (TV, radio, or newspaper) alone or combined with redeemable coupons, door-to-door selling, or free samples in various cities.

Makers of products not for mass distribution generally do not find such testing techniques suitable and must rely on other sources of market information and experience. They usually find it most convenient and economical to turn to professional market research firms. Bumbling on your own can be very costly.

If you plan to use a professional firm to test your market, tell them clearly what you want surveyed. They will then submit a written proposal defining the assignment as they understand it, the names of the people who will handle the operation, and an estimate of the time involved and their charges. Charges are often calculated on a daily or hourly basis, but some consultants and research organizations work on a retainer, or fixed fee, or on a cost-and-percentage basis. In addition, they expect to be reimbursed for certain expenses. These should be specifically defined and agreed to in writing.

Advertising

Few expenses are so wasted as the money spent on advertising. The amount of time you spend on this category of expense should at least equal the proportion of your income spent on it.

An advertising program should convey your message through the medium from which sales will most likely result. Available media include newspapers, magazines, radio, television, direct mail, bill-boards, transportation signs, and business papers and magazines. You may find it effective to utilize several of these or only one or two, experimenting occasionally with the choice of media afterwards.

If you are in a suburban area, you will probably find advertising in a large city newspaper too expensive and its coverage too wide. If a local radio station is available, you may get quick results through spot radio advertising. Make the wording bright and catchy enough to alert the listener within the first 5 or 10 seconds. Trade and business papers are an essential medium for reaching other businesses or dealers. Try leafing through trade journals for ideas that can be adapted to promoting your product.

Notice this: Your advertising dollars may produce nothing in the way of sales. Our counsel is spend money on advertising only on a proof basis. Avoid the euphoria of the advertising game: namely, that having sent out signals to the buying community, they will flock to your merchandise. Experiment. If you use several newspapers or magazines to reach buyers, try scheduling advertisements in different publications in consecutive weeks and check your increase in sales for the corresponding periods. Coupons, games, lotteries (depending upon local law), and discounts are also ways of stimulating and measuring consumer response. A good way in some industries to reach customers is to advertise in trade publications and industry journals. A product with multi-industry applications might be advertised in magazines geared to executives. In certain circumstances you may do well to make use of two different kinds of advertisements: *commodity* and *institutional.*

Commodity advertisements sell more commonly used items. The approach creates interest in an unestablished item. The advertisements direct the customer to a specific brand of goods, whereas mass advertising appeals to a cross section of the population. Or you may consider advertising by class, directing your message toward a special group for which your product may have greatest appeal or use.

Institutional advertising conveys a message about the firm that may have nothing to do with a particular product. It may concern a change in policy on credit, the enlargement of a department, or the acquisition of a new line of goods. Institutional advertising, judiciously placed, can often enhance a business's stature in the community. Some firms identify with a drive for charitable contributions or some other local cause of importance.

Services or atmosphere can be sold in much the same fashion as the product. Suppose you have a store carrying shoes little different from those sold by a store down the street. To attract customers you must establish some apparent difference between the stores by your advertising campaign. For example, your advertising might feature the attentiveness and experience of your sales personnel, your refund policy, your layaway plan, or a special sale on one or two styles that the competition may be unwilling or too late to match.

Another way of gaining a competitive advantage is to segment the market and promote it through advertising. For example, you may choose to specialize in athletic shoes, and decorate your store with an urban motif, high-energy background music, and a modest colored-light system. You must use your judgment to weigh the extra decoration and advertising expenses against the increase in sales brought about by the campaign.

Advertising Costs

What is a suitable amount for a firm to spend on its advertising program? One deciding factor is: How much can you afford? Another is: How much advertising will have proven benefits for you? The two questions may give different answers. On the dollar side alone, some industries devote 1 to 2 percent of sales on advertising. Among retail establishments, furniture stores run highest with 3 to 4 percent, apparel stores average 2.5 percent, and drugstores 1.5 percent. Manufacturers vary even more: Makers of concrete masonry products may spend $\frac{1}{2}$ of 1 percent for advertising while manufacturers of cosmetic products spend 30 percent. But what the relative advantage to each industry for such outlays may be is not clear.

Industries tend to establish standard expense figures for advertising of their products. Reference to trade associations will usually tell you what they are. However, don't feel obligated to follow suit. In your advertising, focus on keeping the message clear and run your ads long enough to be certain that the average shopper will have absorbed their contents. You may end up spending less or more than competitors. But you are also likely to end up being more cost-effective!

Manufacturers, wholesalers, and newspapers can help retailers plan more attractive advertisements. They often provide excellent cuts, mats, and suggested copy slants. The often expertly planned material is usually furnished without charge. Make as much use of it as you can, for the chances are that it will help keep your advertisements up to date, appealing, and effective. Still, don't accept the help blindly. Some of the programs have inferior ability to boost your sales.

Many manufacturers offer cooperative advertising in which they contribute financially to retail-store advertisements calling customers' attention to specials on, for example, hosiery, cosmetics, and items of apparel. Many customers rely heavily on these annual name-brand sales.

Strategic placement of ads in newspapers is essential to capture casual readers' interest. Readers are affected by the position of the advertisement on the pages, its size in relation to surrounding ads, the content of adjacent editorial matter and advertisements, and the qualities of layout and display (for example, the readability and contrasts of the type, the artwork, and borders).

Direct mail, on the other hand, gives you almost unlimited freedom in illustrations and their size and treatment, within limits of the format selected and the reproduction process used. Unlike newspaper advertising, direct mail focuses the recipient's entire attention on your message, no matter how briefly. If the item appeals, your advertising has found a customer. (Direct mail is discussed in Chapter 12.)

A good advertising program promotes items that are timely because of seasons, holidays, local events, or national advertising of manufacturers and producers. Use tempting pictures or descriptive phrases which highlight the characteristics of your merchandise that make it superior to the offerings of other merchants or manufacturers. The use of humor requires a deft touch. But do not attempt it unless the results seem spontaneous and light.

Be certain that you make no misleading statements in your advertising. The Federal Trade Commission has set up trade practice rules which prohibit false advertising, misbranding, and deception.

Use of an Advertising Agency

If you turn your advertising program over to an agency, be sure you choose a firm that is experienced in handling your line of products or services. It is not necessarily true that a small agency will give smaller accounts more attention. A large agency, offering more specialized facilities, may be interested in your business, because of your growth potential, and offer more diverse services (such as market research).

You will find advertising agencies from all over the country listed, together with their accounts, in the *Standard Advertising Register*. You can also use your classified telephone directory to locate local firms. But remember, not all firms listed as advertising agencies are fully equipped to give all types of service. Choose one that is recognized by the various media associations and is free from control of any one advertiser or media owner. It should have a staff of sufficient size, ability, and experience to meet your needs. Evaluate its former work with your type of merchandise to see if its presentation is objective.

Identify Your Sales Channels

There are a number of distinct sales channels through which your product can reach the customer. Each offers unique benefits and costs.

Independent retailers are usually the easiest to sell to. They welcome your salesperson without an appointment, will order from your literature, may pay to reserve products, will regularly attend local shows and one or two select national shows, write orders at the shows, and frequently get their supplies from local distributors. They maintain and adjust inventory levels themselves and will seek out and order new items on the spot.

The buyer for small group stores is often still the owner. Since he or she is occasionally away on business trips, it is wise to make an appointment. Literature is required, but the stores usually have inventory-control systems and reorders come from the system. The buyer seeks out new items at national shows or local shows which are distant from their operations. He or she will try out new items by writing small orders for one of the stores. The buyer will seek discounts, ask for advertising allowance, and return guarantees. The small mail-order house falls in this category.

Medium-sized retail chain stores either buy on their own under the guidance of a central buying office or (increasingly) have most of their buying done by a central office. Their buyers "live by the numbers." Each item must produce a certain revenue in relation to the space it occupies in the store. Samples and literature must be supplied to the buying office, and, therefore, to sell them you must develop presentations in accordance with their buying practices. It is virtually impossible to sell these stores on a cold call basis. Some of the buying is also done at national shows.

Medium-sized mail-order houses operate similarly. Reorders are usually generated by computer which favors existing suppliers. It is therefore difficult for new vendors to gain acceptance. Buyers may demand special terms and, if the new products don't perform well in a short period, they may be quickly dropped.

National chains and large independent merchants have their own buying offices. They use in-house consultants to search out new merchandise. Programs consisting of advertising, special sales, promotional merchandise, store space, and stocking needs are developed in advance.

New items are presented at the buying offices in the form of plans showing anticipated returns based on specific locations in the store. The new items are tried in a small number of stores, and the manufacturer is expected to take back all unsold merchandise at the end of the trial. Frequently, new vendors are required to pass a thorough product and financial evaluation before they can be considered.

Many national chains do not restock shelves from inventory; they expect manufacturers to "count" the inventory and replenish it. Others have direct computer links with the manufacturers. Producers ship new merchandise when the inventory falls to a predetermined level. Increasingly bar code output from checkout counters and shelves are linked with computers which feed reorder information to the manufacturer.

The military maintains stores [called post exchanges (PXs)] for its personnel all over the world. Merchandise for their PXs are bought at central buying offices. After vendors qualify, the central offices develop programs which are specifically tailored for regional locations. After approval, purchase may be made by the PX, the regional buying office, or headquarters. Reorders come to the vendors through either regional or headquarter computers. Military buyers go to national trade shows, but purchases usually follow rigid order-point and order-quantity routines.

These facts show that your sales force should be tailored to each class of buyers. Therefore, do not expect sales representatives who call on PXs or national buying offices to sell efficiently to neighborhood mom-and-pop stores. Similarly, don't expect representatives accustomed to calling on small stores to know how to deal with J.C. Penney or Sears.

Using Independent Sales Agents

Most companies develop a sales strategy and carefully structure their sales organization to match its aims. But only a few of these have their own in-house sales organization. Usually, only large manufacturers can afford their own sales organizations. Most businesses use independent sales agents who are managed and trained by in-house sales managers. In addition, the owner, or president, and a small and specially trained group of in-house sales specialists call on the national accounts with whom the company has close ties.

Independent agents or sales representatives are the most effective means of controlling sales costs. Your independent agent is not your employee. Agents run their own businesses, and your product will be only one of the products they sell and your company only one of a number they represent (exclusive agents exist, but they represent high-dollar volume items only). However, none of the other items should be competitive with yours. Generally, an agent sells to specific areas and industry groups. You will probably get fullest satisfaction from an agent who handles products that are closely related (but not competitive) to yours in type, price, and quality.

Your agreement with an agent usually provides the agent with a commission on sales and the exclusive rights to your products in a specific territory. The agent gets orders for you, but you ship and bill directly to the store. You control prices, terms, credit, and other variables, but the agent may have useful suggestions in dealing with certain customers with whom he or she has had sales and collection experience.

The use of independent agents enables you to reduce the expense of training, recruiting, and supervising a sales force. Except for sales training, supervision, trade shows, advertising, and sales-support material, your selling costs decline automatically when sales drop, since the agent is paid a percentage of sales.

Your own sales force would not find it remunerative to call often on small customers widespread, causing excessive travel costs. If your market is seasonal and yet you need year-round contact or if your product sales volume varies greatly with the economic cycle, you might benefit from the services of an independent agent.

Selecting and Training In-House Sales Personnel

Carefully trained and coached salespersons who are imbued with respect for the company and product(s) they sell will give even the "born" salesperson stiff competition.

Select applicants whose attributes and honesty you respect. They do not necessarily have to be fast talkers. The most successful salespeople want to sell. They become effective when they become convinced of the value of your product and have a thorough grasp of the factors which distinguish your product from others in the same line.

Be sure your sales force has complete understanding of the manufacturing processes used in producing your merchandise. Purchasers often wish to know these details, and salespeople should be able to supply information without fear of misstatement. Establish two-way information links with purchasers located across the nation. However, an agent carrying the lines of a number of manufacturers expects to sell a larger total amount to one of the regular stops in the agent's limited territory. For the new firm, the agent offers the advantage of immediate service without the time and costs of hiring and training one's own sales force.

On the other hand, when the volume of sales becomes high, the agent may not be able to provide the service an in-house sales force can. Also, by putting your own sales people on fixed salaries, you can reduce sales costs as volume rises. A further disadvantage of agents is that you cannot closely control their selling methods. They give you only a part-time selling effort. Furthermore, should you ever break with them, the agent may be able to switch part of your business to your competitor (provided, of course, that the competitor hires your agent).

The decision to use independent agents will be influenced by how fast you need to gain product acceptance and how long it will take to train personnel if the selling requires high technical skills and knowledge. You might need to use an agent if your volume is not sufficient to support your own salesperson(s) or if the market is too thin and too widespread to keep your salespeople informed on any shortages, delayed deliveries, changes in packaging, and discontinued items, so that they can effectively handle criticisms, and complaints, and provide you with any data they obtain from their customers. In addition, schedule frequent face-to-face sales meetings to keep them involved and current, as well as to help make your own production and marketing efforts more profitable.

Develop data on customers and prospects that go beyond a mere record of their prior orders. Certain fundamental information concerning your customers may be of use to you in both sales and marketing strategies. Keep a record of all the business endeavors of a customer, the operations of its subsidiaries, the location of its branches, and for each the floor space, sales volume, and number of employees. Also keep a record of the customer's customers, if you know them, of other suppliers from which the customer buys, and, of course, of the dealings the customer has with your competitors. Salespersons can aid materially in gathering some of this information.

The time spent in contact with prospects is the most productive part of each salesperson's day. Therefore, plan routing carefully, assigning each salesperson a territory which can be efficiently and economically covered. There is real risk in allowing salespersons to follow the tendency to drop in too often on good accounts to the neglect of places which need greater cultivation. Plan just how often you want a salesperson to call back on a customer or prospect.

Controlling Sales Expenses

A sound business establishes a fixed policy on sales expense arrangements. Rules should be established that state how each allowable expense should be reported by the sales force on a form or forms designed for the purpose.

Before establishing the system, consider providing for these expenses in the salary or commission paid each salesperson. That frees salespersons from reporting expenses and you from processing the information. Or you might set up a per diem or other flat-rate system.

If you decide to use a reimbursed-expense system, include instructions clearly stating your policies on hotel bills, meals, tips, use of trains, airplanes, and taxis, automobile costs (mileage rate, insurance, depreciation, parking, etc.), entertainment, club initiation fees and dues, and other receipted bills pertaining to sales effort.

Without clear instructions, reimbursable expenses will soon exceed your budget, cut into profits, and when audited, make for unhappiness with your salesperson. This is not to say that you can eliminate travel-expense audits. Audit of all traveling expense accounts is essential to keep claims on a reasonable, honest basis.

Many businesses are trying to reduce costs by reducing the necessities for travel. More emphasis is being put on trade shows, where many clients and customers can be contacted at once. Better-planned travel routes, more frequent phone contacts, and even the mailing of samples to old, familiar customers are being used to reduce travel expenses, improve timeliness, and make better use of the salespeople.

Working with Your Wholesalers

A cooperative relationship with wholesalers will enable you to operate more efficiently. Wholesalers can buy goods at the time they are produced and store them until they are needed by local retailers or industrial consumers. This greatly reduces the amount of warehouse space and the amount of capital manufacturers need.

The quick cash provided by wholesalers often gives a manufacturer the money with which to continue operations until the season is ended. On certain products a wholesaler or distributor can provide the small manufacturer with national distribution quickly and more thoroughly. Retailers buy more readily from the wholesaler because through past dealings they know the wholesaler is reliable and will not burden them with goods unsuitable to their trade.

Where custom permits it, your wholesaler can be the agent through which you distribute advertising to retailers. In these cases the wholesaler will make your material up into kits, which are given to the sales force to deliver to each of their retail customers. The only cost to the manufacturer is shipping the bulk material to the wholesaler. The cost involved is minute in comparison with the expense of your making up individual kits and mailing them to many retailers.

Operating for Maximum Profit by Reviewing Costs of Sales

You must always be alert to the possibility that a large percentage of customers, orders, or commodities may bring in only a minor proportion of sales. If so, your current marketing efforts are costly. Too frequently, expenses increase in proportion to the number of customers, orders, and commodities, rather than in proportion to the number of actual dollar sales. Thus, a large part of marketing expenditures may secure only a small part of total sales and gross profit.

You must decide whether there is any advantage to you in continuing accounts which entail costs of sales calls, delivery, order processing, and money in excess of the contributions of sales to them.

A survey of physical distribution and storage costs may reveal that some products require such high handling and inventorying costs as to nullify any profit. But before eliminating them, consider if you need to maintain these items as convenience or door openers to customers. In any case, before you drop them, investigate lowering the costs of distribution and storage.

Reassess the ratio of sales to the marketing costs of any part of your business. Are you still using the most economical channel of distribution? Do you still have the best territorial breakdown for the sales organization of specific products? Is your price still viable? If your competitors are claiming a larger share of the market than you are, your research should show you why.

Eliminating unprofitable products or sales is not the only method—or, necessarily the most desirable method—for dealing with unprofitable business. Here are some of the ways a good cost-analysis system helps you convert relatively unprofitable commodities into sources of profit.

Simplify the Line

Reduce the number of sizes, styles, qualities, and price fines. Simplification may result not only in reducing distribution costs and distribution errors but also in increasing sales by permitting concentration of advertising, selling, styling, and design on fewer items. One knitting mill, for example, sharply reduced its storage costs and inventory losses by restricting the variety of articles offered for sale and attributed a rapid increase in sales to that policy. A simplified line will also help you fill reorders faster. You can also reduce production costs while increasing production. But you must be wary not to simplify yourself out of business.

Repackage the Product

A change in packaging may breathe new life into your product by increasing the volume of sales. It may also reduce the direct costs of packing, and the new container may make possible reductions in transportation, storage, and handling costs.

Increase—or Decrease—the Amount of Advertising and Promotion Work

Whether it would be profitable to increase or decrease advertising depends on such factors as the effect of advertising on volume of sales and the effect of the volume of sales on unit production and distribution costs.

Decrease the Price

Sometimes it pays to reduce the price of items that no longer sell well. For some products and at some economic times, a small reduction in price will lead to a substantial increase in sales, and the greater volume will decrease your distribution costs, generating extra profit.

Increase the Price

Failing to raise prices can lead to losses in profits. But price increases do not always lead to reductions in sales or profits. Business people, generally, fear to raise prices, and do so only when competitors do or when forced to by economic necessity. These two reasons do not give you a marketing advantage. Better reasons for raising prices are to bring profits up to standard, improve customer service, reduce stockouts, improve the product, and improve quality. In some cases there may be a slowdown of orders or smaller unit orders. But you might offset this slowdown by temporarily increasing the advertising and promotion of the products on which you raised prices. If you want to hold prices in line, you may be able to do the following to bring costs down:

- Eliminate small and relatively unprofitable orders or establish a special-handling charge for all orders below a minimum size.
- Reduce services offered, such as special storage, free acceptance of returns, and repair services.
- Devise special routines that reduce clerical costs on small orders.
- Establish a minimum-size order that will be handled.
- Turn small orders over to jobbers, brokers, or agents.
- Substitute mail-order solicitation for personal calls on a number of customers of certain classes.

Stay Alert to Product Diversification

You must be constantly alert to innovation and substitutions in packaging, production, and materials. Listen to the information your salespeople pick up on product improvement and criticism. Give someone in your organization specific responsibility for keeping alert to suitable additions to your line.

When you get an order from an unusual source, find out why your product was purchased. The information may disclose a market for your commodity or an application of it that has not occurred to you. If your competitors publish lists of users of their products, study them closely for suggestions of classes of prospects or uses for your merchandise which you have overlooked in your sales work.

Either you or someone you appoint should read the publications of your trade or industry for items regarding new businesses in any of your markets, personnel changes in firms on your prospect list, and news about your competitors.

Your trade association may be another valuable source of information in your profit-improvement program. Many trade groups collect statistics on the industry for use by members and by the government. They print and distribute specialized data on sales promotion, creating markets for the industry's products. They also maintain credit-reporting services that can guide you, and they prepare economic studies on wages, sales, and prices. They act as clearinghouses for technical advice that may be especially helpful to smaller businesses which cannot afford their own technical staffs.

Your trade association will aid you in promoting efficient methods by keeping you informed of government legislation, public events, and technical or trade changes that affect the industry. Detailed manuals on record keeping have been printed for some industries. These are the result of years of familiarity with the problems of the industry and knowledge of the ways adequate records can help solve such problems.

Conducting Business Overseas

With the drop of the U.S. dollar, American products may be becoming more competitive. You owe it to yourself to find out whether your products are affected and whether the drop will open the world market to you. Government assistance in the endeavor is available to small businesses. Contact the Bureau of International Commerce of the U.S. Department of Commerce. The department maintains up-to-date lists of foreign buyers, distributors, and agents for a full range of products in many countries. Their representatives will help you contact foreign businesses and sales agents.

A thorough perusal of Department of Commerce literature will help you decide on your best potential foreign market. Their *Trade List* supplies names and addresses of foreign companies dealing with specific products in 100 countries. The *World Trade Directory Reports* provide exhaustive information about overseas firms—their products, territories, owners, and officers.

To initiate your export program, you might register with the Department of Commerce for inclusion on the *American International Traders Index.* The index contains the names of more than 20,000 American manufacturers who wish to sell in foreign markets, along with data about their products.

To give your product effective foreign exposure you can arrange with the Department of Commerce to have an exhibitor display your commodity at one of the U.S. trade centers overseas. Consult the *Overseas Trade Promotion Calendar* for locations, events, and terms.

Before choosing a country as a market for your product, evaluate its trade restrictions, including tariffs, quotas, import licenses, repatriation policies, and exchange permit requirements. Tariffs imposed by foreign governments on imports may be based on value or quantity, or both. A schedule of tariffs, published by the International Customs Tariffs Bureau in Brussels, Belgium, is on file at your nearest field office of the Department of Commerce. Some groups of countries, such as the European Common Market, publish their own common external tariff schedule. This document may be obtained from the European Economic Community headquarters in Brussels. Be certain that the tariff schedule you obtain is up to date: Changes are made frequently. If your product is difficult to classify, you may have to send a sample to the appropriate authorities to gain a decision on its tariff rates.

Some countries have quota systems which limit the number of a specific item which can be imported within a certain length of time, usually a year. Sometimes the limitations are directed toward specific countries, or they may encompass the entire world. In some cases, where the quota is exceeded, a product is not banned, but a tariff is imposed on any additional items imported into the country.

Import licenses are often used by countries to keep track of their imports or to regulate the amount of importing done. Some countries, when they have balance-of-payment difficulties or shortages of hard currency, may require exchange permits or barter transactions. Exchange permits, which are a form of import licensing enable the government to ration the supply of hard currencies available for imports. Preference is always given to essential items.

Consult with your field office of the Department of Commerce for full information on your requirements.

North American Free Trade Agreement

Keep in mind that the emerging North American Free Trade Agreement (NAFTA), reached by the United States, Canada, and Mexico, may make it easier and lucrative for U.S. companies to transact business in both Canada and Mexico. As a result of a free trade agreement such as NAFTA, many tariffs, quotas, and other barriers to trade among the participating countries are reduced or completely eliminated. In addition, there is generally free movement of goods, services, and capital among the participating countries.

Because of national economic and environmental considerations there are many unsettled issues that may take years to resolve before NAFTA can be fully implemented.

For more information on transacting business abroad you may want to read the *Foreign Trade Reporter,* a newsletter that discusses international business trends.

20

Extending Credit to Your Customers

Credit fuels the American economy. But, in granting credit you should not be carried away because "buy now, pay later" has become a national way of life. Your perspective in extending credit should be no less conservative than in managing any other business activity.

Not all people granted credit will honor their debts. Yet, to do business in the volume that gives the best profit, you may have to give it. In giving it your objective should be to constrain your risk while benefiting from the buying power of the credit society. To do that you must know what it costs you to extend credit and what the impact is on cash flow, and act accordingly. Giving credit will increase your sales, but if the extra volume also erodes cash flow, you may be forced to borrow.

In extending credit, your working capital should be sufficient to carry the accounts receivable, to replenish stock, and to pay operating expenses. If you are a retailer, you will probably need a monthly cash flow of at least three times the outstanding credit balance. As a manufacturer, you will need sufficient funds to operate during the time lag between billings and payment. Therefore, in determining credit policy you also should anticipate and provide against economic recessions that are likely to extend the average length of time that receivables will be outstanding. When the nation hits a slump, slow-paying customers may force your business to seek credit, and, if yours is overextended, they may even jeopardize it. Customer failures are a leading cause of business failure.

Many small business people are guided by the prevailing credit policies of their industries. But the policies yield neither safety nor competitive advantage. The policies are nothing more than the averages for the industry, some of whose members will go bankrupt following them, and to prosper the competition must be surpassed. Because to the typical manager's mind it is a mundane subject, credit offers great prospects for innovation. One area for innovation is in doing all you can to keep people from wanting credit while continuing to want to do business with you. You may offer enhanced discounts on bills paid within a certain period, or give your customers the "baker's dozen" for buying ahead for cash (transactional costs do not rise proportionately). More traditional methods include selling seasonal merchandise by taking payment from a dealer in installments spread over, say, 4 months. That allows the dealer to raise the money to pay you by selling the merchandise.

Cash discount policies may also relieve your credit problems. Customers may find it more advantageous to take out a bank loan to meet the discount terms than ask for credit from you.

Checking the Credit Standing of a Business

Generally speaking, your business should extend credit solely on the basis of present ability to pay. When dealing with another company, however, it pays to keep your credit policies flexible. Business fortunes rise and fall like the stock market. Your best guides are economic trends. In the recovery phase of a business cycle, expand credit; when recession is imminent, reduce it. Of course, prudence has it that you will judge each case on its merits or lack of them.

In determining the amount of credit to extend to a customer, evaluate the character, reputation, and business abilities of those who conduct the business. Collateral circumstances should also be studied. For example, check a prospective credit customer's business location to see if it is an inducement to profitable sales and to see if the customer's insurance coverage against fire is adequate. Are there outside mortgages, liens, or control on the management by other creditors or interested parties? Is the business subject to unusual price cutting and excessive risks? Have others ever had to institute legal action for collection?

Your sales force can also be an important source of information in checking credit. Instruct your salespeople to obtain trade references, names and addresses of banks dealt with, and the financial statement of prospective customers whenever possible. You should become familiar with the financial condition and trade practices of the firm before you commit to selling them on credit. Do not depend on the opinions of your sales department in making these commitments. Salespeople are notorious for their tendencies to extend credit too freely.

Local attorneys often can supply a report on the credit status of a firm you are investigating. They may know of liens, claims, judgments, or actions pending against the debtor. You may also consider paying to have a D&B (Dun & Bradstreet) report run on a prospective credit customer's company. A D&B is a credit check that will provide you with a company's complete credit history. (For more information see "Credit Bureaus," on the next page.

Personal interviews with proposed customers can yield first-rate credit information. Use the meetings to encourage complete openness about prospects, finances, and policies on the part of the customers. Get a financial statement from them, if you can. If the customer makes a false financial statement, knowing that you intend to rely on it for credit purposes, the customer may be subject to prosecution. Know, too, that federal mail statutes make it a crime to send a false statement through the mails.

The financial statements should be certified by reputable independent accountants. (If they are not certified, you have real reasons to question the firm's creditability.) The statements can tell you when an account is approaching its credit limits, and whether the cash position is adequate for anticipated business requirements. How much of the available cash is needed for imminent payment of wages, dividends, bonuses, loans, and purchase commitments or expansion programs? Is the ratio of sales to accounts receivable increasing or decreasing? An increasing ratio may reflect a favorable business trend.

Be sure the statements reflect recent conditions and are sufficiently detailed to provide an analysis of receivables, investments, inventories, and creditors. Hopefully, the information offers comparisons with preceding periods to help you detect trends which may affect your credit decision; if not, ask for statements from preceding years.

A study of notes receivable and trade acceptances should inform you as to what portion is fully negotiable, what portion is restricted, and what notes are worthless and should be written off. Your estimation of inventory should disclose any liability included in accounts payable. Estimate the liquidity of inventories in the event of seasonal changes, priorities, freezing orders, or other factors.

Intelligent analysis of the company's assets, investments, and debts should give you a good notion of its probable risk as a credit customer.

Composite balance sheets and income statements of successful firms of approximately the same size as that of the prospective customer may help. Many such figures are now available through trade associations. Good credit practice compares the ratios of the prospective customer to the significant ratios on composite statements and seeks an explanation of unfavorable variations.

An especially sensitive indicator is the ratio of current assets to current liabilities. When this ratio falls continuously, it is a sign of deterioration. Another important ratio is that of net worth to total debt. If this ratio continues to fall, it may indicate disaster.

Credit Bureaus

The credit bureau acts as a clearinghouse for credit information in the community. It provides a dependable source of information on the credit of local customers. The records reveal the actual trade or credit experiences of individuals with banks, retail stores, automobile dealers, finance companies, physicians, dentists, and hospitals. Credit bureau files include such highly important public records as judgments and deeds, mortgages, chattels, and conditional sales.

Where the bureau also operates a collection department, it provides much information of value to the bureau files.

A reputable merchant or business can pay a local credit bureau for its verification services. Of the almost 2000 credit bureaus in the United States, 95 percent are affiliated with the Associated Credit Bureaus of America, Inc. Through this affiliation, your local bureau exchanges information nationwide, helping to prevent a bad risk somewhere else from taking advantage of businesses in a new locality.

Computerized credit reports will be returned to you, scored on the basis of the answers on the credit application filled out by the customer. Reliance on the computer's weighted score helps prevent the merchant or the credit bureau from being accused of discrimination. The computer is free from prejudice of race or sex, although age is a factor in determining credit risk.

An applicant turned down on the basis of a credit report may, under the law, ask you to find out the source of the negative report. Be aware of the potential for error in the credit report. Customers should be turned down diplomatically and invited to resubmit their application at a later time when their credit is better established.

If there is no credit bureau in the community or when the information developed in the credit investigation does not clearly suggest a decision, certain other factors might be considered before you open or decline the account. You may be able to obtain information from other stores and businesses. Some merchants will base a favorable decision on the good record of the applicant's parents, on a stable employment record, or on the maintenance of a checking or savings account.

Retail Credit Policies

Occupations and income of customers will influence you, as a retailer, in your choice of a cash or a credit policy. In a community made up largely of farmers or ranchers, you may have to give credit until your customers have sold their crops or stock. Lower-income, but steadily employed, families often find it necessary to charge purchases from payday to payday. Buying on credit has long been the preferred method among many higher-income families also. They like to charge purchases, and then pay for all of them at the end of the month. Today, they are joined by the middle-income customer who is in the habit of using various types of credit cards to postpone cash payment.

When you sell for credit, you gain a number of advantages. First, you are able to build a clientele of regular customers. Cash customers are anybody's customers. Charge customers are customers of record. The following are some other important points:

- Charge customers usually are not as concerned with the prices of goods as are those who pay cash. They tend to buy a higher quality of merchandise, and they frequently buy more of it.
- Credit is an accommodation to customers. Because of this, charge customers generally have a feeling of goodwill toward the store.
- Goods can be sent on approval to customers.
- Charge customers provide an excellent mailing and promotion list.
- Adjustments can be made more easily.
- A more intimate relationship can be built up between the customers and the store.

Along with these advantages come disadvantages, which you must also consider:

- Capital is tied up in merchandise charged by customers.
- Credit adds to the interest charges on money borrowed.
- Losses are bound to occur. Credit customers may purchase beyond their ability to pay.

- Credit customers have a greater tendency to return goods than do cash customers.

- Credit adds to the cost of operations since accounts must be maintained and monthly statements prepared and mailed.

Depending on your business, you might run ordinary, *open-end monthly charge accounts* only, or you might also have such variations as *budget accounts,* under which the customer makes a down payment and incurs a service charge for paying for goods on an installment system. In *revolving accounts,* you and the customer agree on a credit ceiling; the customer pays a preset amount each month, plus a service charge. *Option accounts* combine open-end and revolving accounts; if the customer pays in full at the end of the month, there is no service charge, but otherwise a finance charge is assessed, the amount of which depends on the size of the outstanding balances and the monthly payment. (Some stores call this a revolving account. Credit account nomenclature varies.) You may also offer long-term installment contracts, usual in the selling of heavy appliances, furniture, and automobiles.

To change the terms of a credit account you must give 30 days' notice, as required by the federal consumer credit restraint program, and you must explain the changes in the credit program. The consumer may pay off the existing balance under the original terms of the credit account. However, use of the charge account by the consumer after the 30-day period is considered acceptance of the new terms.

Major Credit Card Plans

Whether you are a retailer or in a service business, you will have to consider participation in one or more of the credit card plans. Shall you accept cards issued by clubs, banks, and oil companies and be relieved of billing and collection responsibilities? In a credit card transaction, you will probably receive your payment for the sale or service long before the customer pays the issuer of the credit card. On the debit side, you will have to consider the cost of participation: fees, percentage of sales, charges for imprinting machines, and possibly a point-of-sale checking system. The theft of credit cards generates billions of dollars in losses a year. As schemes for counterfeiting credit cards grow more sophisticated, this total can only increase. Various protection devices exist, ranging from signatures and holograms on the cards to computerized systems of authorization.

You stand to gain more customers through participation in credit card plans. You offer the same convenience in charging that the department store gives, and customers are tempted to spend more when they do not immediately have to lay down cold cash. Business, too, is picked up from travelers and transients who do not wish to carry large sums of money with them.

Before deciding to use credit cards, know that the Fair Billing Act of 1975 allows customers to stop payment on items with which they are dissatisfied. The bank issuing the credit card will automatically deduct the disputed amount from the account of the business. The credit card customer has the legal right not to pay for an item he or she has tried to return or for a defective item that the buyer has tried to get the merchant to correct. This return feature can negate the effects of your sales skills if customers should later decide they do not really want what they bought.

On the other hand, most credit card plans do not require you to refund the money directly to customers returning credit purchases. Give the customer a copy of the slip which you send in with the customer's credit card billing, so the customer is credited from the credit card company. The credit card company then adjusts your account. This gives you the benefit of a free float between the time the item is returned and the time the account is adjusted. Another advantage to credit cards is that the issuers of credit cards will credit payments directly to your bank account.

Discounts for Cash

With the granting of credit, whether through your own billing system or through credit card plans, you will increase your cost of doing business. You have the overhead cost of raising the extra cash necessary to grant credit, plus you may be paying a percentage of the credit card sales to the banks handling the credit cards. Although credit transactions increase your sales volume, there are advantages in doing as much of your business as possible in cash. However, dealing in cash also has drawbacks. In selling cash and credit policies, take care to be consistent and in conformity with the law.

Credit card companies try to discourage you from a cash discount policy because it is contrary to their interests. Their pressures will be subtle, via billing rates or services. Formerly, credit card issuers prohibited the merchants in their programs from giving cash discounts, but Congress prohibited this form of control by law. However, unless a cash discount policy is posted in your store, or you otherwise notify all your customers as to cash discount practices, you are in violation of the Truth in Lending Law. It is also illegal to give different sized discounts to different customers. In effect, a cash discount policy is assessing a finance charge on credit customers; that is why the Truth in Lending Law is applicable.

A way of increasing your cash business without running foul of these restrictions is to have a minimum purchase amount for charges. For example, if credit cards are only allowable on purchases of over $20, a merchant's cash flow will increase. But, be careful to set a limit that will not have an adverse effect on sales volume. One guideline is to set the limit at the amount of cash most of your customers carry in their pockets.

Selling on the Installment Plan

Installment selling facilitates the sale of machinery and durable or "hard" goods, such as refrigerators, ranges, and furniture for the home, which have a long life and a relatively high value. They can be repossessed and resold if the customer fails to make payment.

Any form of credit business entails a larger capital investment than sales offered strictly for cash. Installment-plan selling requires an even larger investment than credit sales of charge account type. Money tied up in installment sales is frozen for a long time unless arrangements are made to transfer the contracts to a sales finance company.

In arranging an installment sale, the down payment should be large enough to make the buyer feel like the owner, not merely the renter, of the merchandise. The actual percentage asked depends on the type of merchandise. It might run from 20 to $33\frac{1}{3}$ percent or more of the total price. Some dealers will sell with no down payment and try to reduce their risk in other ways. Retailers tend to ask a higher down payment on soft goods since they rapidly decrease in value through use, wear, or changes in fashion.

If the article is repossessable, the unpaid balance on it always should be sufficiently below resale value to protect the retailer from loss if repossession becomes necessary.

The monthly payments should be large enough to increase the customer's claim to the article faster than the item will depreciate from time and average use.

Repossessing Property

Check the laws in your city and state on repossession, and also federal law which may supersede local law. The debtor is generally entitled to have a say before the property is seized. A Supreme Court decision prevents state laws from allowing creditors to repossess goods summarily for installment defaults. Repossession can occur only after the debtor has received a fair hearing.

Truth in Lending Law

Credit provided to consumers through open-end credit or installment plans is subject to the federal Truth in Lending Law. The law does not, however, apply to trade or business credit.

Complying with Credit Regulations

Say you are a home-improvement contractor. Your customer wants credit. You must explain the details of the installment contract and also tell the customer that, even after signing, he or she may back out of the contract, provided the cancellation is made within 3 days. Such a grace period—exact periods may vary in different states—is generally effective in door-to-door selling and is sometimes limited to sales above $10, or above $50; again, state regulations vary. If home-solicitation sales are your business, see that your salespeople understand and observe state and federal regulations.

When you offer an installment contract, inform the customer of various points of the credit transaction and include the same information on the instrument presented for signature. Details will vary according to the type of business.

Disclosure

Under the federal Truth in Lending Law, the following information must be included in credit agreements: the cash price of the goods or service, the down payment (include any trade-in), and the difference between the cash price and down payment; all other charges, itemized but not part of the finance charge; the unpaid balance; amounts deducted as prepaid finance charges (or required deposit balances); the amount financed; the total of the cash price, finance charges, and all other charges (which amounts to the deferred payment price); the total dollar amount of the finance charge; the date when the finance charge begins to apply if it is different from the sales date; annual finance charge, expressed as a percentage; the number, amounts, and due dates of payments; total payments; the amount you will charge for delinquency or default, or the method used for calculating the amount; a description of any security; a description of any penalty for prepayment of principal; and an explanation of how the unearned part of the finance charge is calculated in case of prepayment (charges deducted from any rebate must be stated).

If you offer open-end accounts which customers may pay in full or in installments, you again must tell the customer in writing or on a form the terms of the credit offered: the conditions under which a finance charge may be made; the period, such as 30 days, during which no interest is due if payment is made; the method of determining the balance on which a finance charge may be incurred; an explanation of how the actual finance charge due is calculated; the finance charge rates (for example, $1\frac{1}{2}$ percent on the first $500, and 1 percent on amounts over $500); the conditions under which the cost of new purchases is added to the account, and details of how the finance charge is then calculated; a description of any lien that may be made on a customer's property, as, for example, the right to repossess a refrigerator; and the minimum periodic payment you require.

Finally, credit terms on any sale on which the price may be paid in more than four installments must be disclosed. The disclosure is obligatory even if no finance or carrying charge is involved.

Billing Your Credit Customers

You must send out periodic statements (usually once a month) for accounts on which finance charges may be applied or on which there is an unpaid balance of more than $1. You must show the unpaid balance at the beginning of the billing period; the amount and date of each new purchase and a brief description thereof; customer payments and credits; the finance charge (in dollars and cents) and the rates used in calculating it; the annual percentage rate; the unpaid balance on which the finance charge was calculated; the closing date of the billing cycle; and the unpaid balance.

Federal regulations require you to show some of these items on the front of your statement; others may go on the back or on a separate attachment.

The question of what constitutes the balance on which revolving charge account finance charges are computed has been fought in the courts. Retailers like to bill on the *previous balance,* not taking a customer's payments into consideration; customers prefer the *adjusted balance,* under which their payments and credits are deducted before the charge is computed; a compromise, in some cases, is the *average daily balance,* whereby the customer is credited for payments but charged interest in proportion to the time he or she still has not paid. Ascertain state and federal law on this point if you are just setting up charge accounts. Some states have outlawed the previous-balance system, but at this writing federal law covering the practice has yet to be passed.

When mailing a statement to customers, allow plenty of time for them to pay before finance charges become applicable. In many states, the minimum time before such interest can be charged is 30 days. However, a reverse strategy, a discount policy for bills paid promptly, can make your collections easier. For example, offer 2 percent off on bills paid within 10 days and 1 percent off on bills paid within 20 days, with the normal finance charge being assessed after 30 days. Many businesses find this form of positive incentive to be a more effective means of collection than the typical penalty approach.

In response to customer complaints that their open-end credit account bills arrived too late for timely payments to be made, states may also regulate the mailing dates. For example, one state requires that statements be mailed at least 9 days before the end of the next succeeding billing cycle or payment-due date, whichever is earlier. Another state demands 15 days. Be sure to comply with current law.

Collecting Overdue Accounts

A sale beyond the customer's ability to pay can be the unhappy birth of a bad collection problem. If such a problem develops and the customer shows cooperation and honesty in facing it, have him or her start with a token payment to get collection under way. If the buyer is sluggish, prod gently at first, in order to retain the customer's goodwill for future business, and then become increasingly firm. Make the plan of debt payment definite. Exact promises, and press the customer to fulfill them. Get collateral security, notes, dated checks, sureties, or other feasible assurances of payment. Perhaps return of merchandise or extra time allowance would be acceptable. If your customer's business is in serious danger, see if you can give sympathetic help that might let him or her save face. This often spurs the customer's efforts to repay you.

In some businesses, notices of delinquent accounts are sent out, say, 5 to 9 days after the due date. But in many other businesses, the business person just adds a reminder about the overdue balance to the next month's bill, and initiates collection actions if the overdue balance grows to a sizable amount. The first approach to the collection of delinquent accounts should be low-keyed; the customer may have been ill or dealing with urgent family or business matters. If a written approach fails, the retailer may try to reach the customer by telephone. Care must be taken not to harass debtors with continual or untimely phone calls and not to employ bad language. The law has become more stringent on debt-collection practices, frowning on threats of repossession when, in fact, an item could not be repossessed; on threats to damage the customer's credit status with a credit-reporting agency when such action would not be taken; and on threats to have the debtor's wages attached without a court order permitting the action.

Some creditors have fallen afoul of the law by sending out official-looking letters that look as if they came from a government department. Intimidated debtors have imagined that they are about to be jailed for nonpayment.

If you are a retailer, you will probably turn delinquent accounts over to a collection agency 4 to 6 months after the purchase. However, if a customer comes to you with a reasonable explanation and a plan to make regular payments, you may be able to make an arrangement. Be ready to meet the willing debtor halfway; the source of the financial embarrassment may only be temporary—perhaps occasioned by heavy medical bills or a business loss. In the future, the debtor may be a good customer.

Laws Affecting Collection Methods

Certain laws, which your lawyer can explain to you in full, affect collection efforts. For example, the acceptance of a promissory note from a debtor, particularly if it is endorsed by a third party, will usually prevent you from taking action until maturity of the note. Extensions induced by fraud will not be binding. An extension by you may release endorsers, sureties, and guarantors.

If you are using trade acceptances, see that the face of the documents contains a statement that the debt arises from the purchase and sale of merchandise. These documents should include definite orders to pay without any qualifying conditions. If you are having difficulties with a dishonest customer, you may make use of false-statement laws and federal mail statutes if written statements misrepresent material facts. These might deal with the amount and the nature of assets and liabilities, the amount and the terms of sales, the percentage of profit, the amount of goods produced, and the nonexistence of liens and assignments.

In dealing with partnerships, the firm signature is generally equivalent to the signature of all partners. As a rule, it is not necessary to exhaust the firm's assets before proceeding against the individual partners, and you can proceed against a retired partner if you have not received proper notice of retirement and if you had been doing business with the firm prior to the date of his or her retirement. If you are dealing with a limited partnership, not all the partners are personally responsible for the firm's debts.

If you have a judgment against an individual partner, you may levy against the partner's interest in a partnership but not against the firm's assets. The partnership's creditors will get priority over you with respect to the firm's assets, but generally with respect to the partner's private property, the reverse is true: You will get priority over them.

In transactions with social clubs, hospitals, cooperatives, and other unincorporated associations, make sure that the party with whom you deal is authorized to act. Also see that the obligation incurred is within the scope of the organization's purposes.

When dealing with corporations, make sure that the person with whom you deal can bind the corporation. It may become helpful to know that stockholders who have not fully paid for their stock are directly liable to the corporation for any unpaid balance and, therefore, indirectly liable to you, the creditor.

In trying to collect past-due accounts, be sure to keep your statements to debtors private. Avoid repeating statements you have heard that might be slanderous or libelous. Do not imply that the debtor is bankrupt, dishonest, or without credit, especially within the hearing of someone else, including your own employees.

Do not drop the matter when a problem has been turned over to an attorney for collection. Your knowledge of the particular facts will frequently be of great assistance. Inquire about third-party proceedings under which money or property that is due your debtor can be applied to your claim as long as the debtor has an established right to the money or property, or about proceedings when a third party has been given possession of your debtor's money or property through a fraudulent transfer in order to avoid satisfying your claim.

Avoid proceedings in bankruptcy if you can find other and better remedies. See if another plan might not yield a better financial return. You then will keep an honest debtor in business, and you may make up any losses through subsequent dealings. If you want to give your customer a chance to save his or her business, you might make a private agreement with the customer, either with or without the assistance and protection of the courts.

21
Insurance Planning

It is impractical to purchase insurance coverage against every possible contingency. Some small risks can be covered by loss-prevention programs or instruments such as fidelity bonds which guard against losses from employee theft. However, most firms can hope to recover after a major catastrophe only if their loss is covered by commercial insurance.

Major risks confronting a business are losses due to fire, storms, floods, or other natural disasters and losses arising from legal claims for death or injury caused by negligence. Worker's compensation insurance, where applicable, pays benefits to injured employees, but it is not enough to prevent enormous awards for injuries to or the deaths of employees. Only insurance can cover such losses. In addition, almost every business must offer some type of hospitalization, medical, and/or group life insurance to its employees lest it be a disadvantage in attracting and holding desirable workers.

Choosing Your Insurance Company

Four types of insurers compete for the protection policies available to businesses:

1. Stock companies owned by investors who look for profits.

2. Reciprocal exchanges, unincorporated associations in which each member is an insurer of, and is insured by, every other member and provides insurance at cost.

3. Mutual companies cooperatively owned by policyholders who receive dividends.

4. Lloyd's groups (such as Lloyd's of London) composed of individual underwriters who provide coverage on types of risks that other insurance companies refuse to cover. A firm with a record of heavy loss may, at a price, obtain coverage from a Lloyd's group. Many Lloyd's groups deal exclusively with one kind of risk. The Factory Insurance Association, the United States Aircraft Insurance group, Associated Aviation Underwriters, the American Hull Insurance Syndicate, the Oil Insurance Association, and the Food Industries Federation each cover a single industry. Ask your insurance agent if your company should be covered by such a specialized underwriting group.

Since different companies use different formulas for setting rates, it is difficult to appraise their overall economy without a knowledge of their entire spectrum of premiums. You might save in one area to the detriment of another. Be wary of low-premium insurers if they have a very strict claim-settlement policy attached. You may never be able to collect.

Limit the number of agents who handle your insurance needs. Having more than one policy can complicate a claim. Regardless of coverage, you cannot collect more than the price of the damage. When several companies are involved, disputes often arise over which insurer bears the responsibility for settling the claim. Payment is delayed, causing the insured party additional inconvenience.

Guidelines in Buying Insurance

You can check with the state insurance commissioner or your lawyer to determine the financial stability of the companies that want to insure you. Their ratings can be found in books such as *Best's Insurance Reports* (Fire and Marine edition), published by A. M. Best Co. *Best's* gives data on the current year, based on the companies' balance sheets, income statements, and underwriting results. A large public library where there is a technical or an economics division will have this reference volume available. Before contacting an agent or broker, formulate your insurance program with the aid of an insurance consultant. The consultant should be an impartial adviser with a full knowledge of your business needs.

It may be advisable for a small business to buy insurance in a *package policy* that covers everything it needs to cover. The insurance company has less administrative costs in overseeing one large policy instead of several small ones, and its savings can be passed on to you. Some package policies may be specifically designed for specific types of businesses, to give the best coverage possible. Blanket policies for commercial or industrial property will give all-risk protection on stocks of goods against freezing, flood, earthquakes, seepage, landslide, war, radioactivity, dishonesty, etc. Exclusions from blanket coverage will be specifically stated.

The one problem with package policies is that they have one premium. Package buyers may have difficulty evaluating costs against other policies when they seek competitive quotes. When you look into such blanket coverage, try to find out how the premium is computed. Get the price broken down into each type of coverage.

Miscellaneous perils to your business that are not covered by other policies can be covered in one lump in a *difference-of-conditions* policy. This can protect you against anything not covered by fire, boiler, and crime policies and excludes only the specifics you designate. The exclusions keep your rates lower than if you had your policy cover every possible event (falling aircraft, for example).

Deductibles

A deductible is normally a stated dollar amount, although it can be a percentage or even a time period. For instance, in a business interruption policy, the first 24 hours might be deductible; the insurance company would not reimburse you for a loss of business during that time. They would start reimbursing you for your loss of income on the second day. The higher your deductible, the less your insurance cost. You can keep your insurance costs to a minimum by using the deductible to insure just the amount of loss that you cannot afford to bear.

For example, the premium might be $100 for a policy with a $50 deductible as opposed to $70 for a policy with a $100 deductible. For that extra $50 of coverage (the lower deductible) you are paying $30. Unless you make a claim 3 years out of every 5, you are losing money.

There are three different values for each object that can be insured. Make sure your policy covers the amount of value you wish to protect. A policy that covers the cost of an object will not provide enough money to replace the item if the cost has risen in the meantime. A policy covering the tax value of an object is providing even less protection. The tax value is the figure remaining after depreciation has been subtracted from the cost, so even if the object has increased in value, your insurance would pay you less than you originally paid for the asset. The most extensive policy covers replacement cost. This policy provides you with enough money to buy the asset at today's prices so that you can get back in operation right away without the need to raise additional funds. Note that a replacement-value policy may produce gain subject to income tax if the insurance company pays more than the asset's value as carried on your books. However, tax elections may defer tax on the gains.

Coinsurance

This term is used in more than one sense in insurance terminology. It generally implies that the loss is shared by the insured. In health insurance, for example, coinsurance means that the insured is required to bear a percentage of the medical cost. In fire insurance and related lines of insurance, coinsurance means that the insured is required to carry a specific percentage of insurance, based on the property's value; carrying a lower percentage results in the insured bearing the additional loss. For example, if instead of carrying insurance on 80 percent of the value of the property as required, you carry only 60 percent, on loss sustained the insurer would only pay six-eighths, leaving you with two-eighths loss to bear yourself. Coinsurance penalties may be avoided if property is appraised often enough and sufficient insurance maintained.

It is usually possible to obtain a substantial rate reduction under coinsurance.

Stop-Loss Insurance

This is an extension of the deductible concept under which the business becomes a "self-insurer" up to a certain limit in one or more categories of risk. If the loss exceeds that limit, the insurance company pays the excess up to the specified limit of the policy. For example, a $100,000/$1,000,000 stop-loss product liability policy would limit the firm's loss to $100,000 in any settlement up to $1,000,000. The same principle can be applied to other types of risk such as fire, theft, or even employee medical coverage. Substantial savings in premium costs can be realized by firms whose financial condition permits the assumption of this degree of risk.

Buying Fire Insurance

Your fire insurance policy should include protection against fire, lightning, hail, wind, explosion, smoke damage, riot, vandalism, malicious mischief, sprinkler leakage, and aircraft and vehicle damage. These and other extra hazards may be covered by a "difference-of-conditions" policy or by added endorsement to the basic fire policy.

To obtain the most effective coverage, base the amount of protection on the actual replacement value of your property at the time of the fire. Fire insurance policies are customarily written to supply a recovery based on the actual cash value of the damaged property at the time of the loss. This provision, which considers the physical depreciation of the property, will not allow a return sufficient to purchase new equipment. Obtain coverage which can be reviewed at regular intervals to determine whether repayment will be adequate to make the replacements necessitated by fire.

The rates charged will depend on the fire experience and safety conditions in your locality. All cities of 25,000 or more are rated periodically and ranked 1 to 10 according to water supply, efficacy of firefighting equipment, and other circumstances. Companies will also consider the kind of business being operated, the construction of the building, and the nature of adjacent buildings and their occupancy.

You may find it advantageous to insure your inventory separately. In that way, its rates can be adjusted periodically to coincide with its shifting values. While it is not wise to underinsure, there is no advantage in paying excessive premiums on property that has decreased in value. Review coverage regularly.

A good insurance program will not only provide coverage in the event of a disaster but will also serve you by implementing loss-prevention programs. You may be able to obtain lower rates if you install sprinkler systems, keep your property free of trash, have wiring properly installed, maintain fire extinguishers and shelters, and use approved containers for inflammable liquids. You should insist upon strict adherence to "no smoking" rules in prohibited zones.

Your broker may suggest that you fireproof your buildings or install fire escapes, automatic sprinklers, fire extinguishers, or smoke detectors. Your plant might maintain guards and private fire brigades. A good water supply, first-aid rooms in your building, and emergency rooms in nearby hospitals reduce your risk and may also result in lowered rates.

Be sure you understand all the qualifications and exceptions in your coverage. Most fire insurance policies will suspend coverage if an insured building is left vacant for more than 60 days at a time, unless a special endorsement to the policy states otherwise. The comprehensive approach, which automatically covers any newly installed equipment, is strongly recommended. Otherwise, your coverage might be terminated or invalidated on the grounds that your new equipment has created an additional fire hazard on your premises.

When Disaster Interrupts
Your Business

Should your firm suffer the losses of a fire, flood, or other unforeseen calamity, you will need money to pay taxes, interest, utilities, and salaries to key employees while the facilities are being rebuilt. Business interruption insurance will cover these expenses. How long would it take to rebuild your business? Your interruption insurance should give you enough to maintain necessary upkeep during the reconstruction period. Most factory owners arrange for payroll coverage for a 90-day period, but your policy can be written for a longer or shorter time. Extra-expenses insurance is available for industries which must maintain production following a fire, a toxic chemical spill, or other mishap. This kind of insurance is commonly needed by businesses such as newspapers, laundries, and dairies, whose customers depend on them for uninterrupted service.

Make sure you design your interruption insurance to cover a long enough period of time that it will cover a typical interruption for your business. Some companies have run tests of mock computer breakdowns to determine their repairer's response time. Many businesses come to a halt for the length of the computer "downtime," often several days to a week.

Whereas business interruption insurance covers problems that stop your business from operating, contingent-business insurance covers your losses when other businesses stop operating. A fire at your supplier can interrupt your operations, vital material can be held up by a railroad strike, or a bank failure can play havoc with cash flows and start a chain of bankruptcies. Contingent-business interruption insurance costs about half as much as regular business interruption insurance for protection against circumstances beyond your control. Make sure you understand which kinds of situations the two policies cover.

Also, note that business interruption policies may not reimburse you for all expenses to get your business operable again. While the policy may reimburse you for an expense that gets the business going again, it will not usually reimburse your expenses for efforts that fail to start the business again.

Water Damage Insurance

Water damage is almost always written as a separate insurance policy and covers a number of accidents that are likely to beset the small business. Such protection reimburses the insured for damage from overflow of water or steam from plumbing, heating, refrigerating and air-conditioning systems, standpipes for fire hoses, and rain or snow admitted through defective roofs, leaders and spouts, windows, or doors. Again, the premiums can be minimized by proper design and maintenance of the systems.

Flood Insurance

Floods annually cause millions of dollars in property damage in the United States. Yet most private insurance companies do not offer flood insurance because the same localities are threatened year after year, causing the insurer to lose money on underwriting coverage. The federal government has stepped in to provide protection through the National Flood Insurance Program. Contact your local insurer for information. Also, the National Flood Insurers Association serves businesses in flood-struck towns. The SBA helps victims of all kinds of natural disasters, ranging from earthquakes to tornadoes. As a requirement for receiving SBA aid, the business may have to purchase National Flood Insurance.

Power Plant Coverage

If you own your building, plant, or equipment, power plant insurance is essential to cover boilers and machinery. Explosions have resulted in damages to persons and property which have ruined many businesses. Insurance companies further protect plant owners by making periodic inspections to detect cracks, deterioration, and vibrations which could cause explosions.

Insurance companies are increasingly combining boiler insurance with fire coverage in one policy. That eliminates the controversy that can ensue from a loss that was originated by a boiler explosion which resulted in fire.

Liability Insurance

You may be liable for any mishap which occurs through your business operations, maintenance and use of your premises, employees' activities, or the use of your product. Liability can also result from accidents that emanate from the ownership or operation of vehicles used by your business.

Many proprietors tend to limit their liability coverage to the value of the business. This is faulty reasoning. There is no guarantee that an attachment to the assets of the company will not follow after insurance maximums are reached. A recommended method for determining the amount of liability insurance you need involves setting a limit of liability for each person who might be injured on your premises, a limit for a number of people injured at one time, and a limit for property damaged. An alternate method fixes a single limit for all claims that might be brought against you as the result of an accident. An insurance consultant can advise you on the specific amount you will need.

A comprehensive general liability policy protects you against nearly all hazards. (There will always be exceptions; be sure you note them.) With a schedule system, each hazard is insured under a different policy. You will want the comprehensive policy for all liability risks except the ones that can be carried separately.

Automobile coverage, which protects vehicles used by your company, must be purchased separately. However, to avoid confusion in the event of a liability, it is advisable to use the same insurance company for your comprehensive liability and automobile policies. If an accident should occur, for instance, in the loading of your vehicle, there would be no wrangling between companies over which should bear the responsibility for payment.

You may insure each vehicle separately, on a schedule basis, or obtain comprehensive liability coverage which will insure any vehicle operated in the business, even leased ones when not covered by the lessor.

Product liability is a different matter. Costs for such insurance have risen astronomically in recent years and may be beyond the means of fledgling companies to buy. Nevertheless, in view of the fact that there is scarcely any product made which cannot be charged with damages to property or persons, buying product-liability insurance should be looked into. If it cannot be afforded, all representations of the product or products should be reviewed by competent legal counsel.

Malpractice Insurance

Doctors are not the only ones sued for malpractice; many other professionals are liable as well. Lawyers, real estate agents, accountants, insurance agents, engineers, therapists, social workers, architects, and corporate directors have all been held by courts to be responsible for their advice or actions. One out of every three malpractice insurance policies is taken out by a nonphysician.

High rates are usually reserved for doctors because more claims are made against them. Whereas a doctor might pay $30,000 or more for $1 million in coverage, the same coverage might cost an architect $1000 or a lawyer $500.

Many professionals refuse to believe they need such coverage because of the confidence they have in their own ability. However, how much confidence do you have in the ability of your employees? A document misfiled or a deadline missed can lead to a malpractice suit. Forty percent of the claims against professionals are due not to incompetence, but rather to administrative foul-ups.

Worker's Compensation Insurance

State laws obligate the employer to provide personnel with a safe place to work. Employers must limit hazards by hiring competent employees, providing safe tools, and warning employees of existing dangers.

Worker's compensation programs operated by states protect the worker in the event that an injury is sustained while on the job. In some states, laws exempt employers who have only a few workers. Agricultural, domestic, and casual labor are often excluded. Some states do not insist that employers provide worker's compensation for their employees. However, since the expense of settlements in court can be high, most employers choose to carry worker's compensation insurance.

Premiums are determined by payroll, based on an audit. Rates are as low as 0.1 percent for "safe" jobs and as high as 25 percent for dangerous ones. Remember, in determining whether to carry such insurance or not, that judgments against a firm are possible for accidents seemingly not work related, such as an employee being injured after falling asleep at the wheel of a car at night while traveling to a distant customer. The judgment may stand up even if it can be ascertained that alcohol was a contributing factor.

Employee Life, Hospitalization, and Medical Insurance

When contemplating any or all of these as part of an employee benefit package, management must make a number of decisions as to the type and extent of coverage it wishes to provide. There is such a wide variety of choices that inevitably a compromise must be struck between coverage and costs.

Regardless of what is to be offered, a primary consideration is whether to make the plan contributory or noncontributory by employees. While a noncontributory plan has more appeal to the worker, the cost to the employer will be greater, given the same level of benefits.

Frequently a combination of both is settled upon where, say, the business provides group life insurance at no cost to the employee but makes a payroll deduction for a portion of the applicable medical insurance premiums. Another factor to consider in connection with hospital or medical insurance is whether coverage is to be limited to the employee alone or to include his or her dependents as well. After this, the coverage itself must be chosen—benefit limits, deductibles, coinsurance—and cost-benefit comparisons be made for the various options as well as between Blue Cross/Blue Shield and private insurer's plans.

Where health insurance is to be included, serious consideration should be given to a health maintenance organization (HMO) plan if one is available in the general area of the business. As a viable alternative, the cost of membership in a HMO will, in many cases, be less per employee than comparable protection under a major medical policy. Advantages to the employee are the convenience of "one-stop service" for the majority of medical problems plus (usually) an automatic annual checkup. A disadvantage is the loss of freedom to seek a physician of one's choice. Also, there is a vague public conception, sometimes justified, that HMOs offer inferior medical care, tend to skimp on tests, and try to minimize patients' appointments.

In the area of health insurance, expect national legislation to reshape your options, because universal coverage requirements are likely to mandate minimum health insurance protection for all employees.

Crime Insurance

Available statistics indicate that crime equals or exceeds fire as the chief culprit in property loss. Many firms, unprotected by insurance, have had to liquidate their remaining assets after suffering drastic losses through burglaries or robberies. Your insurance should cover the contents of safes and inventoried merchandise. You might investigate the storekeeper's burglary and robbery policy designed specifically for small businesses which covers specific sums for loss from outside robbery, inside robbery, stock and safe burglary, kidnapping of owners, etc. Although larger amounts of coverage are available, the policy does not adapt itself to the medium-size or larger business.

Maintaining an alarm system may seem costly, but it can reduce insurance premiums. The more you do to stop crime, the less risk the insurance company is taking, and they may be able to reflect this in your rates. An alarm system is a kind of insurance, one that may save you grief and money in the long run. In areas where crime insurance is hard to get, the preventive measures you take yourself may be the best protection—dogs, alarms, private security guards, etc.

If you are in a high-crime area and cannot get insurance through normal channels, you may be able to obtain government insurance. Rates will vary according to your geographic location, the crime statistics in your area, and your gross receipts. You will be classified as a not very, moderately, or highly hazard-prone business in paying premiums. Businesses that are not very hazard-prone include barber and beauty shops and children's clothing shops; moderately hazard-prone businesses include grocery stores, drugstores, restaurants, and auto sales and service agencies; and highly hazard-prone businesses include dry cleaners, gas stations, and liquor and jewelry stores.

Federal crime insurance is available in many states. This insurance policy cannot be canceled no matter how many claims are made, assuming none of the claims is fraudulent. If your business is in a high-crime area, where insurance coverage is unavailable, you can contact a local insurance agent who can provide you with more information.

Fidelity Bonds

Although burglary, robbery, and theft account for substantial business losses each year, the largest crime losses arise from employee dishonesty. Small amounts are sometimes drained from the company over a period of years until losses reach thousands of dollars. Fidelity bonds which protect you against employee dishonesty are a wise investment.

The bond concerns three parties: the employee, the firm, and the bonding corporation. You may get *individual* bonds to cover each employee separately, *schedule* bonds which list all names or positions to be covered, and *blanket* bonds which cover the entire labor force. Some companies make the mistake of bonding only the workers who directly handle money. However, it has been no rare occurrence for a supervisor, for instance, to make out orders to fictitious names and collect on them.

The bonding company further aids the business owner by conducting a check on employees for any record of dishonesty. The bonded employee tends to adhere to more scrupulous practices.

Bonds are continuous until canceled by either party.

Special-Purpose Coverages

Sometimes a standard insurance policy does not cover a particular risk in a business. Insurers will often design special contracts to meet such needs. For example, you may need *credit life insurance.* Such a policy can be tailored to meet your specific need.

Credit life insurance may be required if you are a retailer selling goods on credit, particularly on installment terms. Should a customer die, his or her debt is covered by this plan; you, the retailer, receive payment, and the debtor's estate is also free of obligation. Small loan companies also use this type of insurance.

Commercial credit insurance covers you if you extend open account credit to buyers of merchandise for commercial purposes. It does not apply to retailers, but it might be beneficial if you sell extensively to relatively few customers.

Profits and commissions insurance will cover a manufacturer or selling agent who might lose substantially in expected profits or commissions should a large stock of goods be destroyed. Fire insurance might cover the cost of replacement, but not the profit that will not be realized. This type of insurance is applicable in business in which goods could not be speedily replaced.

Accounts receivable insurance reimburses you for customer billings that prove uncollectible. Such an insurance reimbursement is more valuable to you than the tax deduction for bad debts.

Valuable papers insurance will protect your business against damages caused by the destruction of important documents.

Consult with your insurance adviser for special coverage that might be necessary in your type of business.

Reducing the Need for Insurance

Take advantage of any loss-prevention program or other device which reduces your need for heavy insurance premiums. One method of avoiding insurance involves a transfer of risk to another party. For example, you might lease vehicles under an agreement whereby the lessor maintains the insurance. Use services that perform your operation whenever possible, rather than hire personnel. In this way you fix the supplier of the service with the responsibility for loss or liability. The cost of insuring inventory can be shifted to manufacturers or wholesalers by "hand-to-mouth buying," through which you avoid maintaining large inventories.

Use of Life Insurance in Business

Business life insurance meets the hazards of loss to a business from the death of someone associated with it. The insurance is a modified basic life policy, but requires special application to meet the problems peculiar to the business. The many legal, financial, tax, and technical complications require careful study by experts.

Key-Employee Insurance

Almost every business has one or more men or women upon whom it depends heavily for its success. Frequently, it is the proprietor or manager. It might be the financial expert, the sales manager, or in the case of the retail shop the leading salesperson. It might be a chemist, an engineer, or a scientist whose technical efforts produce the firm's lifeblood of ideas. If key-employee insurance is taken out because it is required by a bank or other lender to protect a business loan, the cost of the insurance is not a tax-deductible business expense.

Partnership Insurance

A partnership automatically dissolves after the death of one of its partners. There is a vital need, therefore, for life insurance protection to safeguard the business against forced liquidation. Adequate partnership insurance will enable surviving partners to reorganize at once and continue the business. It will liquidate the interest of the deceased partner without loss, enabling the beneficiaries to secure full, fair value for the partner's interest in the firm. It also lends support to the credit standing of the firm.

Corporation Insurance

The death of a major shareholder may not have dire consequences for a business, but there are distinct hazards. Sometimes with the transfer of the deceased's shares, new shareholders unknown and hostile to management may gain control. A shareholder's death can deal a severe blow to a firm's credit. A corporation insurance program helps reduce the shocks of these changeovers. It gives the deceased shareholder's heirs the full value of their inherited interest at once. Knowledge of such insurance reduces the chances of the heirs looking to sell the shares elsewhere.

Proprietorship Insurance

This provides for maintenance of a business upon the death of a sole proprietor. Provisions should be written into the policy to meet the conditions of a will or trust agreement concerning the sale or liquidation of the business.

One plan may call for the sale of the business to specified employees, with the purchase money provided by the insurance. Another may provide that the business will be run by the executor of the heirs. Or a trust company may be named as beneficiary, and management control may be established. However, the plan must be specific. Many a small business flounders upon the death of the sole owner because the proprietor did not provide the business with insurance to maintain it.

Proprietorship insurance can also aid the firm's credit status by covering the new owner or key person during the period of a loan or a mortgage on property held.

Considerations in Purchasing
Business Life Insurance

Most businesses choose life insurance plans that have cash values. These provide the firm with a valuable reserve for emergencies in the event of any sharp dislocation in business conditions. When necessary, the policy's cash values can be used as the basis for inexpensive and assured loans.

Before selecting a business life insurance plan, consult at least three experts to make certain that every angle of the firm's interests is being safeguarded: your accountant, your attorney, and your life insurance agent. The first two provide the essential information on which the plan is based, and they double-check it when it is completed. Your agent will give you technical advice on the arrangement of the policies.

Tax factors, both income and estate, are involved in almost all business life insurance arrangements. Avoid plans which will necessitate additional taxes. On the other hand, tax laws often change, and the plan set up today on the basis of a certain tax advantage may prove to be disadvantageous next year. Periodically the business life insurance plan should receive a checkup by relevant professionals. Valuations of the interests of the owners are never constant. Revaluations should be written in whenever necessary on partnership and corporation policies.

Index

About the Author

The J.K. Lasser Institute brings together the combined talents of tax attorneys, accountants, financial analysts, and business writers to prepare authoritative tax and business advisory publications for professionals and nonprofessionals alike. Its renowned tax preparation guide, *J.K. Lasser's Your Income Tax*, has sold well over 30 million copies to date.